IMAGES
of America

ALONG THE HUERFANO RIVER

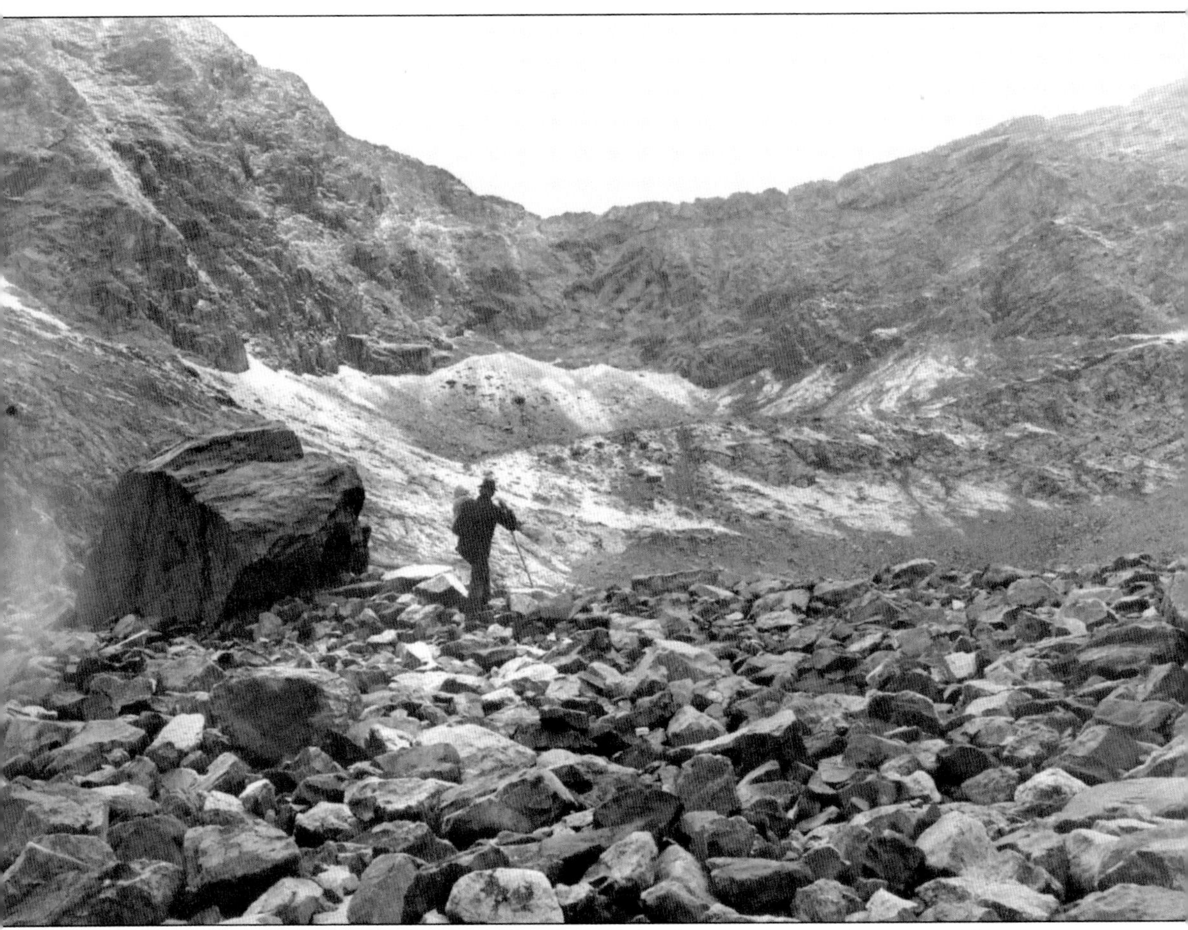

Headwaters of the Huerfano, c. 1968. Carrying his daughter in his arms, Alfred Newman Jr. climbs the north face of Mount Blanca. He approached the top of the mountain by way of the Lily Lake Trail. Today, this area is part of the Sangre de Cristo National Wilderness. (Carolyn Newman.)

On the Cover: The Thatchers' Chuck Wagon. Ranchers in southern Colorado raised thousands of cows during the 1870s and 1880s. Two of the wealthiest livestock owners were John Albert Thatcher and his brother Mahlon D. Thatcher. Here, the grandson of John Albert stands beside a chuck wagon that boldly displays the Thatcher brand. For more details, see page 54. (Pueblo County Historical Society.)

IMAGES
of America

ALONG THE HUERFANO RIVER

Kay Beth Faris Avery

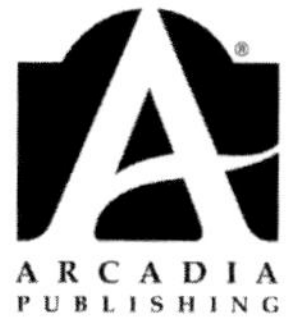

ISBN 978-1-4671-1700-5

Published by Arcadia Publishing
Charleston, South Carolina

Printed in the United States of America

Library of Congress Control Number:

For all general information, please contact Arcadia Publishing:
Telephone 843-853-2070
Fax 843-853-0044
E-mail sales@arcadiapublishing.com
For customer service and orders:
Toll-Free 1-888-313-2665

Visit us on the Internet at www.arcadiapublishing.com

To Carolyn Newman, who offered so much assistance in the making of this book, and to my husband, Charles W. Avery.

Contents

ACKNOWLEDGMENTS

I wish to extend my appreciation to all who contributed images and information to this project. I am especially grateful to those individuals who offered materials from their private collections. Each of them has been noted beneath the particular image they contributed.

In addition, I must thank local historian Carolyn Newman, Huerfano County Historical Society president Sharon Vezzani, chapter nine consultant David Perkins, Nancy Christofferson at the Francisco Fort Museum, William Bechaver at the Alton Tirey Local History Center, Pat Schall at the Monte Vista Historical Society, Christopher J. Schreck at the Steelworks Center of the West, Marie Steinbach at the Pueblo County Historical Society, Emily Brock at the New Mexico History Museum, Coi Drummond-Gehrig at the Denver Public Library, and Maria E. Tucker, Tammi Moe, and Charlene Garcia Simms at the Rawlings Library within the Pueblo City-County Library District.

Images for which no courtesy line has been provided come from the author's collection. In addition to material from private collections, images also appear courtesy of Huerfano County Historical Society/Alton Tirey Local History Center (HCHS/ATC); Huerfano County Historical Society/Francisco Fort Museum (HCHS/FFM); Huerfano County Historical Society/Walsenburg Mining Museum (HCHS/WMM); Pueblo City-County Library District, Special Collections (PCCLD); Pueblo County Historical Society (PCHS); Steelworks Center of the West (Steelworks); Monte Vista Historical Society (MVHS); Denver Public Library Western History Collection (DPL), US Library of Congress (LOC); US Geological Survey Denver Library Photographic Collection (USGS); and Palace of the Governors Photo Archives New Mexico History Museum/Digital Collection Archives (NMHM/DCA).

Introduction

The 113-mile-long Huerfano River originates at Lily Lake on Blanca Peak in the Sangre de Cristo Mountains of Colorado and joins the Arkansas River in Pueblo County just south of Boone. It is a short tributary by most standards, but the historic trail that winds along its banks boasts a rich and varied history much older than the state of Colorado.

In the millennium prior to Europeans entering the Southwest, Utes, Apaches, and other Native American tribes used the trail along the Huerfano for hunting game or raiding one another's camps. By the late 1300s, the Pueblo Indians around Taos, New Mexico, had a well-established system of hunting and trading trails extending into southern Colorado, including the one that wound north into the San Luis Valley, ascended Sangre de Cristo Pass east of Blanca Peak, snaked down Oak Creek on the north side of the pass, and followed the Huerfano to its confluence with the Arkansas.

By the 18th century, Spanish explorers were quite familiar with the Sangre de Cristo Pass Trail and all routes that crossed over the Huerfano River. In 1806, Lt. Zebulon Pike became the first American explorer to enter Colorado. After erecting a temporary stockade at the site of present-day Pueblo, Colorado, and making an unsuccessful attempt to scale the mountain that now bears his name, Pike followed the Arkansas River to about the Twin Lakes area, descended into the Royal George, and in the dead of winter trekked painstakingly mile by mile through this chasm until his men at last climbed back to level ground near present-day Cañon City.

Leaving a string of starved, half-frozen men along the way, Pike marched up Grape Creek into the Wet Mountain Valley, traversed Medano Pass, skirted the Great Sand Dunes, and reached the mouth of the Conejos River, where he built temporary shelter and awaited rescue. Eventually Spanish dragoons found him, rounded up all his men, placed them under arrest, and took them to Santa Fe for questioning. They spent several months incarcerated at a prison in Chihuahua before they were finally allowed to return to the United States.

Zebulon Pike's intrusion into Nuevo Mexico alarmed the Spanish viceroy in Mexico City so thoroughly that he suggested the building of a military lookout post to protect against American intruders. Gov. Fecundo Melgares established this Spanish fort in 1819 on South Oak Creek near the top of the Sangre de Cristo Pass, less than five miles above the Huerfano River. It lasted only a few months before the Spanish soldiers manning it were overrun by Indians.

Two years later, in January 1822, Jacob Fowler wrote in his journal about passing by the remains of this fort. Fowler was taking a trapping crew from the upper Arkansas River to Taos, New Mexico, by way of the Huerfano River and Sangre de Cristo Pass. He and his partner, Hugh Glenn, had come west to trap beaver so they could pay off debts they had accumulated during the financial panic of 1819. Many more adventurers would follow in their footsteps. In fact, so many mountain men frequented the trail over Sangre de Cristo Pass that it became known as "the Trappers' Trail." Travelers taking this route often wanted to avoid customs officials in Santa Fe as they smuggled trade goods into Taos and smuggled out their pelts.

After Mexico gained independence from Spain in 1821, the citizens of New Mexico welcomed American-made merchandise into their country. William Becknell, as the first American vendor to reach Santa Fe in the spring of 1822, managed to exchange $300 worth of trade goods for $6,000 of Mexican silver. Becknell's dazzling profits inspired other businessmen to attempt the long and hazardous journey along the Santa Fe Trail from Missouri to New Mexico. By 1843, annual traffic had swelled to 230 wagons hauling merchandise as far south as Chihuahua.

A key element of the expanding commerce was a booming business in beaver pelts and buffalo robes. To acquire these products, American fur traders began building trading posts along southern Colorado's waterways. John Gantt constructed an adobe fort on the Arkansas River. However, Gantt's venture was soon dwarfed by the Bent brothers' success. William and Charles Bent, in partnership with Ceran St. Vrain, established a larger, more popular adobe fort at a site near modern-day La Junta in 1833.

Bent's Fort became the center of a huge trading empire catering to Plains Indians, mountain men, and Santa Fe traders. Wagon caravans frequenting Bent's Fort passed down the Arkansas River to Timpas Creek, moved southeast to the Purgatoire River, and then rolled over Raton Pass to Santa Fe. This route became known as the Mountain Branch of the Santa Fe Trail. However, many adventurers still continued to follow the Arkansas to its juncture with the Huerfano River, travel the Trappers' Trail over Sangre de Cristo Pass, and head south within the San Luis Valley. Horseback riders taking this route from Bent's Fort could reach Fernando de Taos in three days or less.

In 1842, George Simpson and several other independent traders worked together to build El Pueblo at the site where Fountain Creek joins the Arkansas River. By then, beaver pelts had declined sharply in value, and former trappers were looking for ways to get into a more lucrative trade in buffalo robes. For these coveted bison hides, the owners of Fort Pueblo offered horses, guns, ammunition, coffee, sugar, flour, corn, copper kettles, cast iron skillets, cotton cloth, thread, buttons, shawls, knives, axes, farming tools, and whiskey (which the locals called Taos Lightning).

The population in and around Fort Pueblo dramatically increased during the Mexican-American War when Gen. Stephen Kearney ordered three detachments from the Mormon Battalion to winter there in 1846. However, trade at Fort Pueblo steadily declined after the war, as angry Utes and other hostile Native American tribes decided to drive the whites out of the Rocky Mountains. The only hardy pioneers moving into southern Colorado in the 1850s were farmers searching for fertile soil and a future prosperity growing corn, wheat, beans, chilies, sheep, and a few cattle.

Then 20 troy ounces of shiny yellow nuggets were discovered on Little Dry Creek in northern Colorado. By the spring of 1859, the initial find on a tributary of the South Platte River had transformed into the Colorado Gold Rush, as thousands of would-be prospectors packed their covered wagons and hastened across the Great Plains to cries of "Pikes Peak or Bust!" Boom towns materialized almost overnight, some becoming regional supply centers supporting shopkeepers, saloon operators, gamblers, laundresses, waitresses, boardinghouse proprietors, clergymen, and all sorts of skilled laborers. The farmers in southern Colorado began to prosper, too, as they sent flour, meat, and fresh produce into the Denver area.

In February 1861, the US Congress voted to separate the Kansas Territory into two parts, with the western portion renamed the Colorado Territory. By then, the nation's census recorded Colorado's non-native population at 34, 277. "Huerfano" became the name of one of the 17 original counties of the Colorado Territory. The four-million-acre tract that composed this county in 1861 included all or part of modern-day Pueblo, Huerfano, Las Animas, Bent, Baca, Otero, Prowers, Crowley, and Kiowa Counties. The region's vast expanse contained about 50 eligible voters (an average of one voter per 150 square miles).

America's first transcontinental railroad was completed in 1869, but southern Colorado did not boast railroad tracks until 1871, when William J. Palmer built a narrow-gauge rail line from Denver south to Colorado Springs. Palmer extended his railway another 50 miles to Pueblo in 1872 and into Huerfano County during 1875. Next, the Denver & Rio Grande Railroad (D&RG) stockholders purchased land from John Francisco at Francisco Plaza and established the town of

La Veta. The line was completed to Mule Shoe Curve by May 30, 1877, and to Alamosa by July 4, 1878. As the tracks extended farther and farther into the San Luis Valley, so did the saloons, gambling houses, dance halls, bordellos, outlaws, and railroad wars.

By late 1878, the executives of the standard-gauge Atchison, Topeka & Santa Fe Railroad were attempting to build rail lines in all of the D&RG's most productive territory. The vicious rivalry between the two railroads very nearly destroyed both, but a compromise was finally reached in 1880. The settlement gave the D&RG a monopoly over the coal and mineral traffic along Colorado's continental divide. Then Palmer's railroad headed even farther west to Salt Lake City, a destination that was reached in 1883. At its height, around 1890, the D&RG had the largest operating narrow-gauge network in North America.

Although the railroads had bypassed Badito and the trail along the Huerfano River, cattle ranchers and sheep growers in the county still managed to make money. The larger outfits were particularly good at taking advantage of the region's expansive grasslands, its best watering holes, and cheap labor (furnished by cowboys who earned the going rate of $30 a month, plus room and board). To consolidate their hold on much of the land in the county, the ranchers on the Huerfano organized the Cuerno Verde Livestock Association. This alliance proved very successful at protecting brands, rounding up rustlers, and increasing bargaining power with government agencies.

By 1913, there were people from 31 different countries living in Huerfano County, speaking 27 different languages. Whether working for railroads or coal companies or livestock growers, these laborers and their families managed to hold onto old traditions. Worshiping together on Sundays provided a tie to the Old World and a renewed hope for God's blessing on future endeavors. Many of the churches they built are still in use today.

The social experiments taking place in America's cities during the Vietnam War era came to Huerfano County in 1968. It was in this year that a group of counterculture artists established the community of Libre in the foothills of Greenhorn Mountain, not far from Turkey Creek and the Huerfano River. Soon afterwards, other "hippies" seeking an alternative way of doing things formed four additional communes in the upper Huerfano Valley. Each was unique in form and structure, but together they left a mark upon the land.

Over the past five decades, Huerfano County has lost many of its former industries. The coal mines have shut down. Railroad operations have slowed to a few freight trains that pass through Walsenburg each day without coming to a full stop to load or unload cargo. A ski resort that looked promising in the 1980s and 1990s has been closed for more than a decade. Many of yesterday's ranchers have sold their land and their water rights to oil companies or developers as their children move elsewhere to seek employment.

Yet the scenery along the Huerfano and in its vicinity is still as alluring as ever. From the windswept plains south of Pueblo to the pristine lakes near the summit of Mount Blanca, the land along the Huerfano continues to offer much to visitors. In fact, some sightseers who plan on passing through on a quick heritage tour find themselves coming again and again, until at last they admit to themselves that they have fallen in love with the area's broad expanses and beautiful mountains.

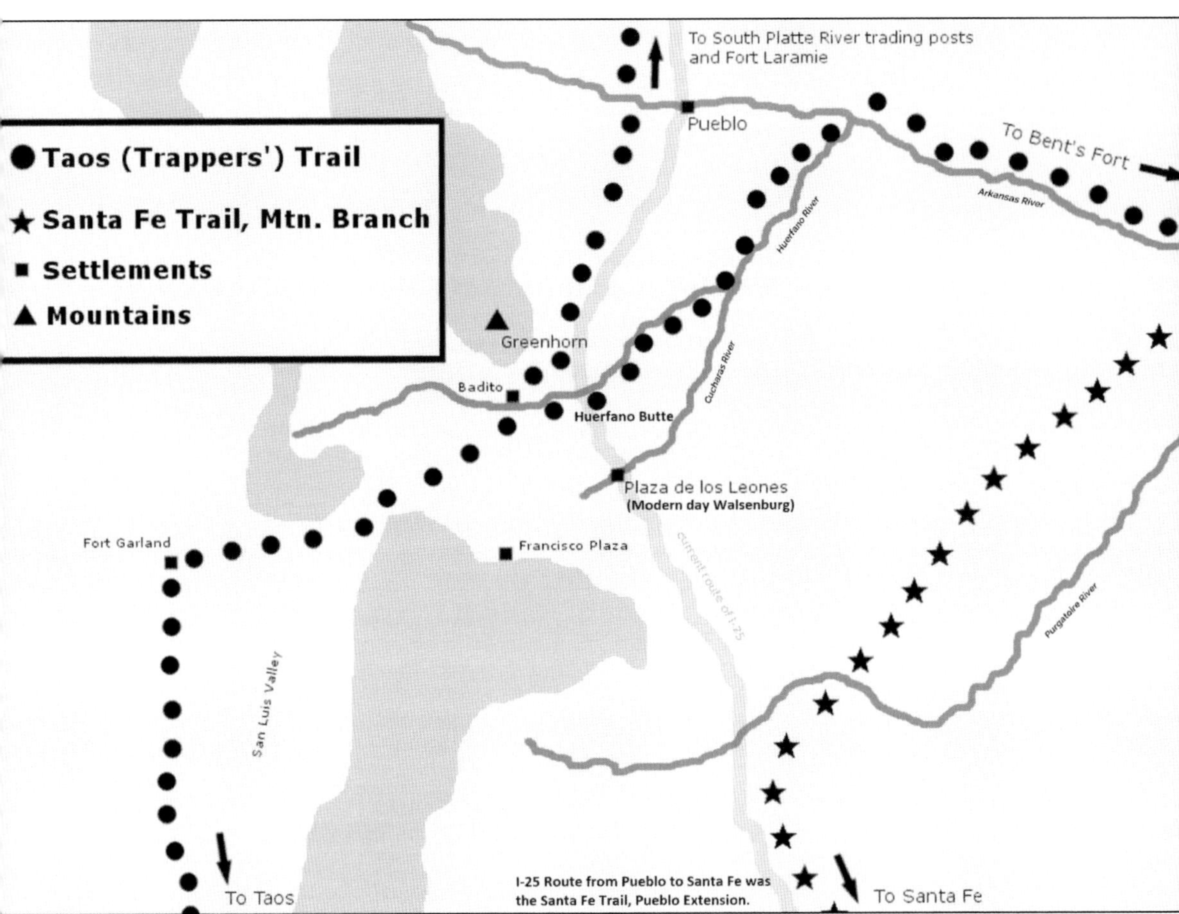

Two Frontier Routes. This map compares the trail over Sangre de Cristo Pass (also known as the Taos or Trappers' Trail) with the Mountain Branch of the Santa Fe Trail. Both routes were extremely important in the development of southeastern Colorado. (Ruth Orr at the *Huerfano World Journal in Walsenburg.*)

One

Early Explorers

The trails curling north from Taos were popular routes for Spanish colonials. Don Juan Oñate's nephew Vicente de Zaldivar traveled into the San Luis Valley in 1598 searching for buffalo herds. In 1706, Capt. Juan de Ulibarri and his 140-member expedition trekked over Sangre de Cristo Pass after runaway Picuris Indians who had fled to prairie lands east of modern-day Pueblo. Gov. Juan Bautista de Anza used this trail to return to Taos in September 1779 after defeating the Comanche chief Cuerno Verde near Greenhorn Mountain.

By 1800, the Colorado Sangres had become the strategic link between the Arkansas River and the Rio Grande. In October of that year, Spain ceded this area to France through the Treaty of San Ildefonso. To finance an ongoing war, the cash-strapped Napoleon Bonaparte then sold all of France's claims in North America to the United States for $15 million. Pres. Thomas Jefferson commissioned the Lewis and Clark Expedition to explore and map this vast new territory of 828,000 square miles. The American explorers departed St. Louis in May 1804, journeyed to the Pacific Ocean via the Missouri and Columbia Rivers over the next 19 months, and returned to St. Louis in September 1806.

Also in 1806, Capt. Zebulon Pike was sent into the southwestern region of the Louisiana Purchase to spy on activities within the Spanish borderlands of what is today southern Colorado and northern New Mexico. In his account of his expeditions, published in 1810, Pike described many of Colorado's geological wonders, including the "grand peak" near Colorado Springs that now bears his name, the Royal Gorge on the Arkansas River, and the Great Sand Dunes in the San Luis Valley.

Pike's excursion into the Rocky Mountains was followed by Maj. Stephen Long's 1820 expedition, which was commissioned to explore the Platte, Arkansas, and Red Rivers. Major Long failed to locate the source of the Red River but found instead the upper Cimarron and hundreds of miles of desert in which his men nearly perished from hunger and thirst.

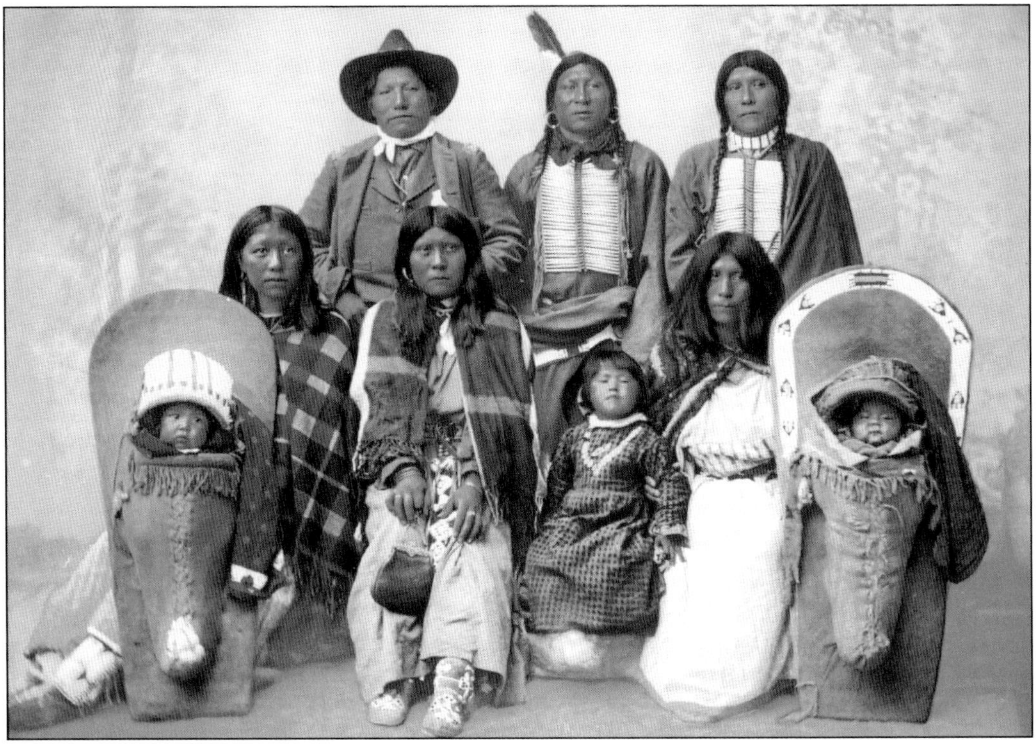

CHIEF SEVERO AND FAMILY, c. 1885. The trails along the Arkansas and Huerfano Rivers were frequented for centuries by Native American tribes, including the Ute, Arapahoe, Comanche, Cheyenne, Pawnee, Kiowa, Sioux, Shoshone, and Jicarilla Apache. Note that the photographer Charles A. Nast captured this image at a time when Ute women still made ornate cradleboards and Ute men wore long braids plus hair pipe breastplates. (DPL, no. X-30721.)

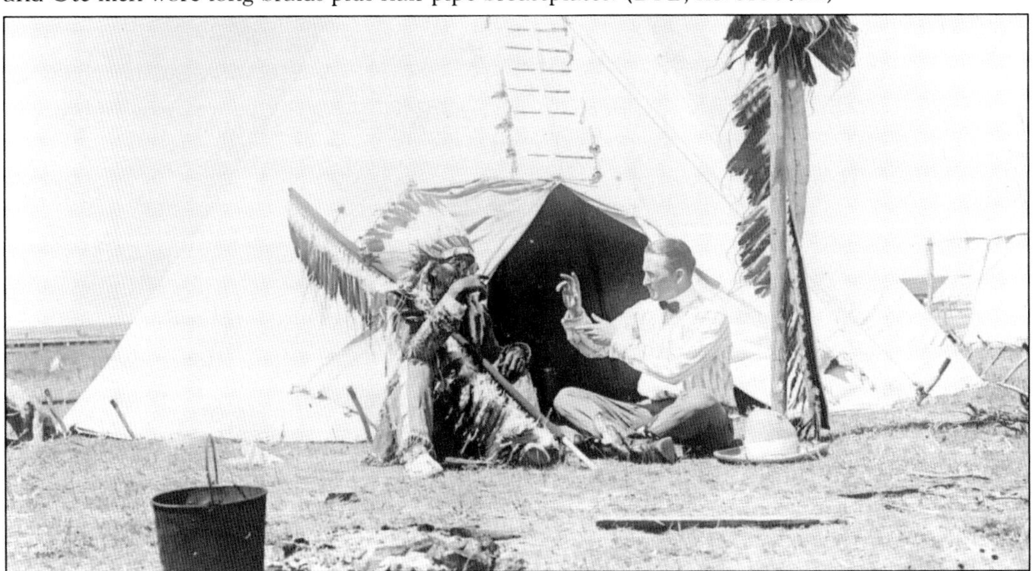

TWO CULTURES, ONE SIGN LANGUAGE, 1923. Maj. F.J. McCoy attempted to communicate with an Arapahoe chief, but Major McCoy did not speak Arapahoe, and the chief did not speak English. The pair managed rudimentary understanding through Native American sign language. (LOC.)

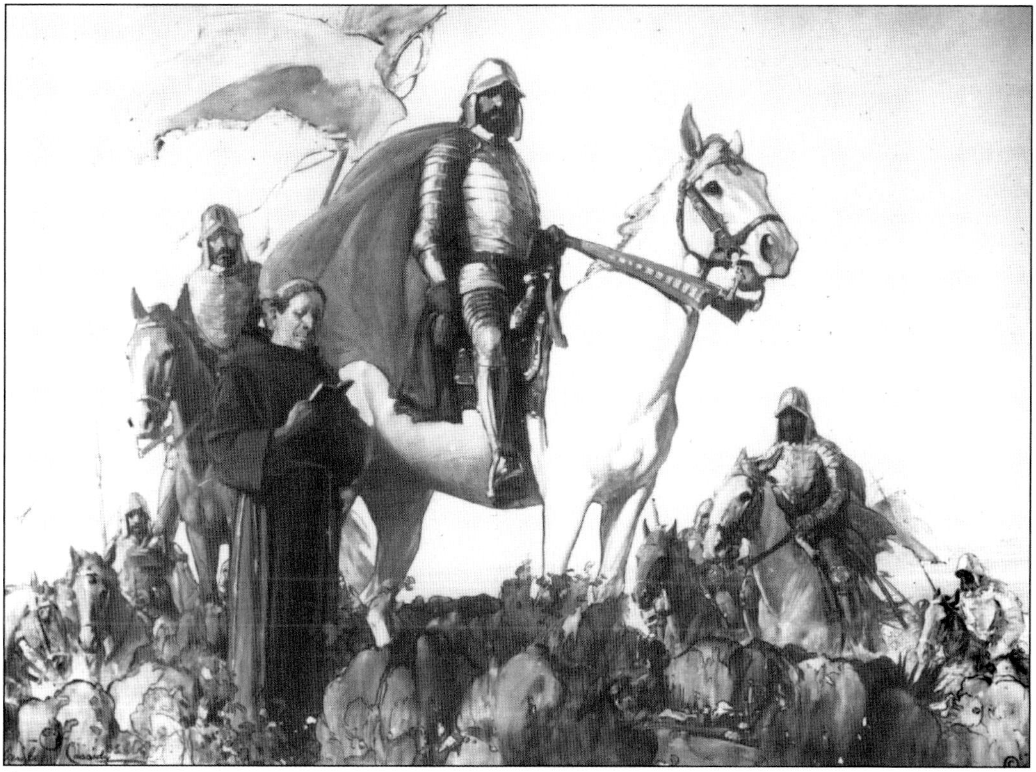

Coronado Murals, 1921. Although Francisco Vasquez de Coronado never ventured over Sangre de Cristo Pass, his travels through America's Southwest in the early 1540s set the stage for the conquistadors who came later. Gerald Cassidy painted his conceptions of the Coronado expedition for the Onate Theater in Coronado, New Mexico. (Palace of the Governors Photo Archives [NMHM/DCA], no. 020206).

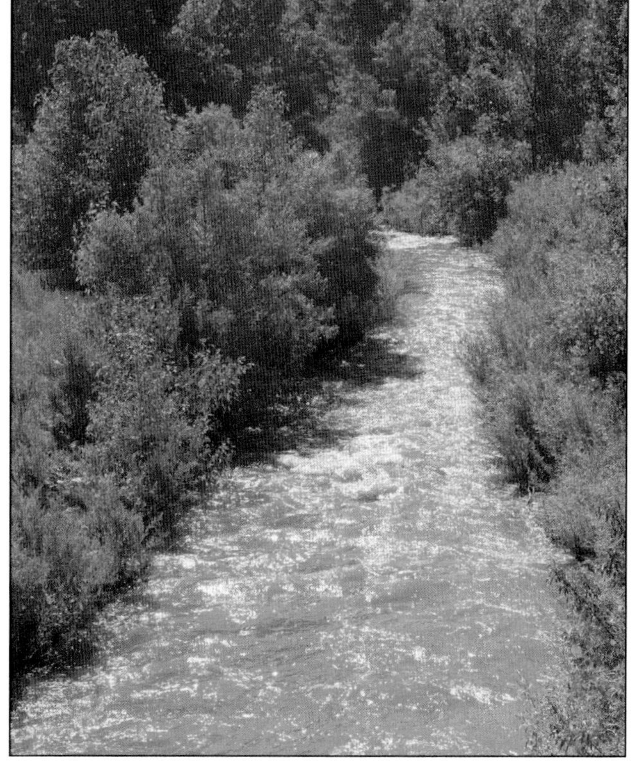

A Rose by Any Other Name. The Huerfano River has been called many things over the past four centuries. The Apache named it Chiopo. Valverde in 1719 chose the name Rio San Antonio, while Anza in 1779 decided it must be the Rio Dolores. Other names include Second Fork on the Arkansas (Pike, 1806); Third Fork on the Arkansas (Choteau, 1815); Wharf Creek (Long, 1823); and Rio Wolfano (Farnham, 1839).

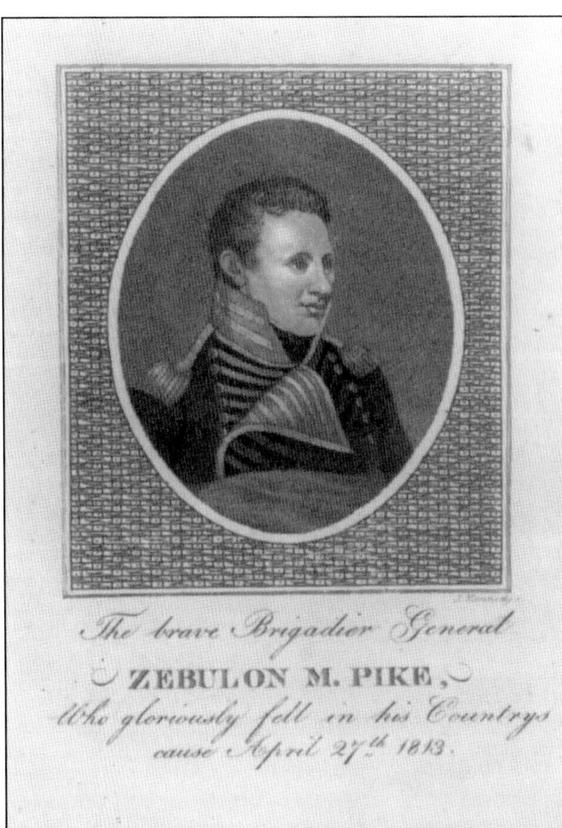

ZEBULON M. PIKE. In January 1807, Pike hiked through a corner of Huerfano County as he was ascending Medano Pass. After leading an expedition up the Mississippi River to find its source and another expedition into the southwestern region of the Louisiana Purchase, Pike was eventually promoted to brigadier general. He died in the Battle of York at the site of modern-day Toronto, Canada, on April 27, 1813. (LOC.)

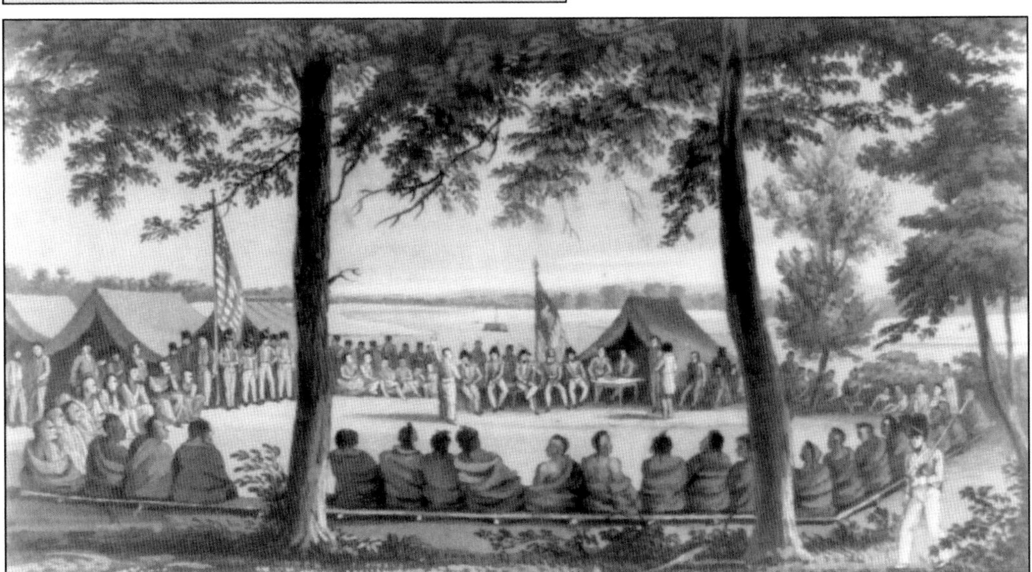

PAWNEE COUNCIL; PAINTED BY SAMUEL SEYMOUR. Maj. Stephen H. Long engaged in a parley with the Pawnee tribe near Council Bluffs, Iowa, during the winter of 1819. The following summer, Major Long ascended the Platte and South Platte Rivers, trekked south to the Arkansas watershed, and headed into New Mexico, where he searched for a route that would return him to Fort Smith, Arkansas. (LOC.)

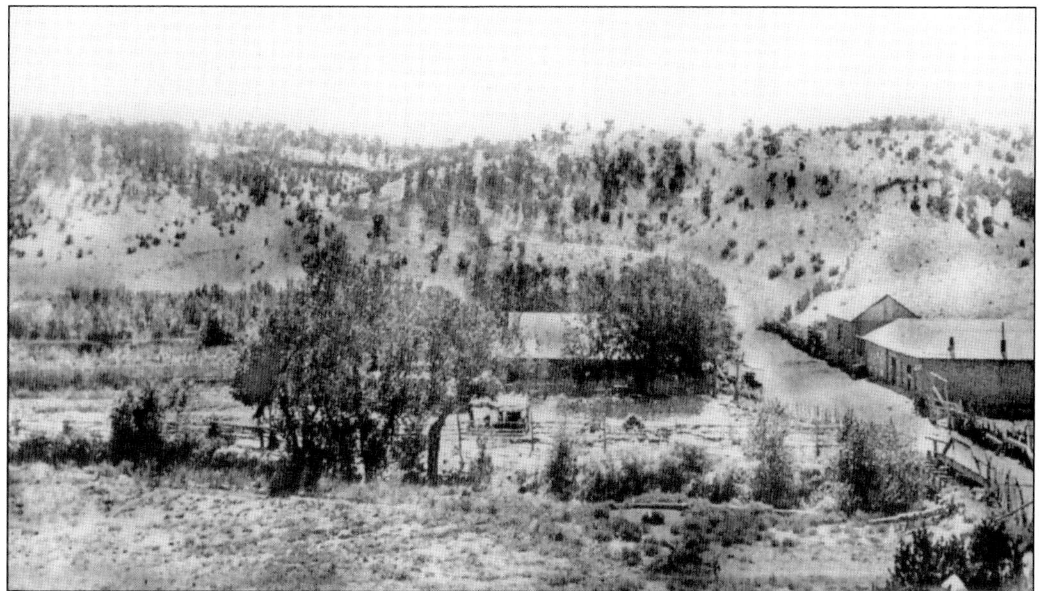

Looking South from Badito. Badito is a corruption of the Spanish word *vado*, meaning "little ford." The settlement marked the site where an ancient trail across Sangre de Cristo Pass left the Huerfano River and climbed toward the pass summit. The Badito area began to prosper in the 1850s and boasted nearly 500 residents in the late 1860s. (HCHS/FFM.)

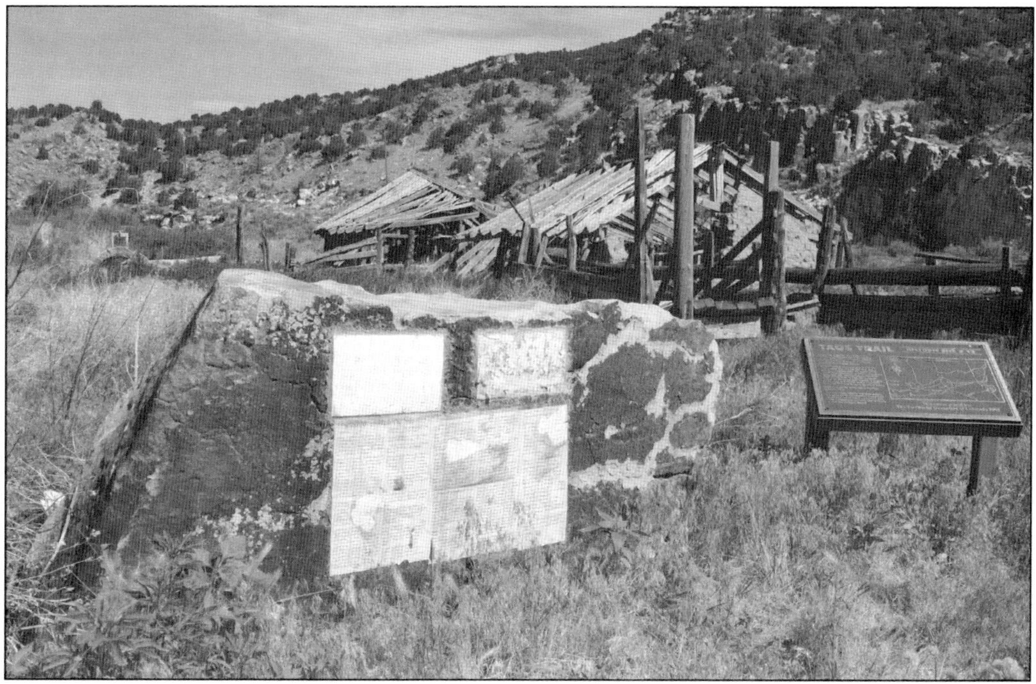

The Ruins at Badito. Badito became the administrative center for Huerfano County in 1867, but an adobe courthouse was not erected there until 1872, only a few months before the county seat was moved to Walsenburg. The courthouse at Badito then served as a general store and post office for many years. All that remains of the town today is a collapsing livery stable and a crumbling adobe hotel.

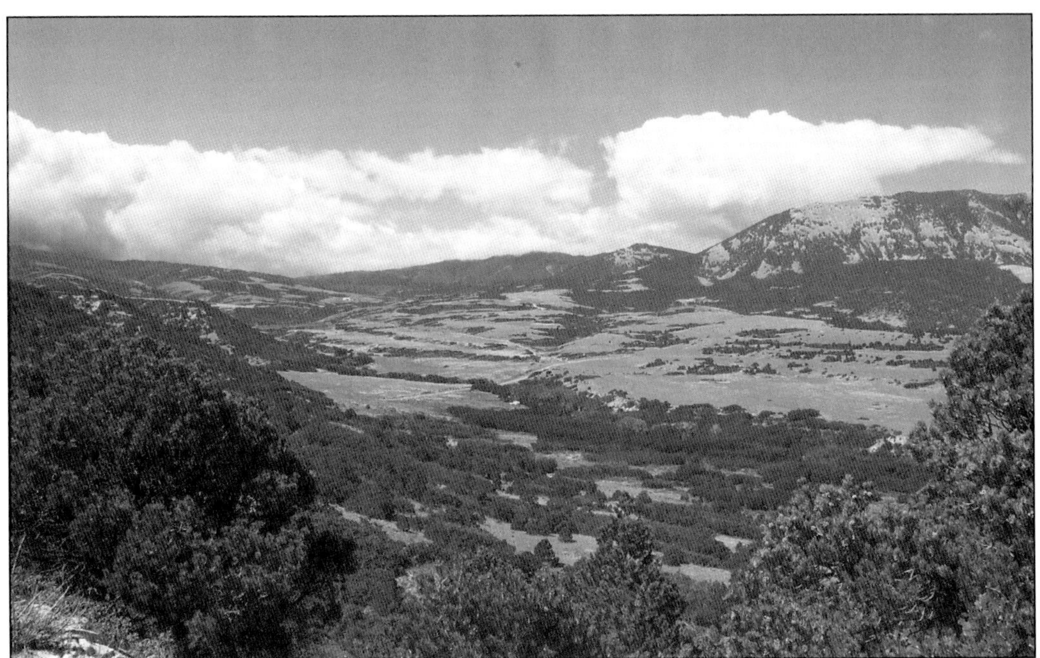

Summit of the Sangre De Cristo Pass Trail. Lying south of Badito, between Colorado Highway 69 and US Highway 160, this portion of the old trail is on private property. The trail intersects US 160 near the top of La Veta Pass at the boundary line between Costilla and Huerfano Counties. (John Van Keuren.)

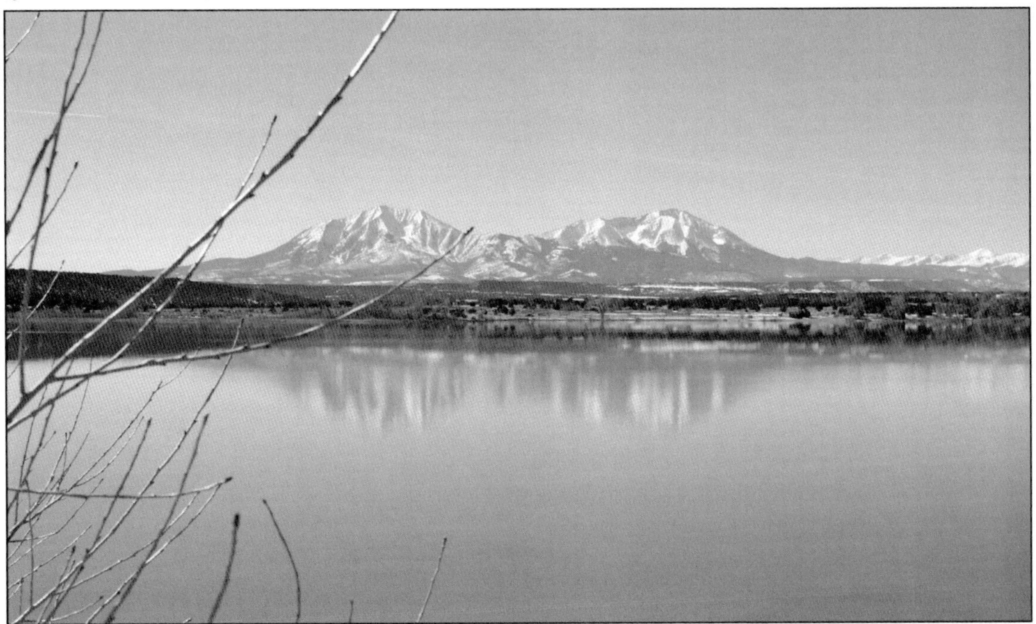

The Spanish Peaks. These twin crests were mentioned in the journals of many early explorers, who called them by various names, including the Wahatoyas (breasts of the earth), Dos Hermanos (two brothers), and the Mexican Mountains. The first recorded Europeans to explore the Spanish Peaks region came north from Santa Fe in 1706, one hundred years before Zebulon Pike discovered Pikes Peak.

Two

Fur Trappers and Traders

Throughout the first two decades of the 19th century, Spanish officials frowned upon US citizens intruding into Mexico to exchange trade goods for beaver pelts. Trappers who were caught trading illegally were jailed and their furs confiscated. Robert McKnight in 1812 and Jules de Munn in 1817 suffered these punishments.

After Mexico gained independence from Spain in 1821, New Mexicans developed a different attitude as they wholeheartedly welcomed American-made merchandise into their cities. Despite the heavy tariff of $500 per wagon, trade between the United States and Mexico increased rapidly over the next quarter-century. Within a single seven-month traveling season in 1831, a million dollars in commodities flowed west from Missouri (freight valued at more than 20 times this amount in today's currency).

Most traffic from the plains moved on the Santa Fe Trail over Raton Pass, but some adventurers went up the Huerfano River over Sangre de Cristo Pass on the trail that headed into Taos. Many of the Americans taking this route trapped beaver in the San Luis Valley. Among the most famous were Jacob Fowler, Isaac Slover, William Wolfskill, Kit Carson, the Robidoux brothers, and "Old Bill" Williams.

By 1833, the trappers had depleted the best streams in the Rocky Mountains, so haberdashers turned to South American muskrat to serve as a cheap substitute. At the same time, changing fashion dictated a new preference for silk top hats instead of the formerly chic felted beaver. In just one year, the worth of prime pelts dropped from $6 a pound to $3.50 a pound on the St. Louis market. Prices fell even further in 1834, while buffalo hides gained in value.

The demand for tanned buffalo robes brought about the establishment of trading posts on the upper Arkansas River, including Bent's Fort and El Pueblo (also called Fort Pueblo). In these adobe-walled plazas, trading post operators purchased hides with coveted manufactured goods, food, horses, or illegal whiskey. The whiskey was hauled from Simeon Turley's distillery near Taos by way of the trail over Sangre de Cristo Pass.

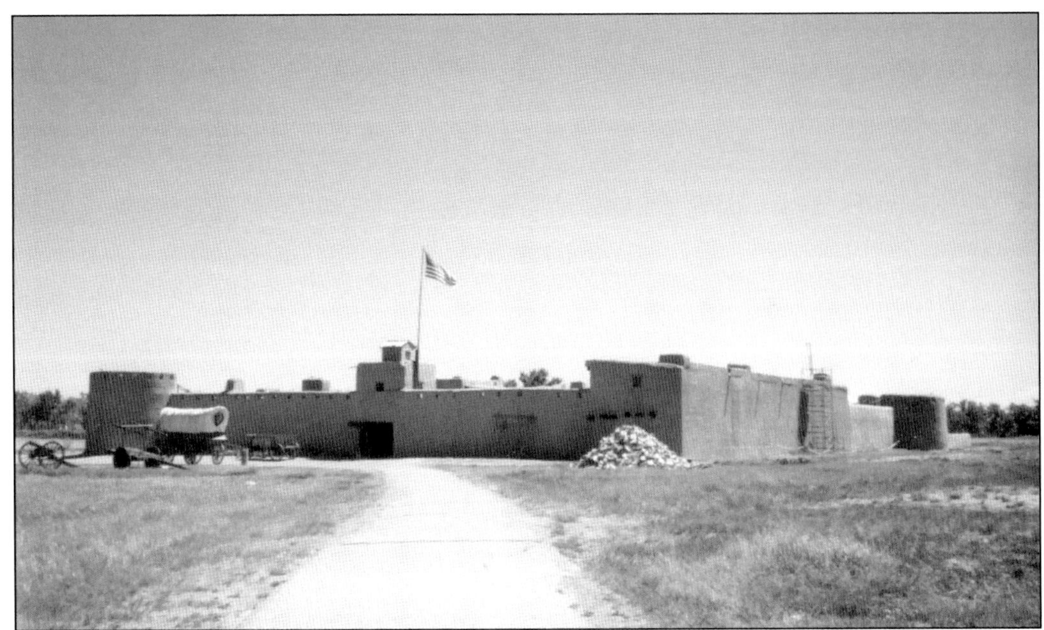

Reconstruction of Bent's Old Fort. Sometimes referred to as Fort William, the actual trading post was owned by Bent, St. Vrain, and Company. It was a rendezvous point for mountain men seeking to sell their pelts, a cultural crossroads for Native Americans bartering buffalo robes, a waystation for emigrants traveling farther west, and even a supply depot for US soldiers under orders to fortify the region. (PCCLD, no. Ph-C-159-01_001.)

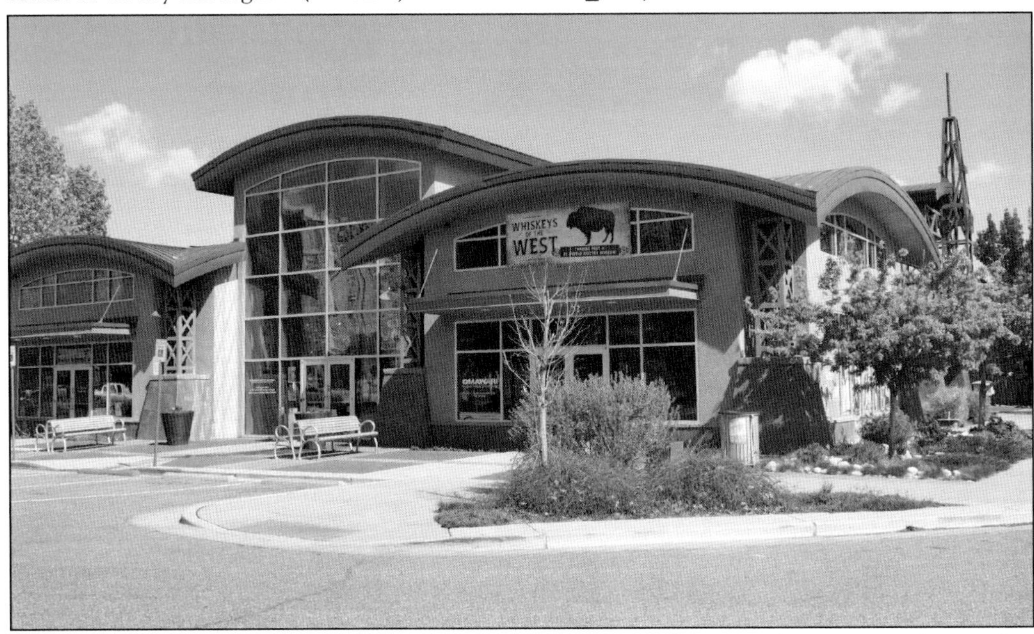

El Pueblo History Museum. This attraction showcases the region's past, together with a multidimensional view of the community's cultural and ethnic diversity. The property includes a re-created 1842 adobe trading post and an archaeological excavation of the original post. It is located in the heart of Pueblo's City Center, within walking distance of the Historic Arkansas Riverwalk and the Union Avenue Historic District.

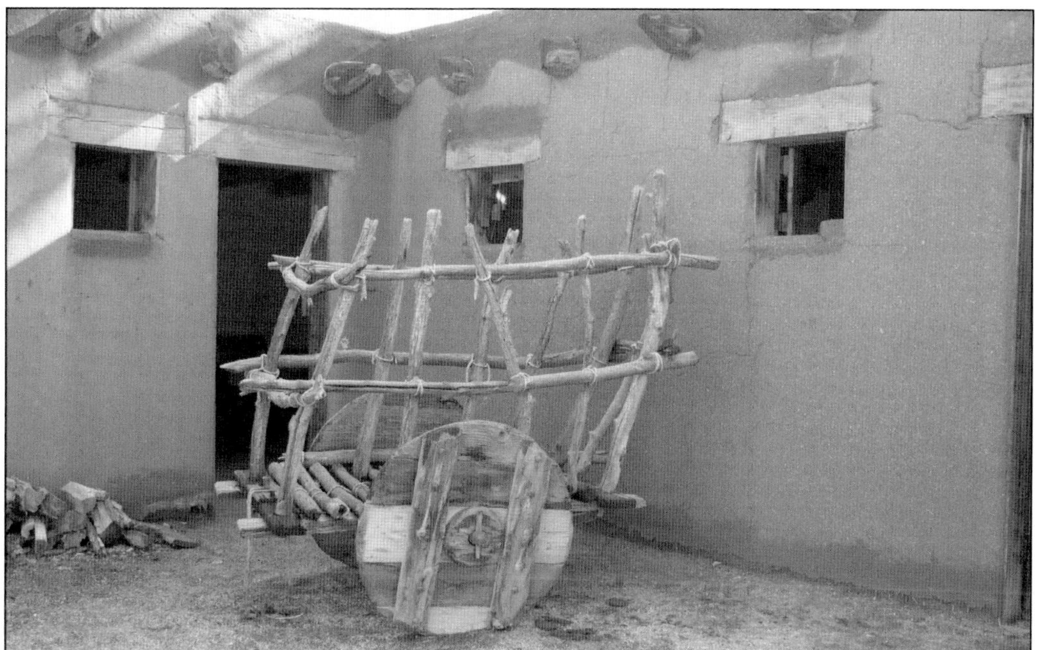

The Carreta. Because only Missouri traders and rich Mexican merchants could afford to own a Conestoga wagon, most New Mexicans hauled heavy loads on pack animals or in simple, two-wheeled ox carts similar to the one pictured here at the El Pueblo Museum.

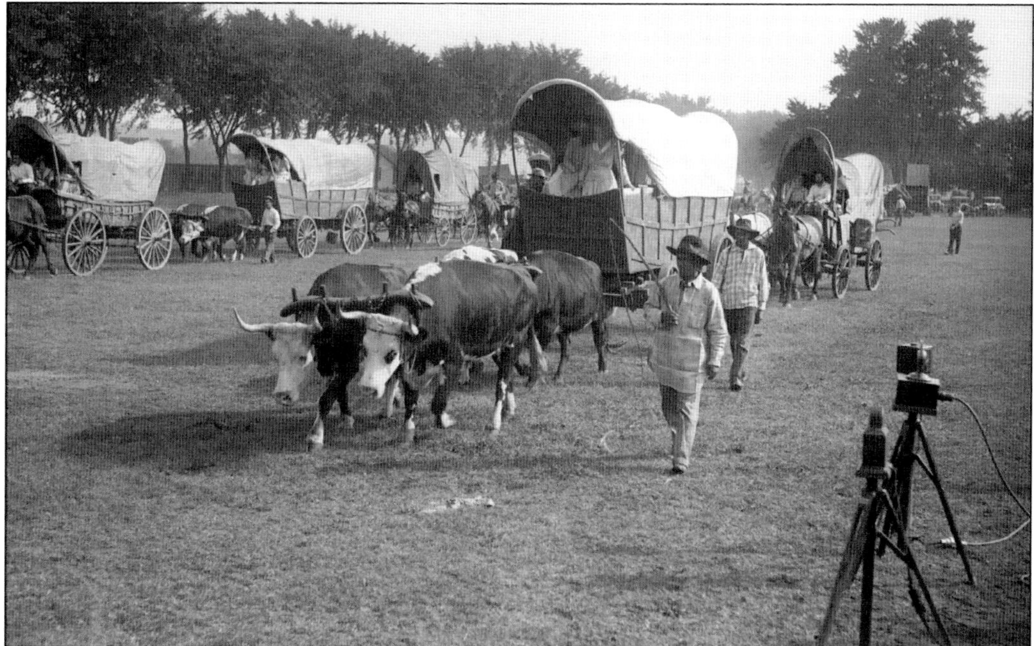

Oxen Pulling a Covered Wagon, c. 1930. From 1822 to 1880, thousands of wagons carrying fortunes in trade goods rolled over the Santa Fe Trail. The trail was the equivalent of today's interstate highways and the wagons traveling on it analogous to freight-hauling tractor-trailers. In this photograph, employees working for the Harris and Ewing Studio capture the appearance of an authentic wagon train. (LOC.)

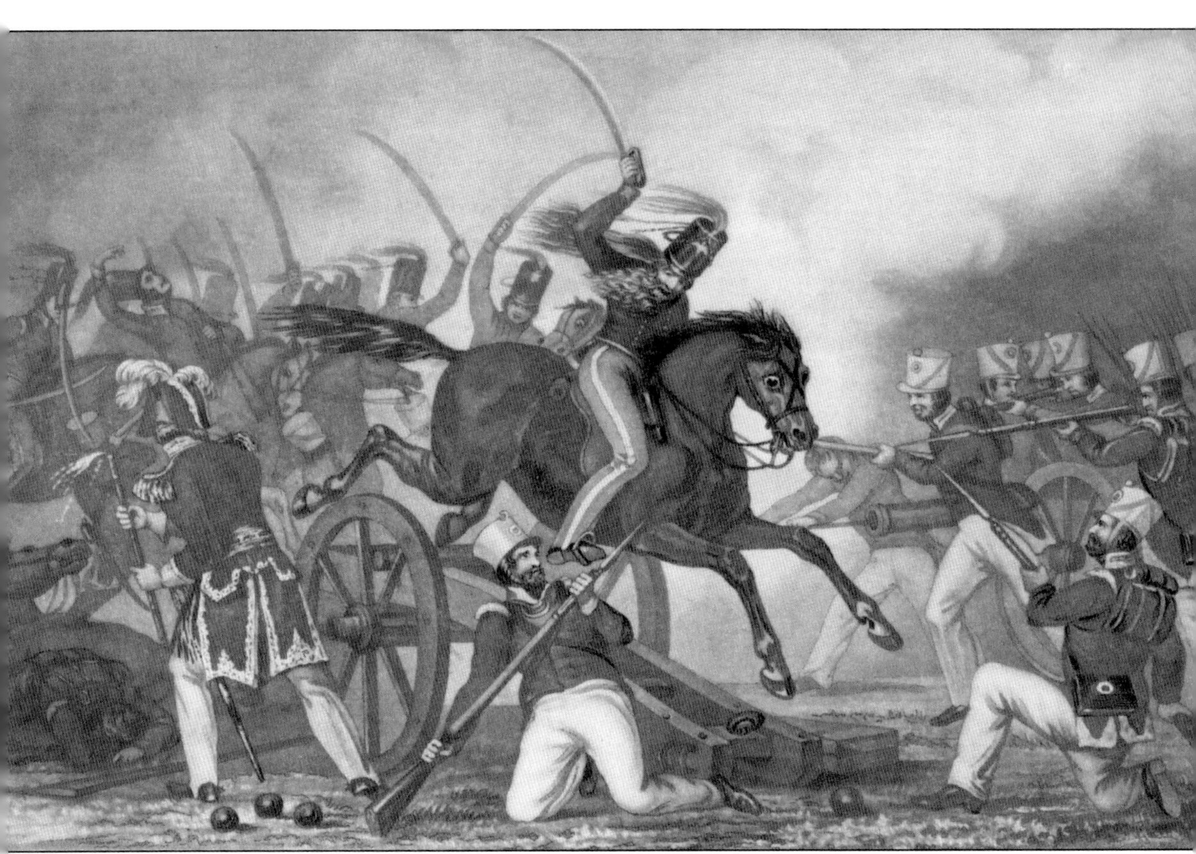

An Outpost for Manifest Destiny. Bent's Fort was constructed on the north bank of the Upper Arkansas River when the Arkansas served as an international boundary separating the United States from Mexico. Because of its strategic location, national policy makers considered the fort an ideal jumping-off place for western expansion. In the summer of 1846, Gen. Stephen Watts Kearney marched 2,500 soldiers from Fort Leavenworth, Kansas, to Bent's Fort as he prepared to invade New Mexico and convert it into a US territory. In Henry S. Sadd's engraving, Capt. Charles May leads a charge at the Battle of Resaca de la Palma on May 9, 1846, as he defends another critical frontier outpost, this one on the Rio Grande near Brownsville, Texas. (LOC.)

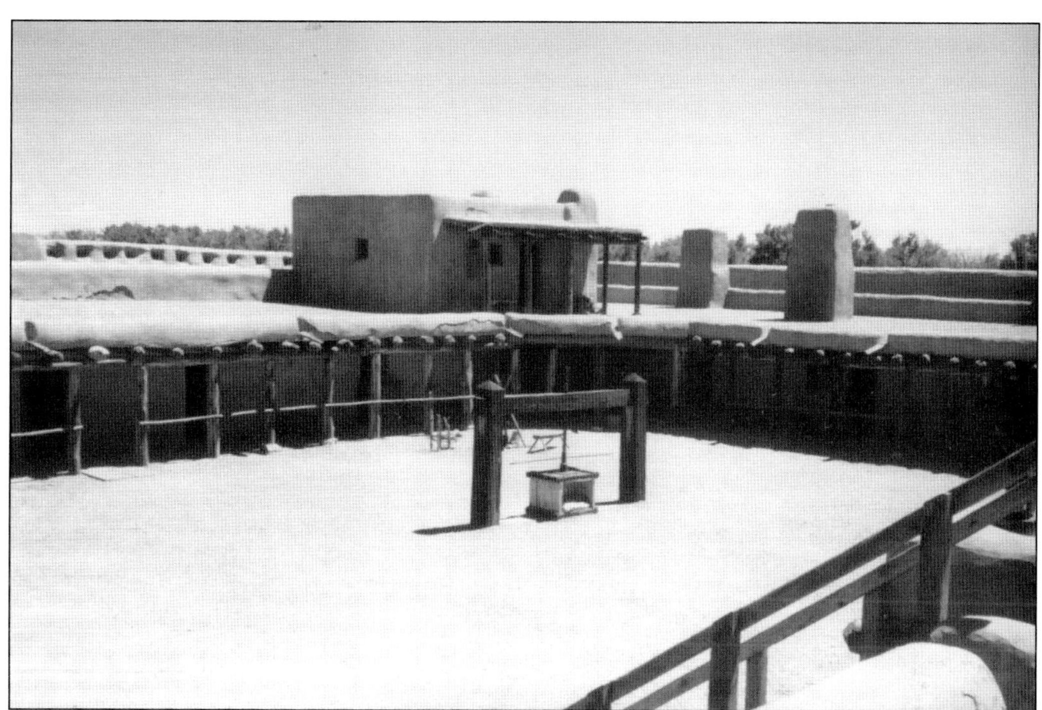

The Fur Press. This device is prominently displayed in the courtyard at Bent's Old Fort National Historic Site near La Junta, Colorado. The fur press was an essential tool in the fur trade. It was used to squeeze thick stacks of buffalo robes into compacted 90-pound bales. (PCCLD, no. Ph-C-159-01_002.)

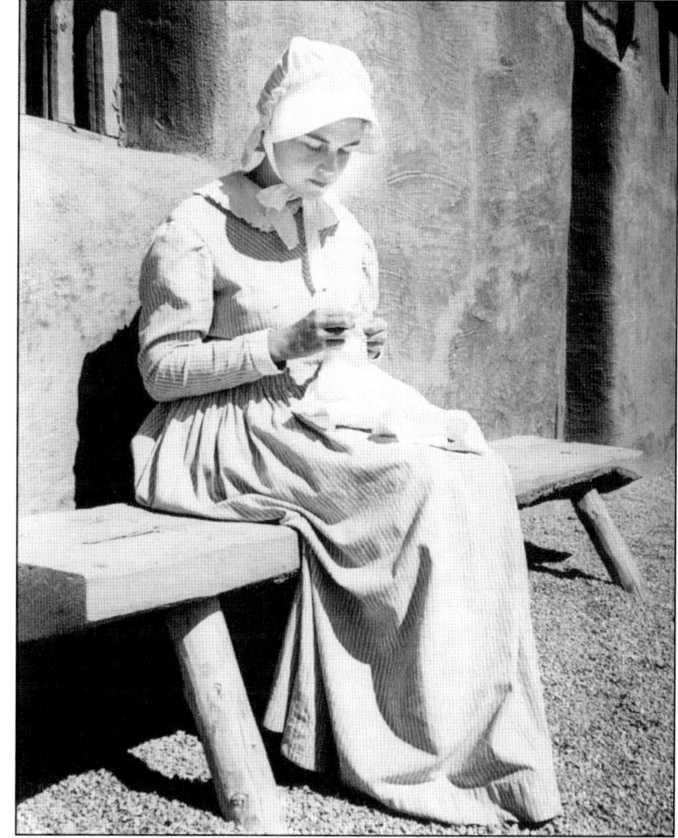

Reenactor at Bents Fort. Women who moved west on the Santa Fe Trail faced all sorts of dangers: Indian attacks, disease, prairie fires, lightning storms, buffalo stampedes, rattlesnakes, swollen rivers laden with quicksand, prolonged thirst on long stretches of arid desert, and even accidental falls from overturning wagons. Nineteen-year-old Susan Magoffin spent most of her short stay at Bent's Fort in bed, recuperating from a miscarriage. (PCCLD, no. Ph-C-159-01_001.)

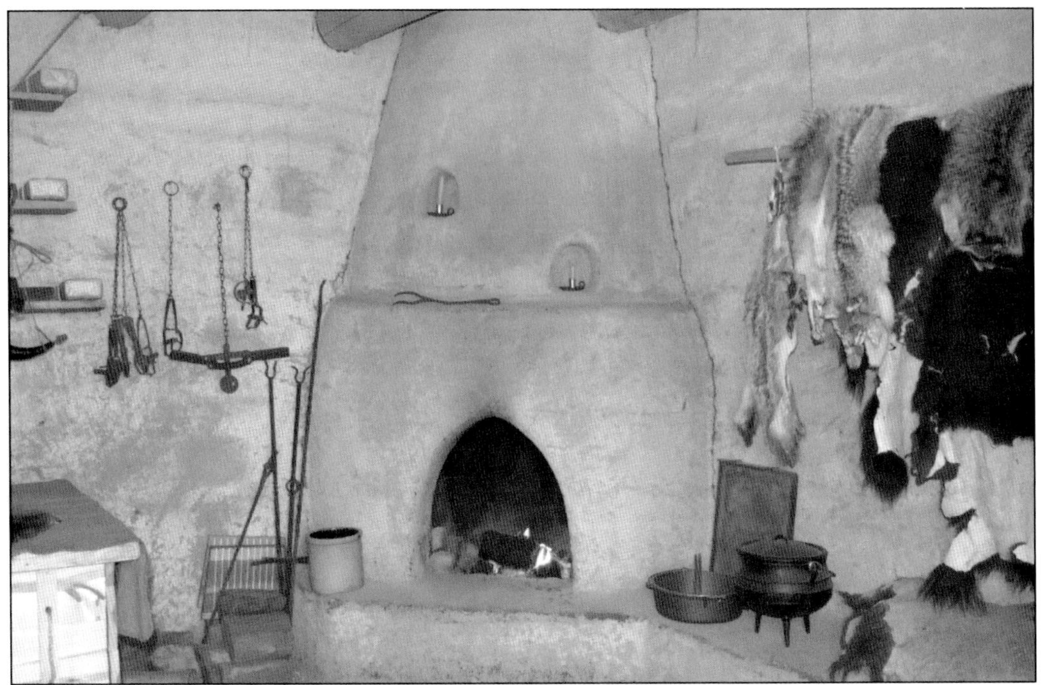

Fur Trapper's Lodgings. This room inside the recreated El Pueblo Trading Post was furnished to look as if a fur trapper resided there. Note the adobe fireplace, the cast iron pots sitting on the hearth, the numerous tanned hides, and the metal traps decorating the walls.

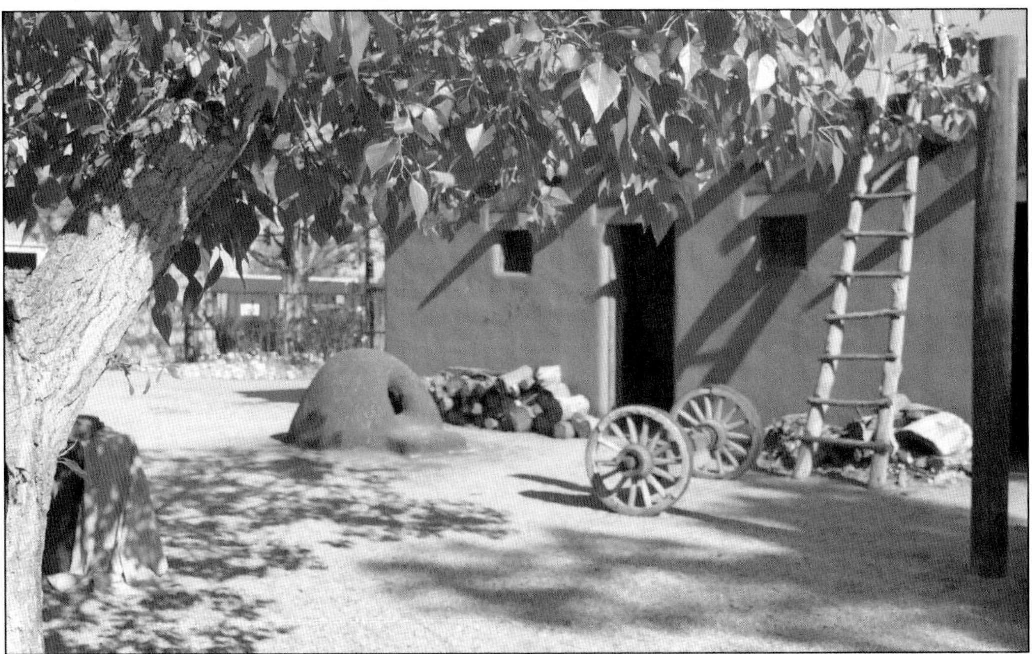

Courtyard Interior. The courtyard at the recreated El Pueblo Trading Post has the appearance of the average New Mexican plaza, complete with adobe walls, a ladder for climbing onto the roof, and *hornos*. In these beehive-shaped outdoor ovens, Mexican and Native American women baked bread and roasted ears of corn.

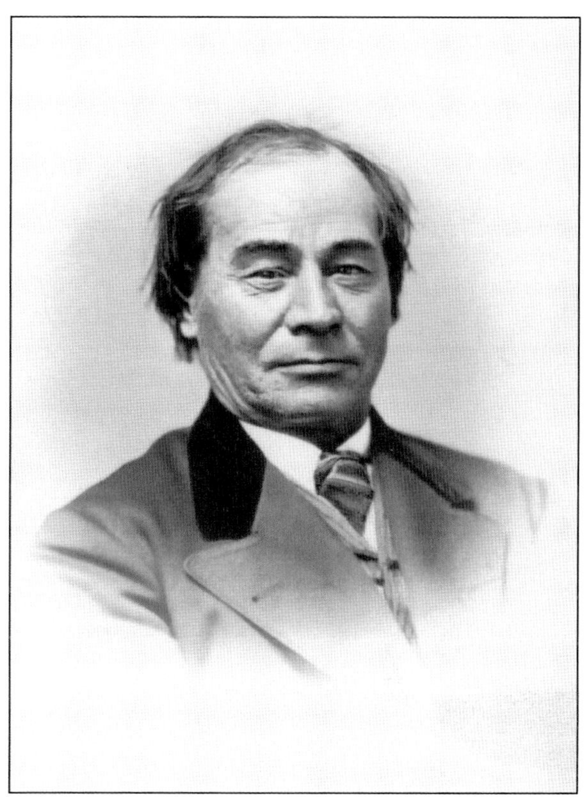

William Bent. With financial assistance supplied by Charles Bent and Ceran St. Vrain, William Bent erected his adobe fort on the Arkansas River in 1833. Bent's castle on the plains eventually became the epicenter of a fur trade empire stretching from Wyoming to Santa Fe. His marriage to a Cheyenne woman and his untiring efforts to negotiate peace treaties with various North American tribes further strengthened his influence in the region. (PCHS.)

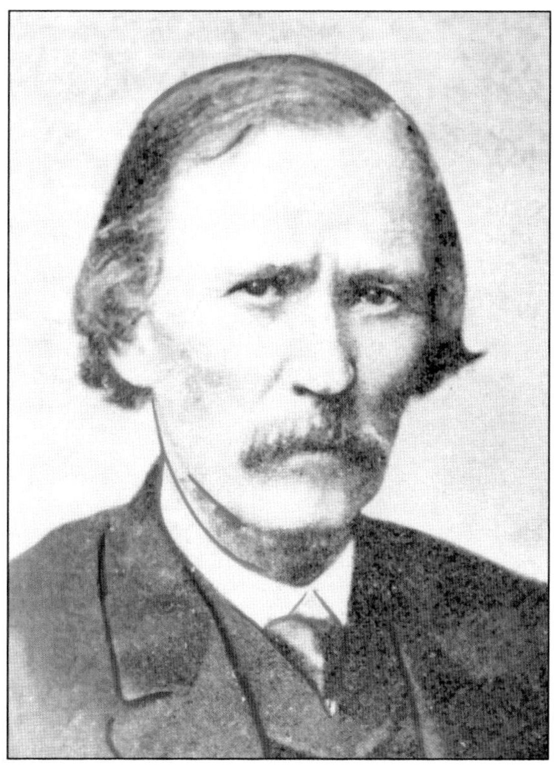

Kit Carson. Christopher "Kit" Houston Carson was employed as a hunter by the Bent brothers in 1841 and regularly visited Bent's Fort throughout the 1840s. During his lifetime, Carson had many careers: mountain man, wilderness guide, Indian agent, and Army officer. He gained national recognition as the capable scout who led John C. Fremont's first three expeditions into California and Oregon between 1842 and 1848. (PCCLD, no. Ph-B-92-01_001.)

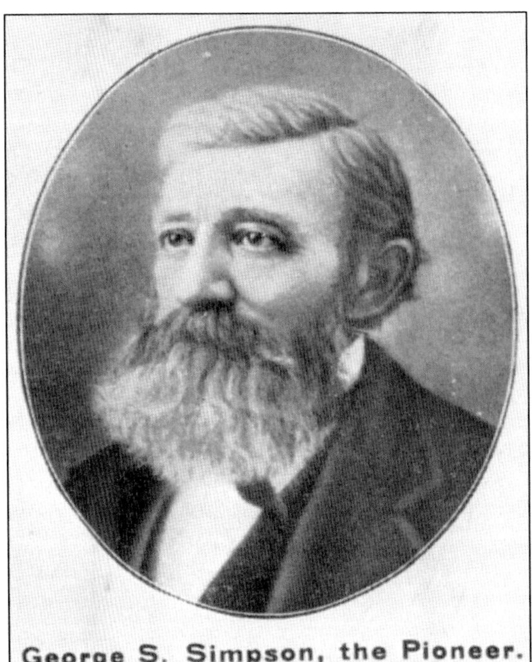

George S. Simpson, the Pioneer.

George S. Simpson. He was a son of a St. Louis merchant and one of the few formally educated adventurers who came west in the early 1840s. Simpson partnered with Mathew Kinkead, Robert Fisher, and a group of other independent traders to construct El Pueblo. This frontiersman was buried near Trinidad, atop a rugged cliff that now bears the name Simpson's Rest. (PCCLD, no. Ph-B-398-01_001.)

James P. Beckwourth, El Pueblo Museum. This former slave turned fur trapper lived with the Crow Indians in the 1820s. He also participated in the Florida Seminole Wars, fought in California during the 1846 war with Mexico, and blazed a trail over Beckwourth Pass in the Sierra Nevada during the California Gold Rush. Perhaps he is best known as one of the cofounders of Fort Pueblo.

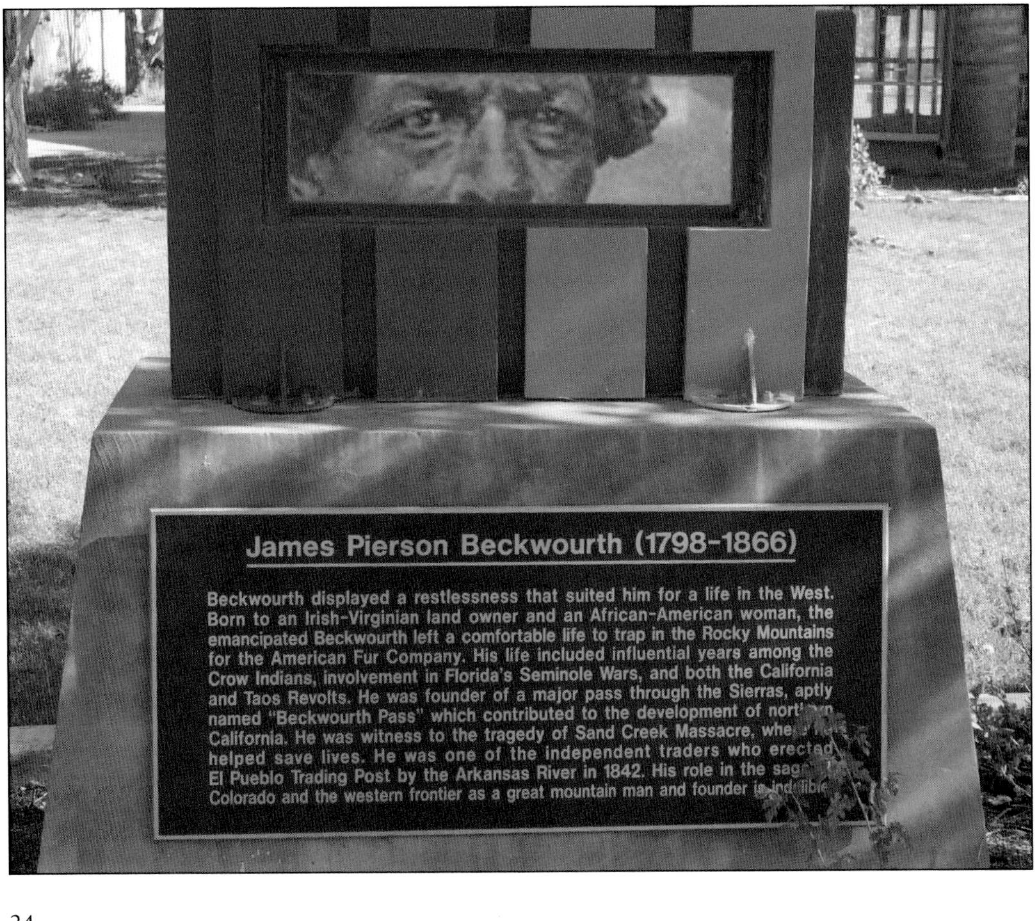

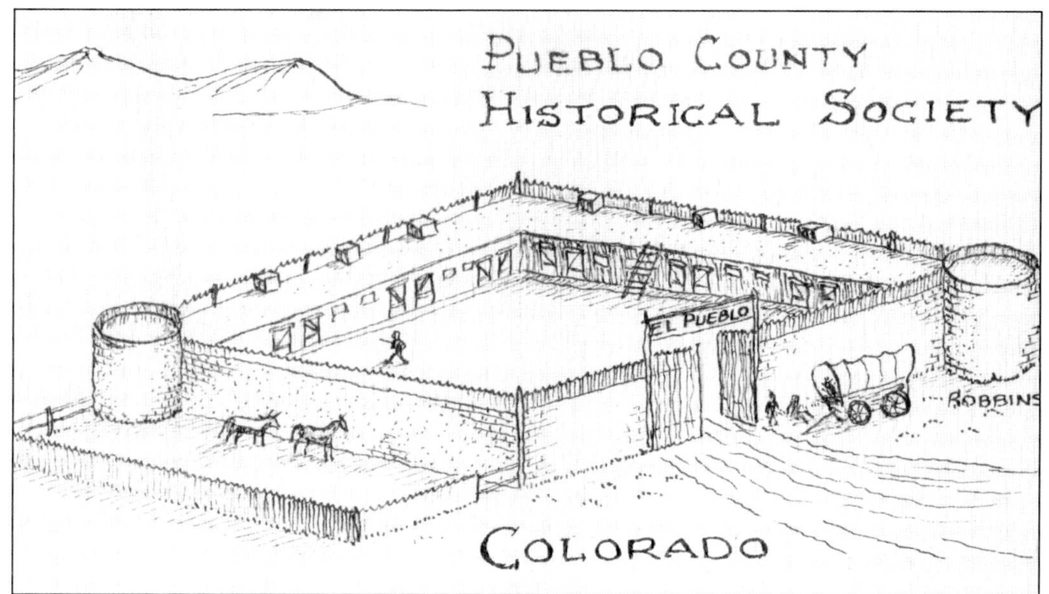

The Pueblo County Historical Society Logo. This rendition of the El Pueblo fortress may not be entirely accurate. For example, the corner bastions look suspiciously like the ones at Bent's Fort. The actual fort, positioned close to the confluence of the Arkansas and Fountain Rivers, was approximately 180 feet square. The post population varied from about 150 in 1847 to about 24 in 1854. (PCHS.)

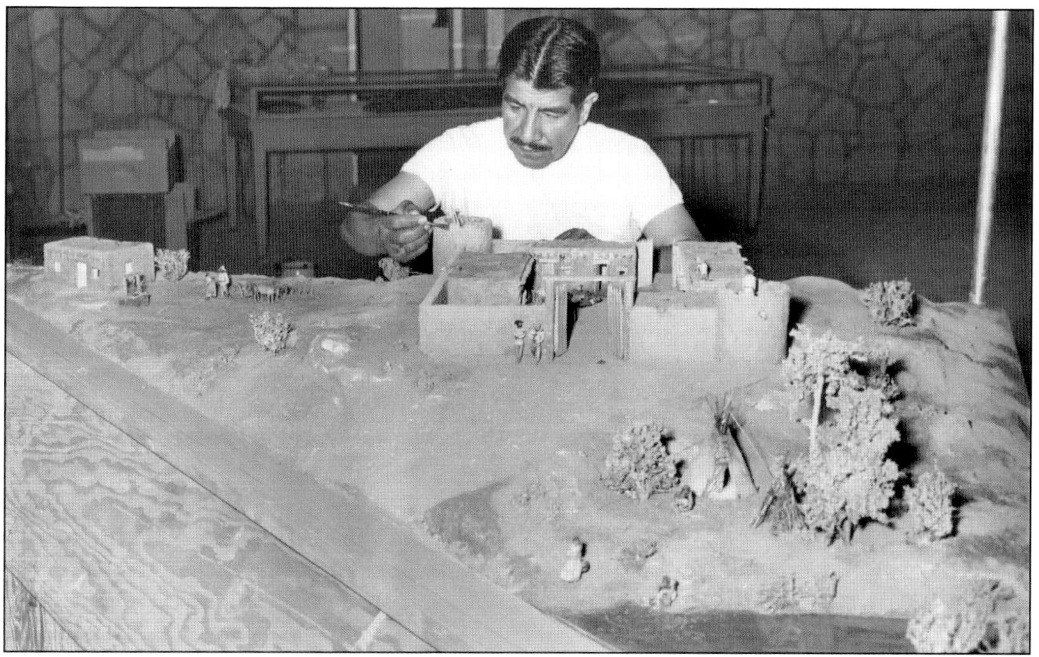

Miniature of El Pueblo Trading Post. The Mexican-American War, increasing debts, a decline in the fur trade, and an outbreak of cholera motivated William Bent to abandon his fort in 1849, but the El Pueblo fortress remained in use until December 24, 1854. On this day, Tierra Blanca and his Ute warriors overran the fort and killed or kidnapped everyone on the premises. (PCCLD, no. Ph-P-398-03_002.)

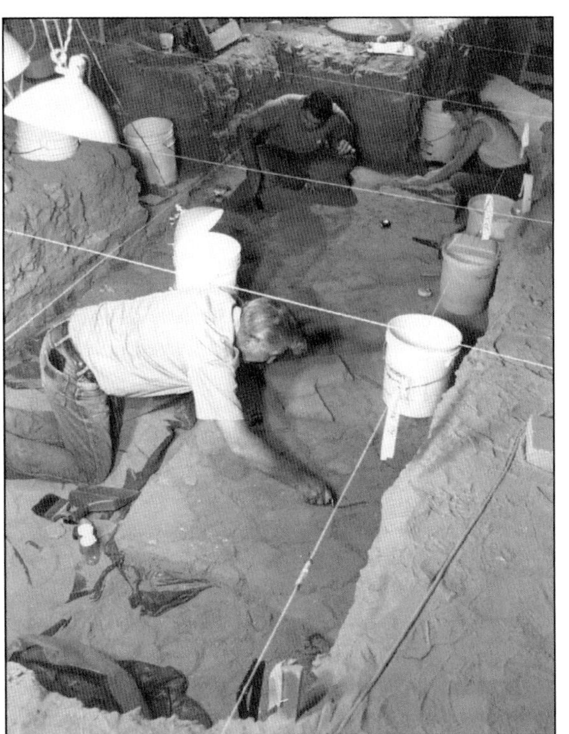

El Pueblo Archaeological Excavation. The original fort remained buried under rubble for many years. Then, in 1988, Dr. William Buckles of the University of Southern Colorado–Pueblo began an archaeological excavation to locate the remains of the original trading post. The facility, which is administered by History Colorado, was listed in the National Register of Historic Places in 1996. (PCCLD, no. Ph-P-388-02_001.)

Mormon Battalion Memorial, 1946. Dignitaries stand before the memorial and a plaque that reads, in part: "The Mormon Battalion in the Mexican War spent the winter of 1846-47 near this site. With their families and Mormon immigrants from Mississippi they formed a settlement of 275 persons. They constructed a church and rows of dwellings of cottonwood logs. Here were born the first white children in Colorado." (PCCLD, no. Ph-P-322-02_007.)

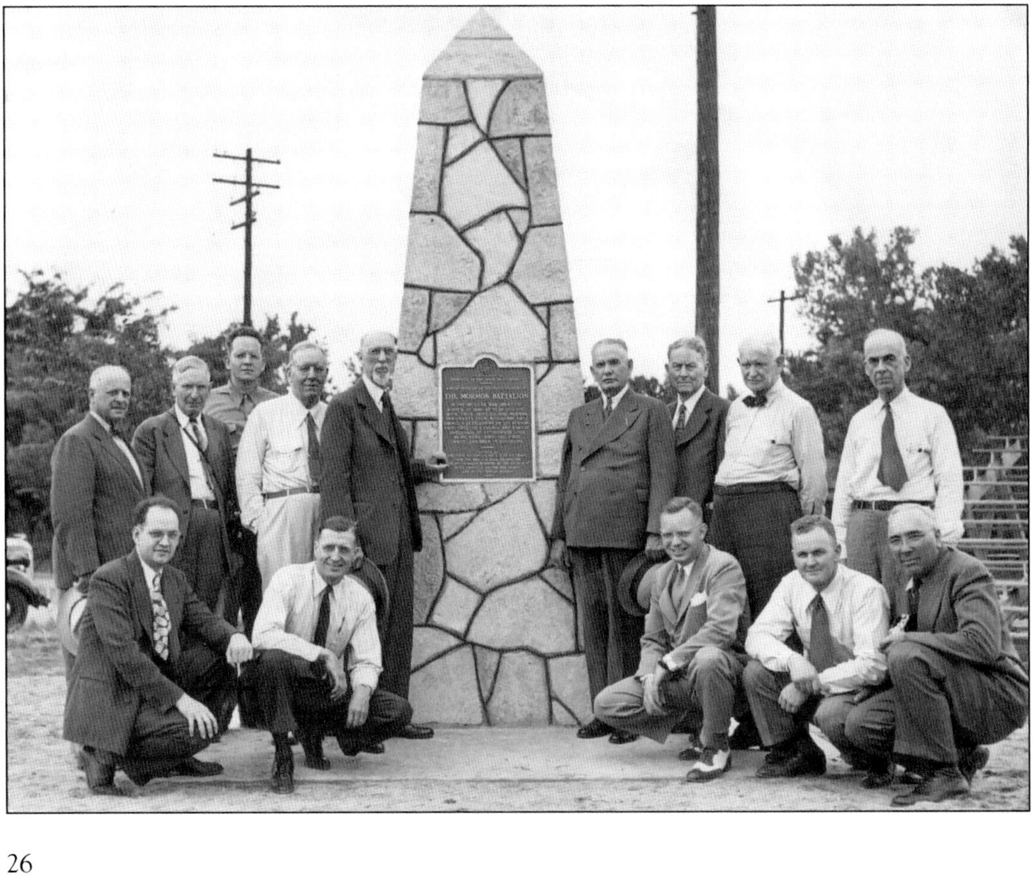

Three

Pikes Peakers and Early Agrarians

In May 1858, William Green Russell brought a colony of mining men from the state of Georgia to the Rocky Mountain wilderness 85 miles north of Pikes Peak in what was then the Kansas Territory. The miners set up camp on the South Platte River near its convergence with Cherry Creek and started panning for gold. After three weeks of disappointing results, some of the men decided to return home, leaving Russell and 11 of his comrades behind to continue their search. When Russell finally happened upon "good diggings" at the mouth of Little Dry Creek in early July, he managed to collect more than 20 troy ounces of gold.

News of his success traveled fast, moving down the Front Range to Autobees Plaza on the Huerfano, finding its way across the Santa Fe Trail, and spreading all over the eastern half of the United States before Christmas. By the spring of 1859, the initial find on the South Platte River had transformed into the Colorado Gold Rush as thousands of would-be prospectors packed their covered wagons and hastened across the Great Plains toward the villages of Auraria, St. Charles, and Denver City.

Pikes Peakers streaming into the Kansas Territory exploded the population from 8,600 in 1855 to 143,000 by 1861. Some of the new settlements disappeared almost as quickly as they had come into existence, but others grew into flourishing towns and cities. The farmers in southern Colorado began to prosper, too, as they sent cattle and fresh produce into the Denver area. By 1863, Joseph Doyle had 600 acres of Huerfano River bottomlands planted in corn and other irrigated crops. Ceran St. Vrain began selling half-mile parcels along the Huerfano River to friends and acquaintances he convinced to settle on the Vigil–St. Vrain Land Grant. This four-million-acre grant had been awarded to him and Cornelio Vigil prior to the Mexican-American War and was pending before the US Congress. In 1861, the perimeter of this huge expanse became the boundary lines of the original Huerfano County.

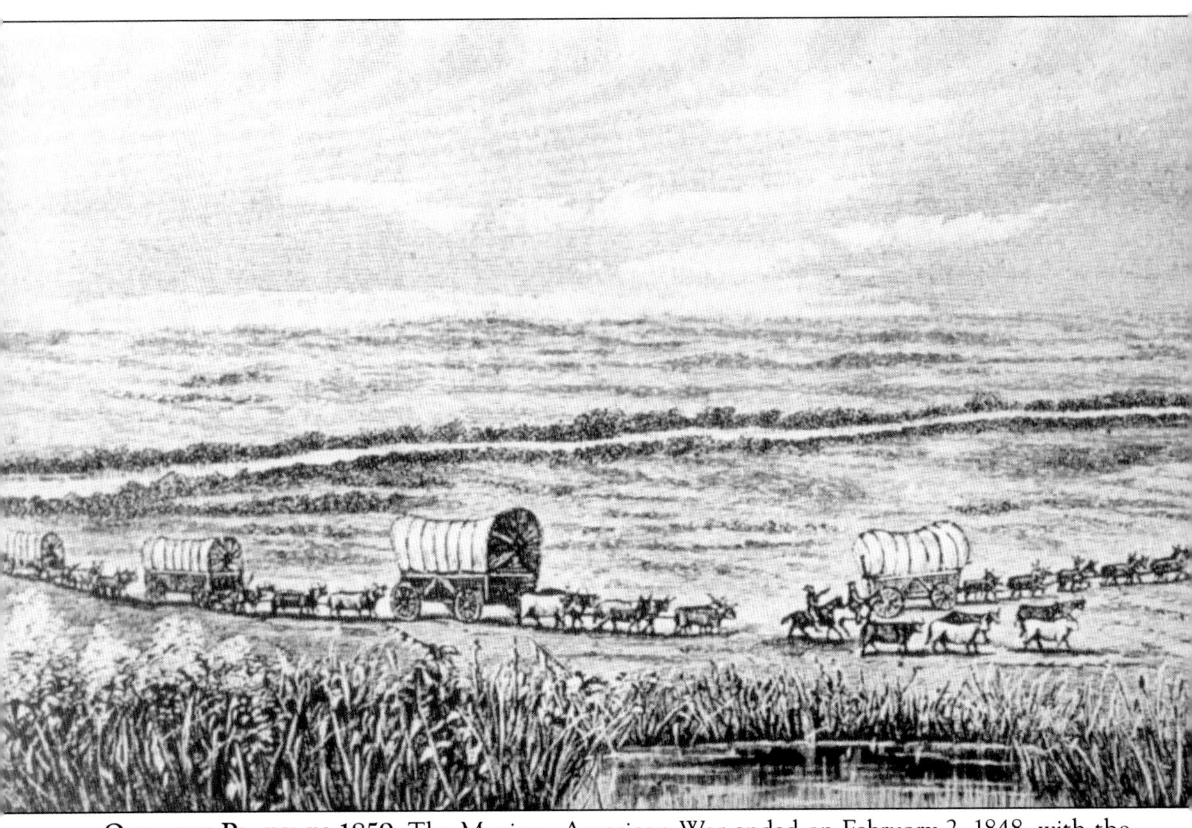

Over the Plains in 1859. The Mexican-American War ended on February 2, 1848, with the signing of the Treaty of Guadalupe Hidalgo, which ceded 525,000 square miles of Mexican territory to the United States. This land eventually became all or part of present-day California, New Mexico, Nevada, Utah, Arizona, Colorado, and Wyoming. Throughout the 1850s and 1860s, the number of wagon trains moving westward into this large region continued to steadily increase. By 1865, annual traffic on the Santa Fe Trail had grown to more than 5,000 wagons hauling merchandise worth $40 million. Many of the wagons were pulled by muscular, slow-plodding oxen, but mules like the ones pictured in this *Harper's Weekly* engraving also remained popular beasts of burden. (PCHS.)

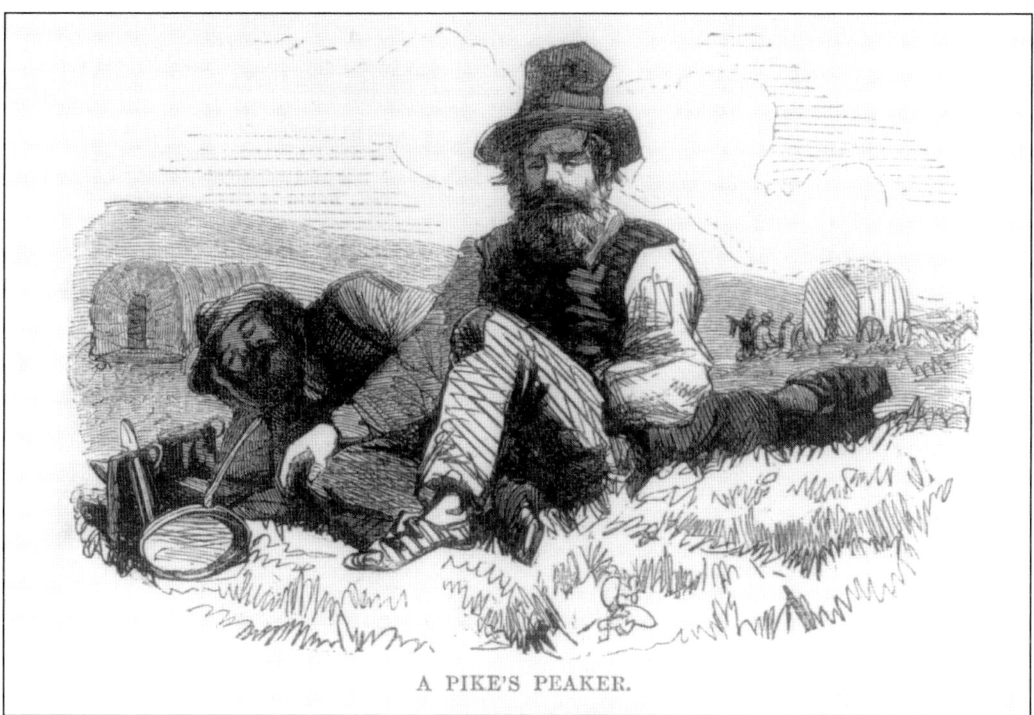

A Pikes Peaker. This illustration from an 1859 issue of *Harper's Weekly* shows a disheveled man seated by a wagon train campfire. An estimated 100,000 gold seekers took part in the Colorado Gold Rush, many of them motivated by the famous slogan "Pike's Peak or Bust." In truth, the location of the first gold discovery was 85 miles north of Pike's Peak on a creek that runs through modern-day Denver. (LOC.)

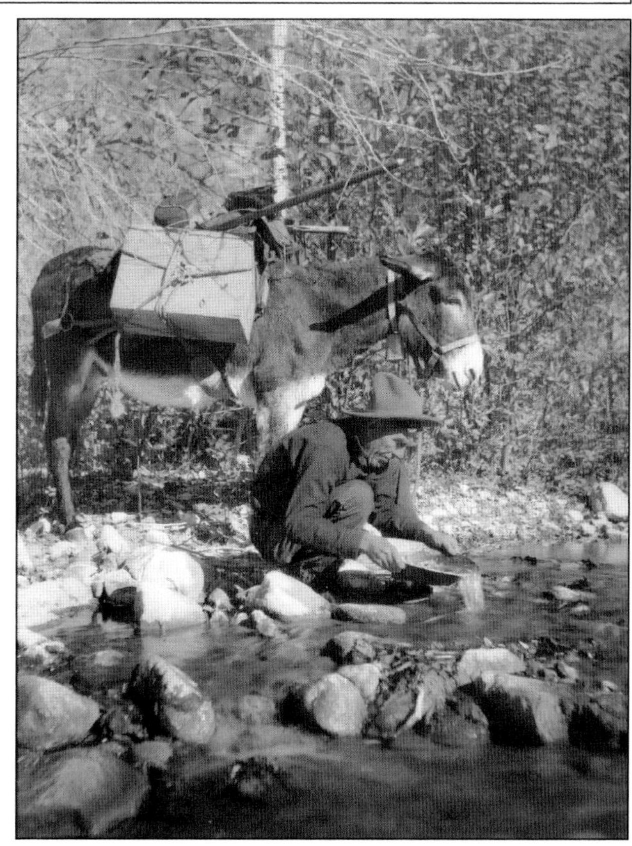

Prospecting for Gold. A miner kneels at an unidentified creek and pans for gold. The donkey standing behind him is loaded with the man's equipment, including a wooden supply box, a cast iron pan, and a pick axe. This photograph was taken between 1890 and 1915. (DPL, no. Z-1049.)

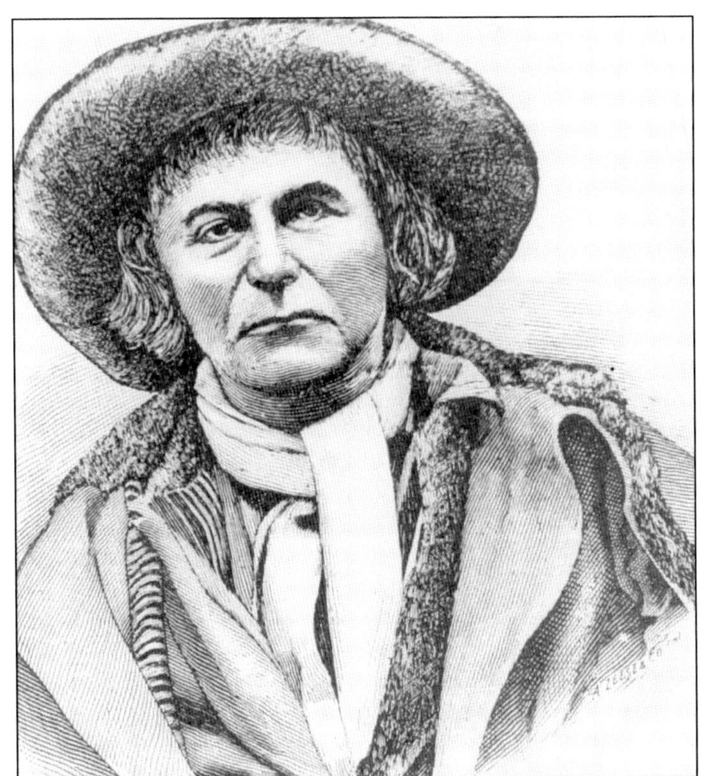

Richens Lacey Wootton ("Uncle Dick"). When he was 19, Wootton joined a wagon train owned by Bent, St. Vrain, and Company. Over the next six decades, he found work as a trader, trapper, buffalo hunter, frontier guide, military scout, rancher, and toll road builder. In 1853, he settled near El Pueblo on the Arkansas River, where he raised cattle and continued to trade with Plains Indians. (PCCLD, no. Ph-B-475-02_003.)

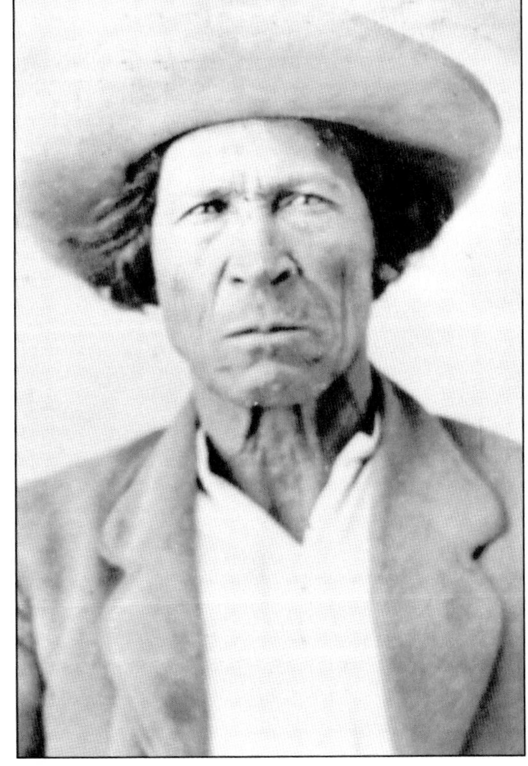

Charles Autobees. Prior to the Mexican-American War, Autobees hauled whiskey from Simeon Turley's distillery 10 miles north of Taos to trading posts along the Trappers' Trail. In 1856, he started a settlement known as Autobees Plaza at the junction of the Arkansas and Huerfano Rivers. In 1868, he added a ferry service across the Arkansas and a saloon that became popular with the soldiers stationed nearby at Fort Reynolds. (PCHS.)

Joseph Bainbridge Doyle. In the 1840s, Doyle was one of the builders of Fort Pueblo. During the 1859 gold rush, he freighted wagons of food, clothing, and supplies to Denver City. The profits he made hauling freight allowed him to enlarge his farm and increase his herd to nearly a thousand cattle. Doyle was elected a Huerfano County commissioner in 1861 and a territorial legislator in 1864. (PCCLD, no. Ph-B-127-01_001.)

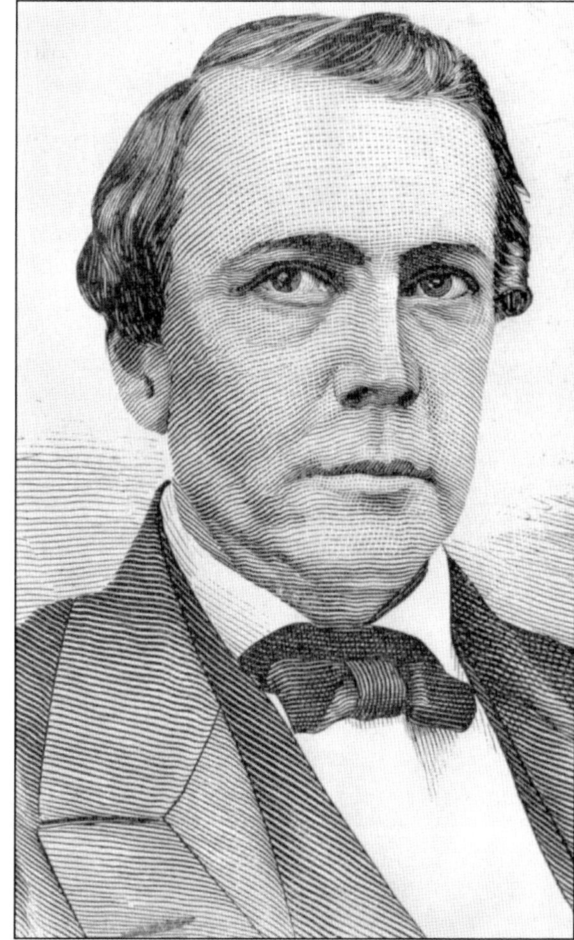

Casa Blanca, Erected c. 1860, Burned 1942. At his settlement on the Huerfano, Doyle built a two-story home where he lived with his children and his wife, Maria de la Cruz "Cruzita" Suaso. The house lumber was shipped in by wagon from Kansas City. When he died of a heart attack in 1864 at the age of 46, Doyle was considered the richest man in the Colorado Territory. (PCHS.)

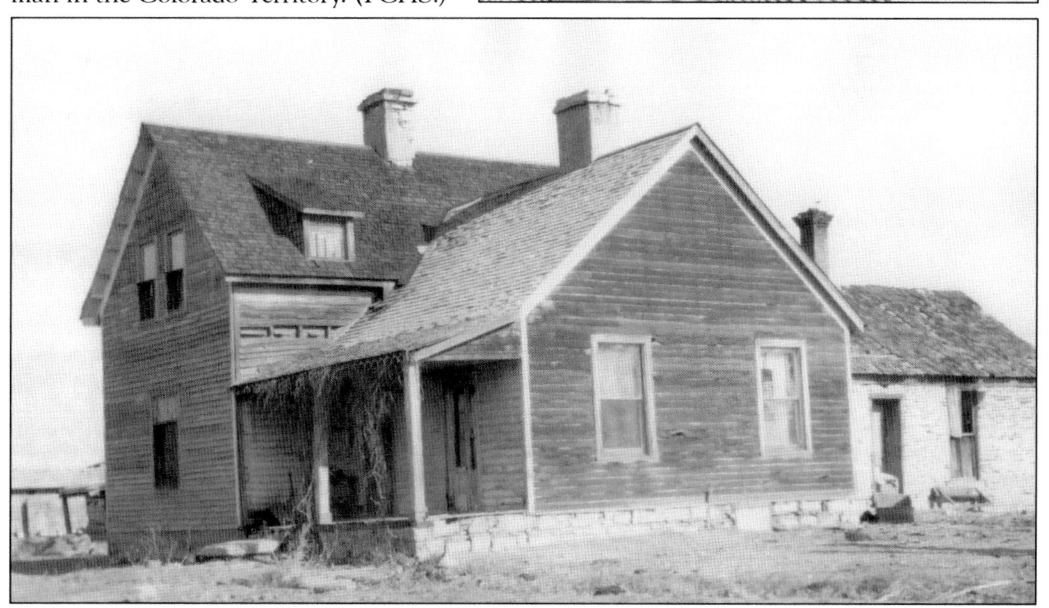

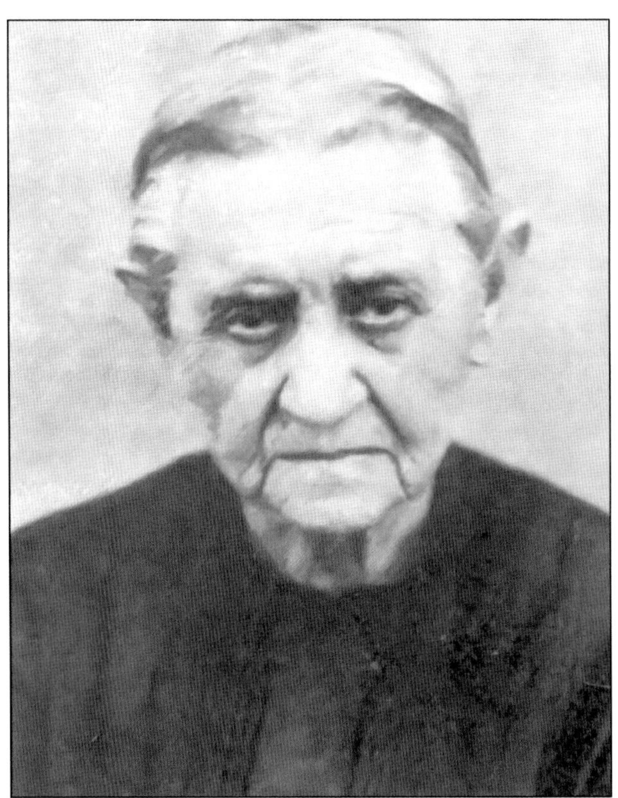

Estafana Bent Hicklin. Her father, Charles Bent, had served as the first territorial governor of New Mexico under US rule, but in January 1847, Governor Bent was killed in Taos by insurgents rebelling against the new territorial government. Three-year-old Estafana witnessed her father's violent death. Life was hard on the frontier. Estafana married Alexander "Zan" Hicklin at age 13 and bore her first child at 16. (PCCLD, no. Ph-B-200-01_001.)

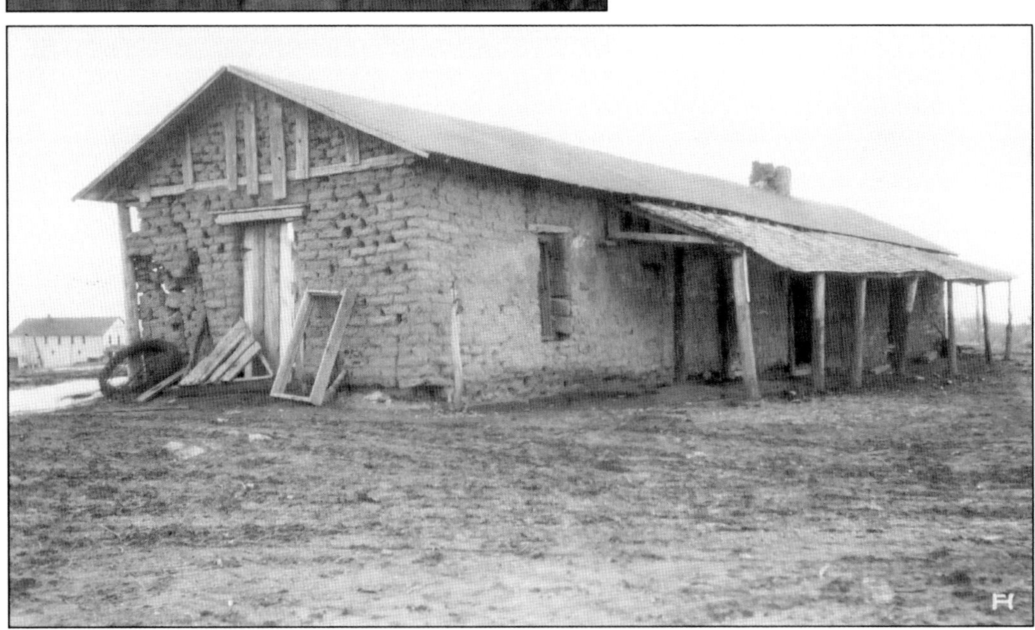

Hicklin's Adobe Home. In September 1859, the Hicklins moved into Colorado's Greenhorn Valley to settle on the Vigil–St. Vrain Mexican Land Grant. Estafana, Zan, and their growing family then lived in this four-room adobe home as they strove to expand their livestock herds and increase their grain harvests. In 1874, Zan contracted pneumonia and died. Estafana struggled to keep his holdings intact but eventually lost this battle. (PCCLD, no. Ph-C-199-01_003.)

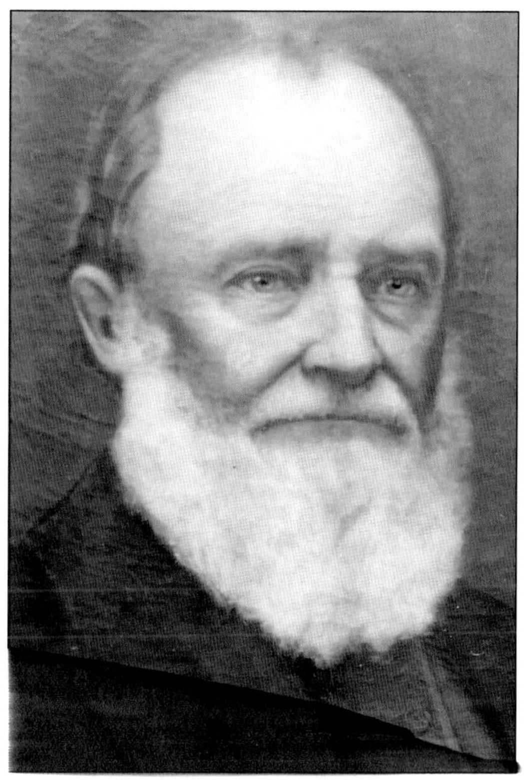

ALBERT GALLATIN BOONE. The town of Boone was founded as Booneville during the Pike's Peak Gold Rush by Albert Gallatin Boone. He was the grandson of Daniel Boone. In 1860, President Buchanan appointed Boone to draft a treaty with the Cheyenne and Arapahoe. Boone also worked for President Grant to draft treaties with the Kiowa, Comanche, Cheyenne, and Sioux tribes. (PCCLD, no. Ph-B-51-02_001.)

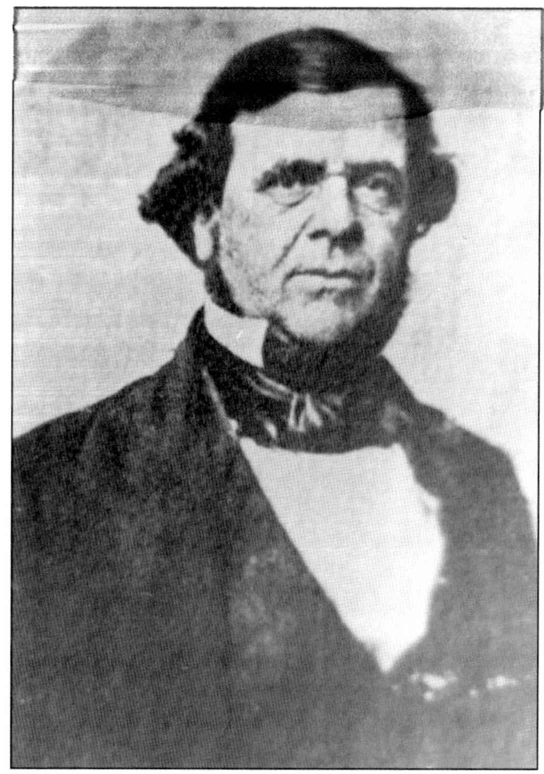

CERAN DE HAULT DE LASSUS DE ST. VRAIN (CERAN ST. VRAIN). After Charles Bent was scalped alive and murdered in his own home, St. Vrain helped to avenge his business partner's death during the Siege of Pueblo de Taos. St. Vrain dissolved his partnership with William Bent in 1850, but he continued to diversify his other business interests until his death in 1870. (PCCLD, no. Ph-B-409-01_001.)

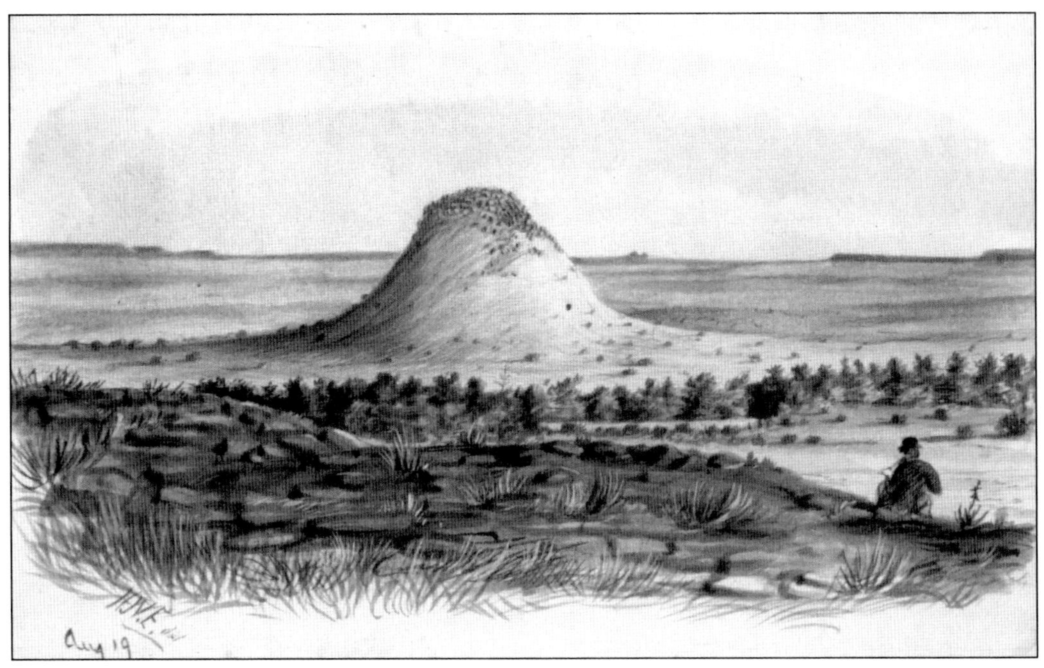

HUERFANO BUTTE. Ceran St. Vrain moved his son Felix to the Huerfano Butte area in 1865. Near this same location, St. Vrain employees operated a stage station and a general store. Five miles upriver stood the settlement of St. Mary's Plaza. Henry T. Sefton built a store, hotel, and blacksmith shop here in the late 1860s. Next door to St. Mary's was Patterson's Plaza, a community named after Joseph Decatur "Kate" Patterson. Patterson had been with the William Green Russell party when gold was discovered in 1858. After the Civil War, Patterson and Russell worked together to bring hundreds of displaced Southerners into Huerfano County. The image above, Henry W. Elliott's sketch of Huerfano Butte, was created on August 19, 1869, during the Hayden Expedition. The photograph below shows Huerfano Butte as it looks today. (Above, USGS.)

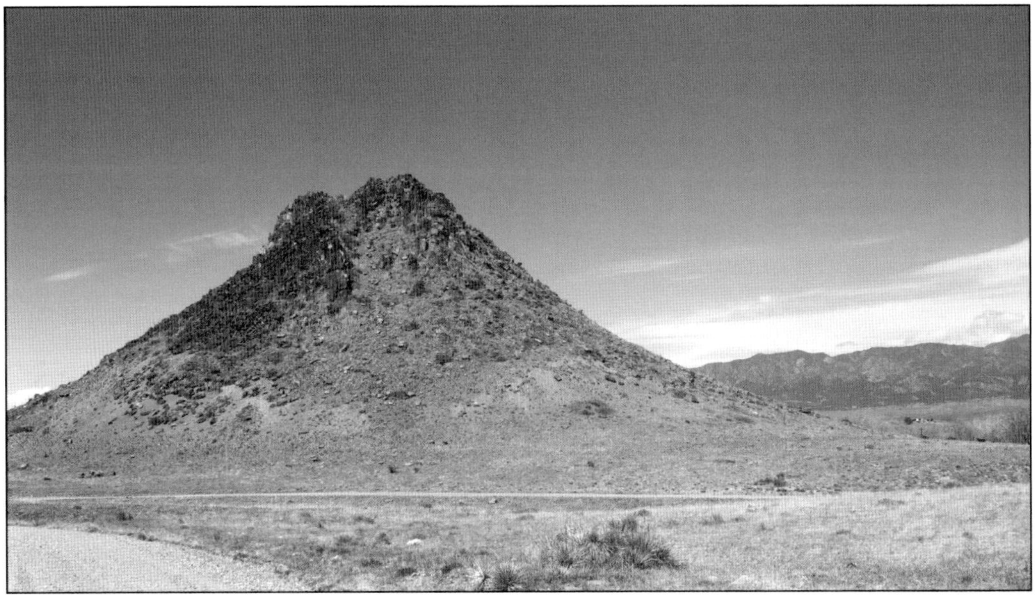

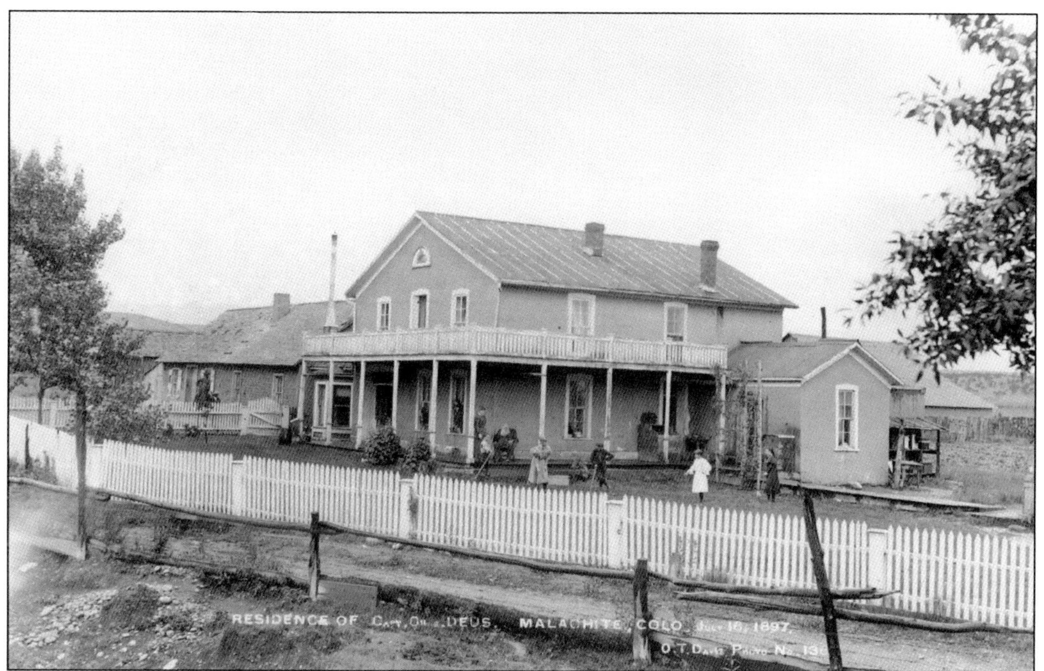

Residence of Capt. Richard Charles Deus, 1897. In this photograph, taken by O.T. Davis, Captain Deus sits on the first-floor porch of his 10-room adobe home while children play croquet in the yard. In 1870, Captain Deus and William Thomas Sharp established the settlement of Malachite. The town was named after a copper-laden ore found on Pass Creek. (DPL, no. X-12261.)

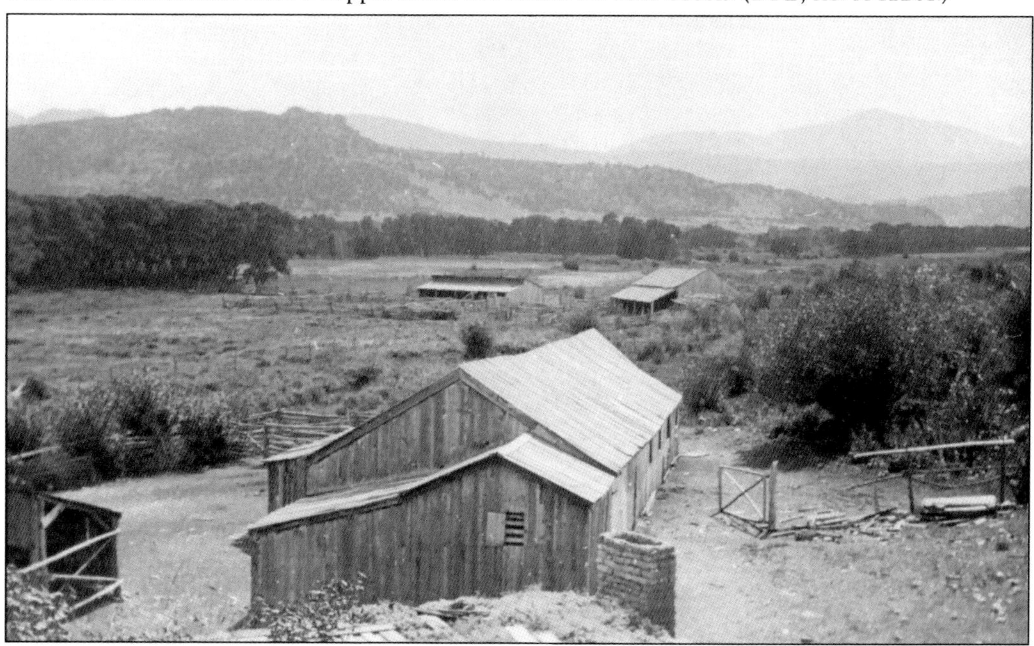

Pass Creek Trading Post. These barns and outbuildings lay at the foot of Mosca Pass on the Old Ute Trail. The site is near William Thomas Sharp's Trading Post, where Chief Ouray used to come in the 1860s to exchange his tanned hides for coveted trade goods. A stamp mill for refining copper was built near the trading post. (PCCLD, no. Ph-C-400-02_001.)

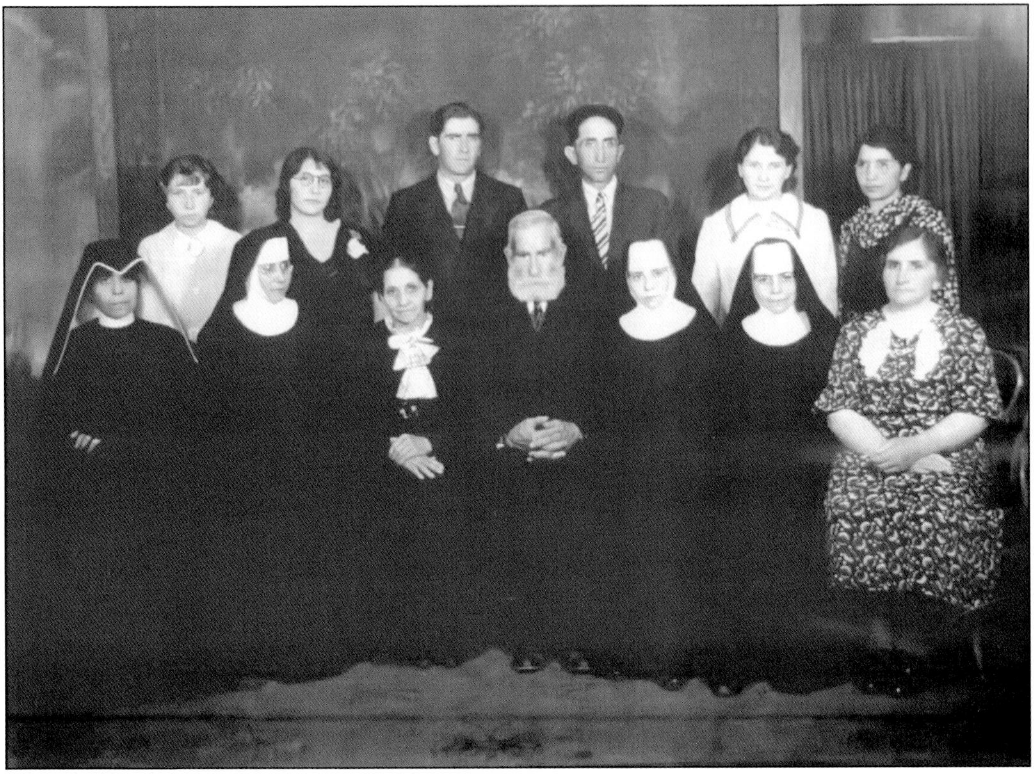

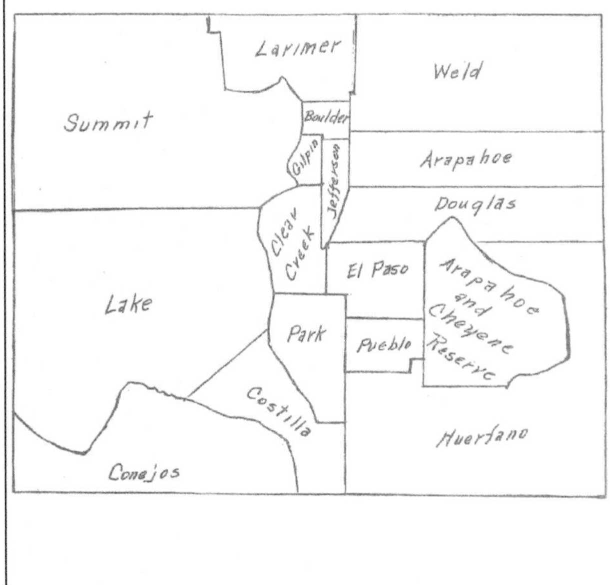

Garcia Family and Colorado Territorial Map. Pedro Jose Garcia and his wife, Gabriela, were still spending winters in Los Lentes, New Mexico, when their son Catedra was born on January 18, 1863. The family moved permanently onto the upper Huerfano in 1866, where they helped to establish Fort Talpa (an early settlement also known as Huerfano Canon and renamed Farisita in 1923). The Garcia ditch, which boasts one of the first water rights in the state of Colorado, was appropriated in 1867. Above, Catedra and his wife, Manuelita, are surrounded by some of their 14 children. The photograph was taken shortly before Catedra's death in May 1941. The map at left shows the 17 Colorado counties in existence at the time of Catedra's birth. (Above, Ray and Alfred Garcia, great-grandsons of Catedra and Manuelita.)

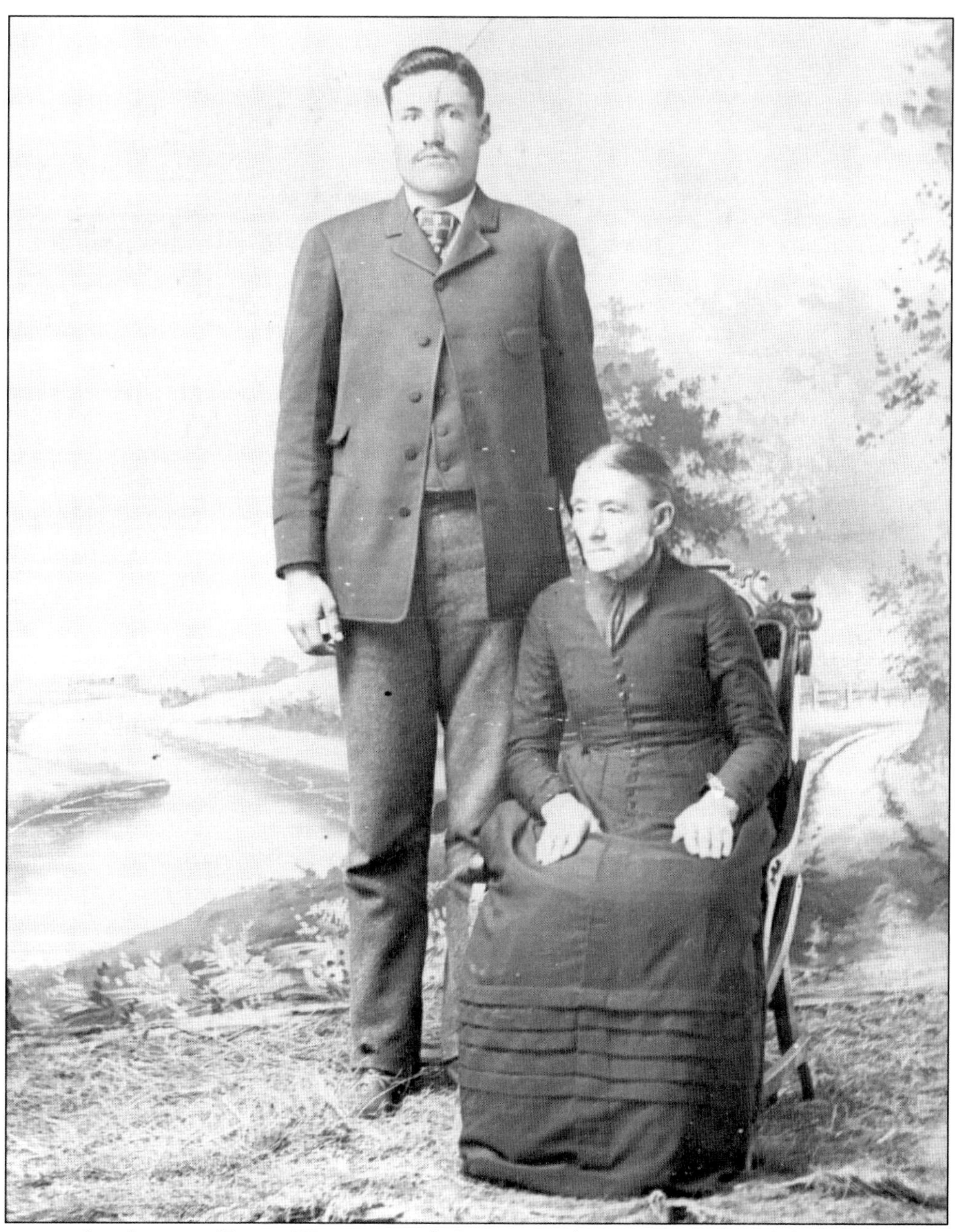

PLAZA DE LOS LEONES (EARLY WALSENBURG). Don Miguel Antonio Leon and the Atencio family founded this Hispanic settlement on the north side of the Cucharas River in the late 1850s. They laid out the lots using the Spanish *acequia* (irrigation ditch) system of subdividing the land. The lots (*tiras*) were long and angled so that each family in the village got a strip of good land by the river and drier land farther away from the river. The emphasis was on "fair" and "functional." "Fair" meant each family was assured river access for growing crops and watering livestock. "Functional" meant that each of the long, narrow lots had to be oriented downhill for good irrigation flow, because irrigation was vital for growing crops in an arid climate. In this photograph, Rumalda Martinez Atencio, wife of one of the settlement's cofounders, rests in a chair while her nephew stands beside her. (PCCLD, no. Ph-C-400-08_010.)

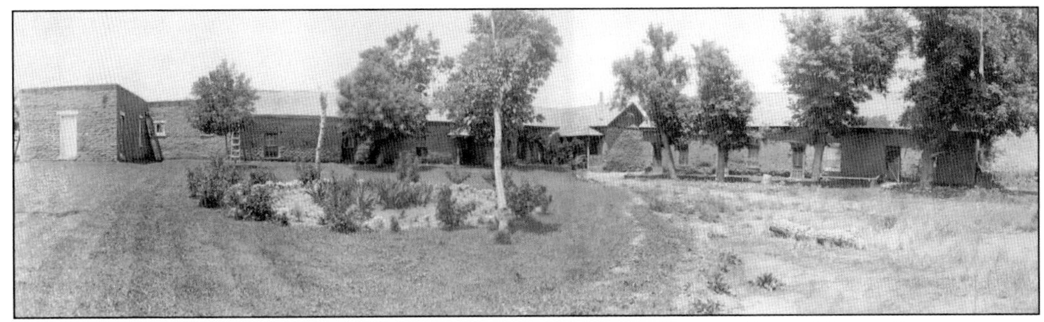

Francisco Fort, c. 1930. Col. John M. Francisco and his partner, Judge Henry Daigre, began building Francisco Fort in the 1860s on land purchased from the Vigil–St. Vrain Land Grant for $37,710. To pay for the land, they contracted to supply the Denver mining camps with cattle, sheep, hogs, flour, barley hay, beans, and other vegetables. (HCHS/FFM.)

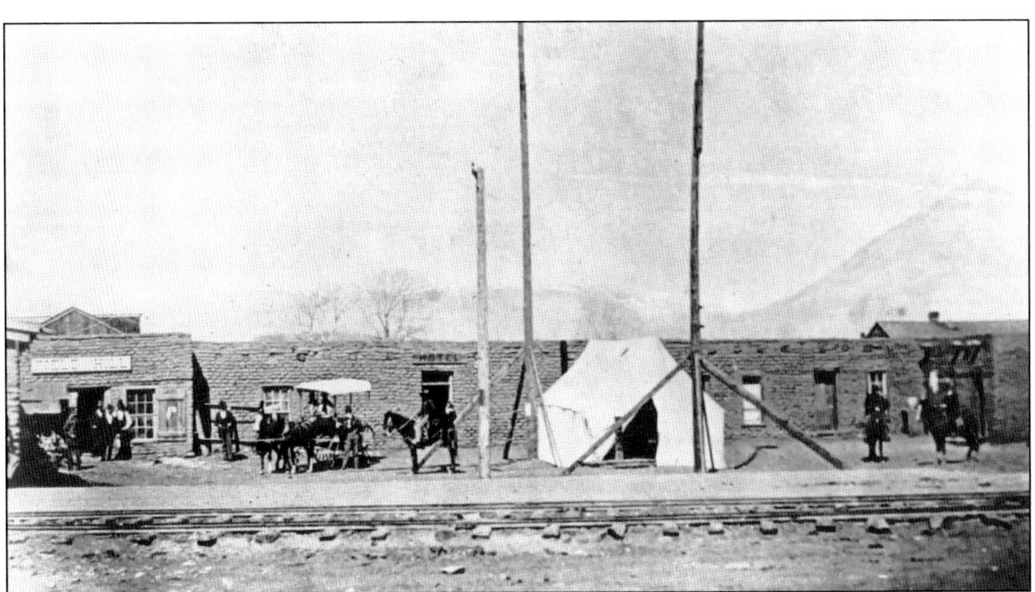

Francisco Fort, 1876. The Denver & Rio Grande Railway Company platted the town of La Veta and built a narrow-gauge railroad to it in 1876. At the time, the tracks passed directly in front of the fort. Currently the Francisco Fort Museum holds a variety of exhibits, including a country store, one-room schoolhouse, saloon, blacksmith shop, doctor's office, gun collection, and many Native American artifacts. (HCHS/FFM.)

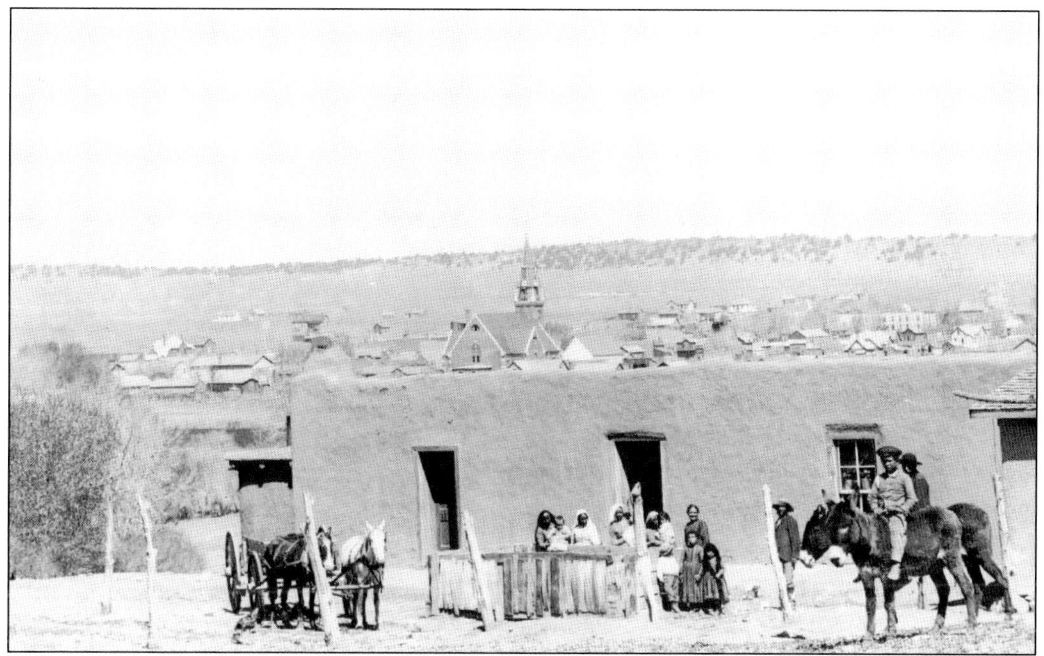

MEXICAN HOME NEAR WALSENBURG, 1889. Some of the first settlers to come searching for fertile soil and future prosperity moved to Huerfano County from the San Luis Valley or from Mora County, New Mexico. This photograph features one of those homes. It was constructed of adobe and topped with a dirt-covered roof. (MVHS/O.T. Davis Collection.)

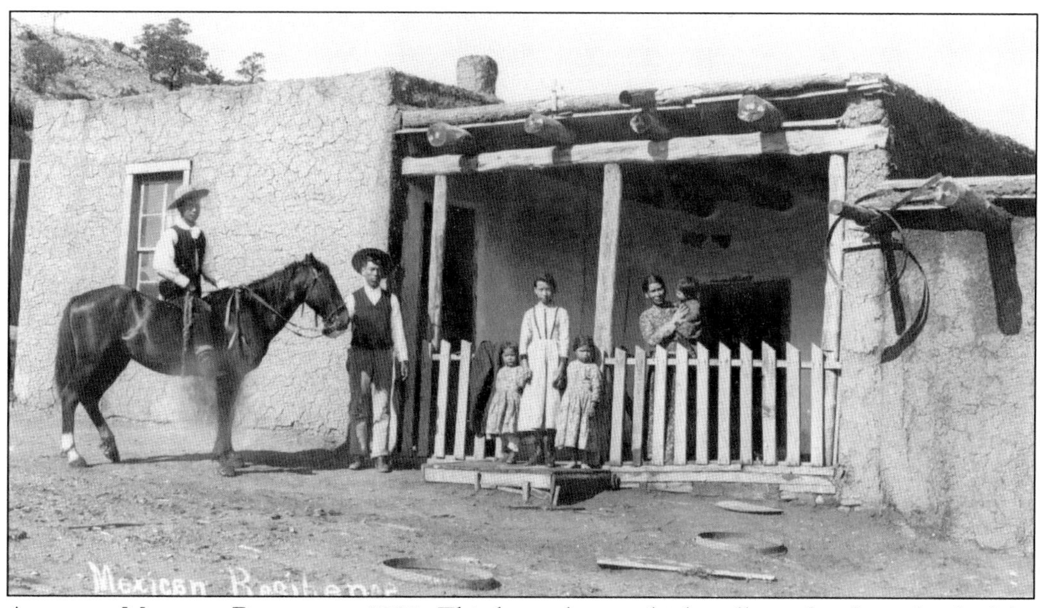

ANOTHER MEXICAN RESIDENCE, 1881. This home boasts thick walls made of sun-dried adobe bricks, log roof beams called *vigas*, aspen or cedar laths called *latillas*, and horizontal timber supports that serve as wooden lintels. The headers over the windows, doorways, and porch opening are examples of lintels typifying this style of architecture. (MVHS/O.T. Davis Collection.)

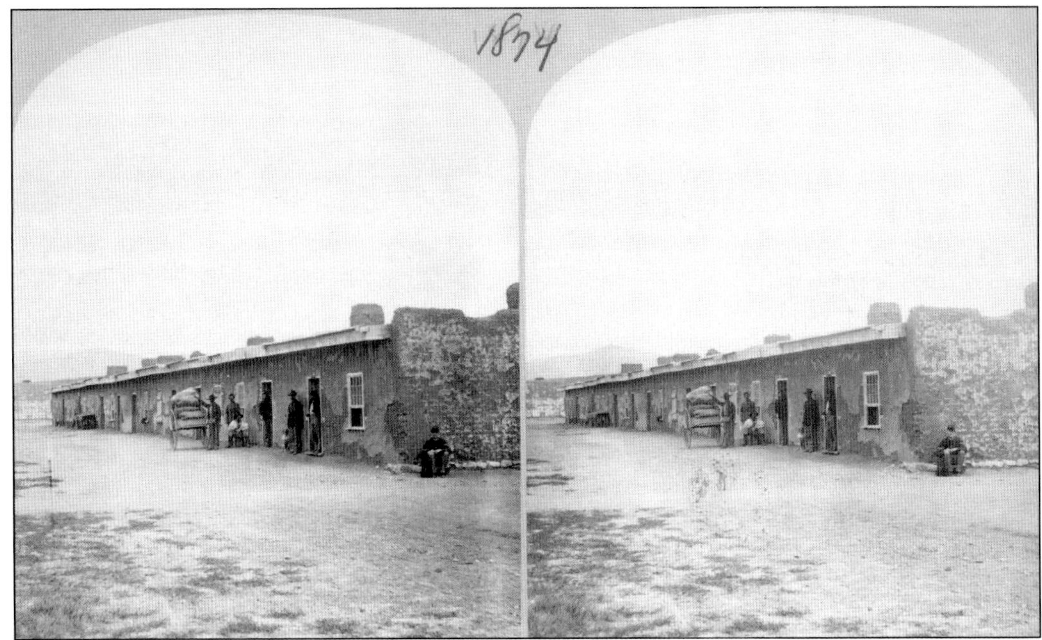

Fort Garland, 1874. To protect travelers coming over Sangre de Cristo Pass and settlers moving into the San Luis Valley, the US Army built Fort Massachusetts along Ute Creek at the base of Mount Blanca. Unfortunately, this fortress was badly placed, both for defense of its own garrison and for defense of the new settlements. Six years later, in 1858, the Army constructed a new stronghold six miles south of the old one and named it Fort Garland. (LOC/Timothy H. O'Sullivan Collection)

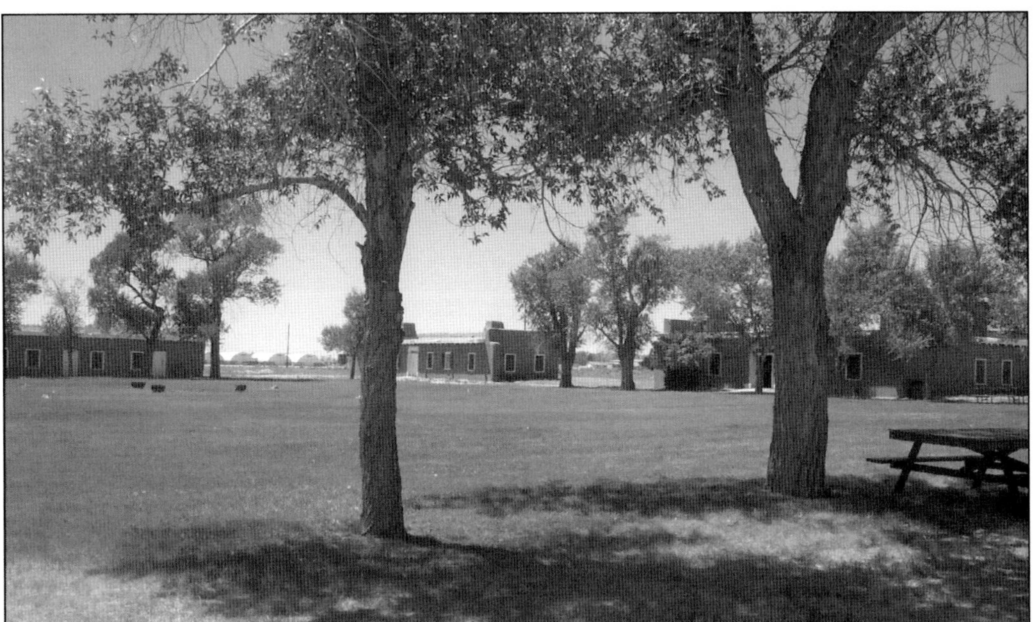

Fort Garland, 2003. This sprawling adobe post could accommodate as many as seven officers and two companies of soldiers. It remained in operation from 1858 to 1883. The Colorado Historical Society restored many of the buildings and opened the Fort Garland Museum in 1950.

Four

Surveyors and Railroaders

The country's first transcontinental railroad was completed on May 10, 1869. It routed east from San Francisco along the 42nd parallel, through Promontory, Utah; Cheyenne, Wyoming; and Council Bluffs, Iowa, bypassing Colorado altogether. With assistance from East Coast investors, Denver citizens financed the Denver Pacific Railroad, a branch line connecting Cheyenne to Denver. It reached the Mile-High City on June 24, 1870.

During the following year, William J. Palmer founded the Denver & Rio Grande Railroad. By October, his company had managed to lay three-foot-wide, narrow-gauge track southward from Denver to the new town of Colorado Springs. The first coal-driven steam engines on Palmer's rail line chugged along at an average pace of 15 miles per hour. Even so, this new mode of transportation was faster than a stagecoach. D&RG passengers could leave Denver at 7:30 a.m., eat lunch in Colorado Springs, and return to Denver by 6:30 p.m., just in time for dinner.

Palmer extended his railroad 50 miles south to Pueblo in 1872. Then the economic panic of 1873 hit hard, drastically slowing railroad construction. After inaugurating an intensive publicity effort to gain new stockholders, Palmer finally accumulated sufficient funds to build into Huerfano County. The 50-mile segment from Pueblo to Old Cucharas was completed on February 22, 1875.

Within the next three months, Palmer's workers built westward six miles to the 17-year-old settlement of Plaza de Los Leones, which had been renamed Walsenburg in honor of the German-born entrepreneur Fred Walsen. By then, Walsenburg's founding fathers had agreed to deed to the railroad half of all town lots in exchange for a downtown depot and side railing from the main track to the depot.

Palmer's employees finished the line to La Veta in July 1876 and in November began laying track up the eastern slope of the Sangre de Cristo Mountain Range to the top of La Veta Pass. The stretch at Mule Shoe Curve proved particularly challenging, as the tracks ascended Dump Mountain by way of two sharp hairpin curves that appeared both thrilling and dangerous to passengers on board.

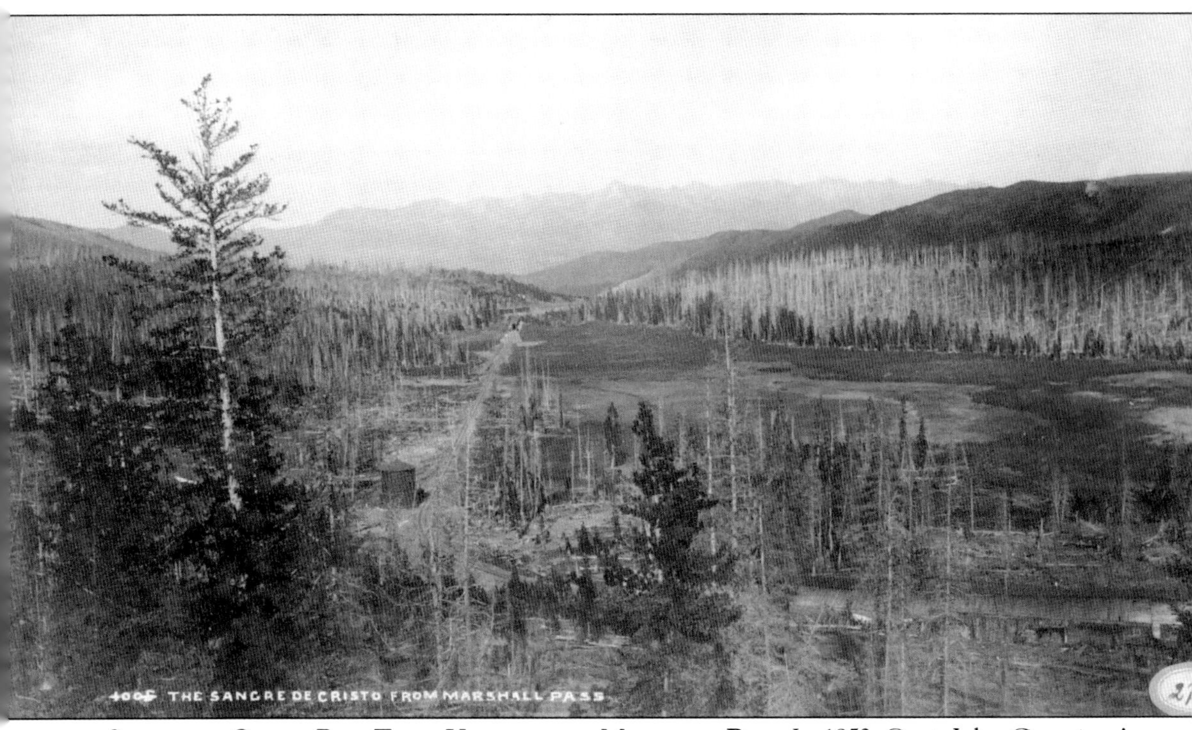

Sangre de Cristo Pass Trail Viewed from Marshall Pass. In 1853, Capt. John Gunnison's expedition entered the Rocky Mountains via the Huerfano River. Gunnison then built a wagon road over Sangre de Cristo Pass, crossed the San Juans at Cochetopa Pass, and continued west into central Utah, where he was attacked and killed by a band of Pahvant Utes. Four months later, John C. Fremont followed approximately the same route on his fifth and final expedition through the Rocky Mountains and the Sierra Nevada. Fremont's exploration party finally reached San Francisco on April 16, 1854. Despite the tremendous efforts of both Gunnison and Fremont, the first continental rail line was not built along the 38th parallel. This photograph of the trail over Sangre de Cristo Pass was taken by W.H. Jackson sometime between 1882 and 1890. (DPL, no. WHJ-465.)

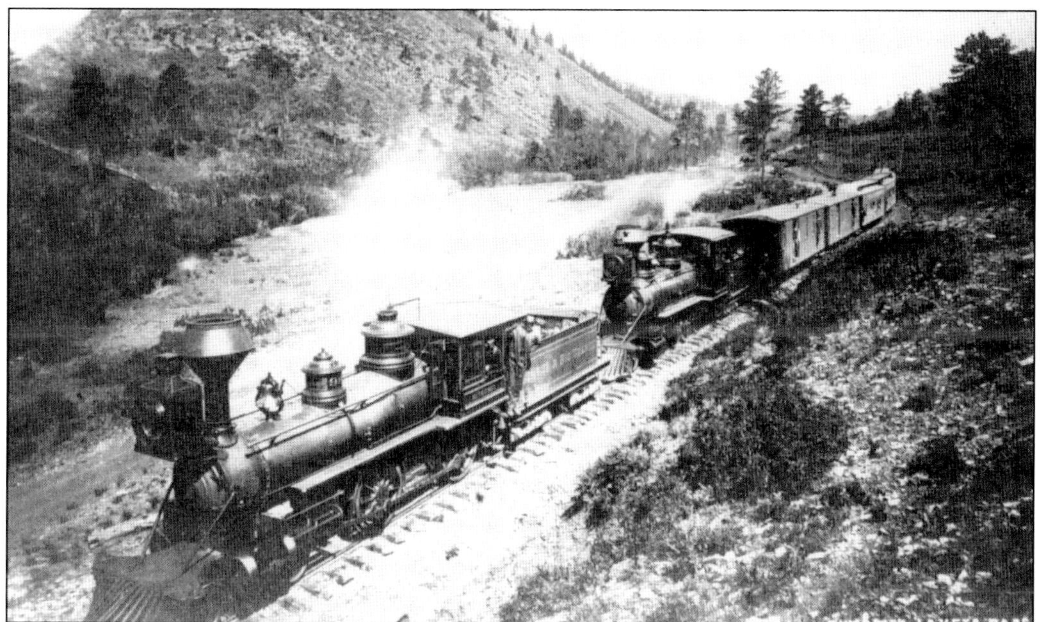

The D&RG on La Veta Pass, c. 1880. Locomotives No. 99 and 46 descend Veta Pass below Dump Mountain, eastbound toward Walsenburg. Both William Henry Jackson and L.L. McClure have been given credit for this photograph, but it was probably taken by O.T. Davis. In fact, it is part of the O.T. Davis Collection, housed at the Monte Vista Historical Society building at 111 Jefferson Street in Monte Vista. (MVHS/O.T. Davis Collection.)

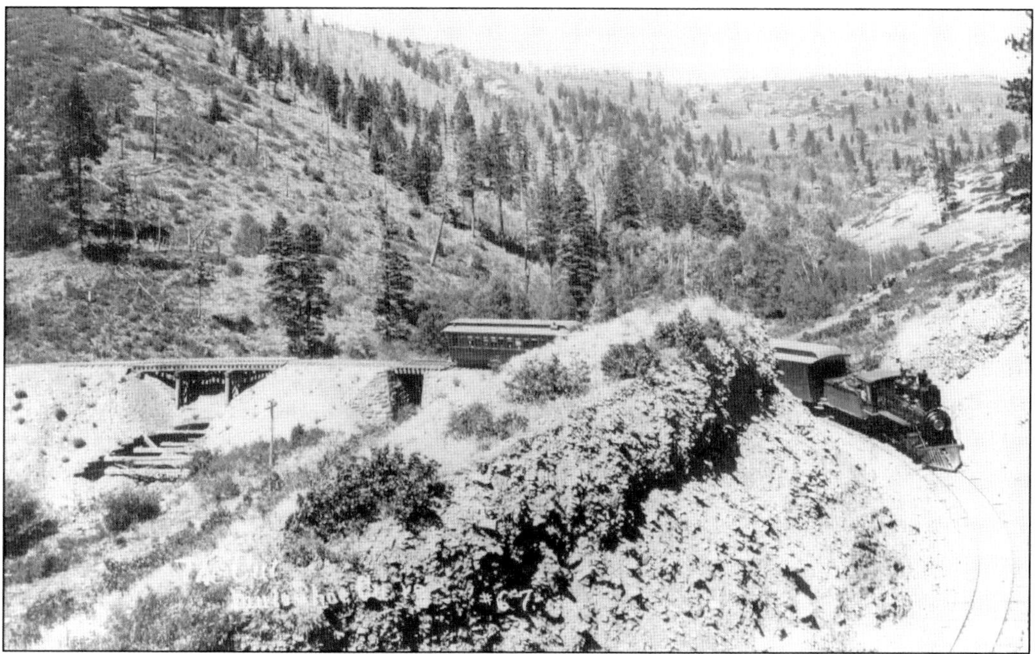

D&RG Passenger Train on Mule Shoe Curve, 1887. This dangerous curve reversed direction almost 180 degrees as it crossed over the Baldy Scott Toll Road. West of the curve, the tracks climbed Dump Mountain at a very steep grade to reach the pass summit, which boasted an altitude of 9,382 feet above sea level. (MVHS/O.T. Davis Collection.)

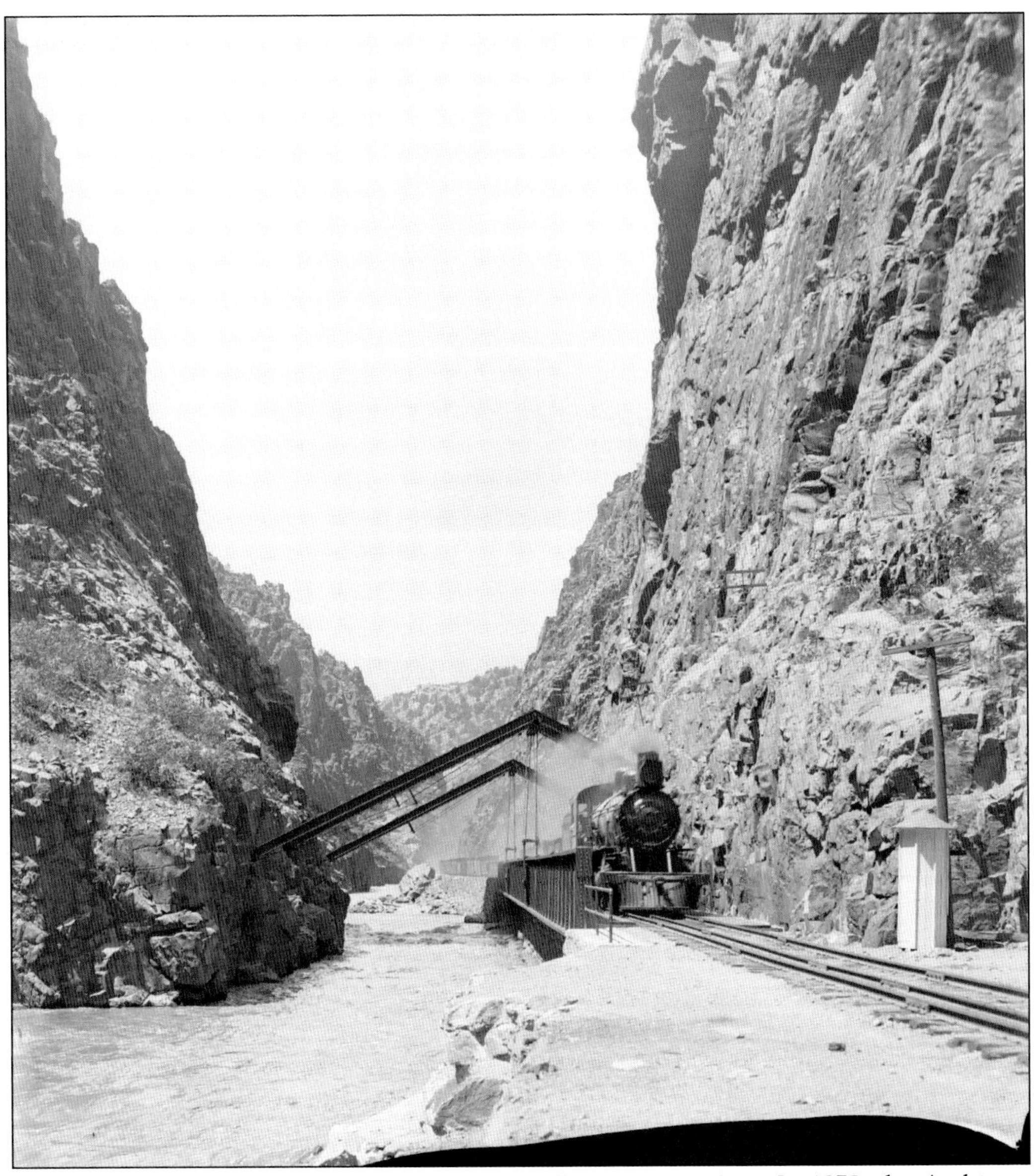

In the Royal Gorge, Rio Grande Southern Railway, c. 1900. In 1878, the Atchison, Topeka & Santa Fe Railroad (AT&SF) obtained a court injunction prohibiting the D&RG from building into New Mexico by way of Raton Pass. Barred from constructing south on the old Mountain Branch of the Santa Fe Trail, William Palmer chose to race west into the Royal Gorge on a direct route to the silver-rich town of Leadville. Angered by this decision, AT&SF directors deployed hired guns to Cañon City, and both sides prepared for war. After a physical standoff and a prolonged battle in the courts, a settlement was finally reached in 1880. Through this agreement, the D&RG was prevented from building farther south than the town of Española, New Mexico, while its rival gave up control of the Royal Gorge and all routes heading west into Colorado's Rocky Mountains. (LOC/William Henry Jackson Collection.)

Garland City, 1877. This temporary town was a construction camp while D&RG track layers were building into the San Luis Valley. The narrow-gauge rail into Alamosa was completed on June 22, 1878. Soon afterwards, Garland City's prefabricated buildings were loaded onto a train, shipped to Alamosa, and reassembled in less than a day. (DPL, no. X-8587.)

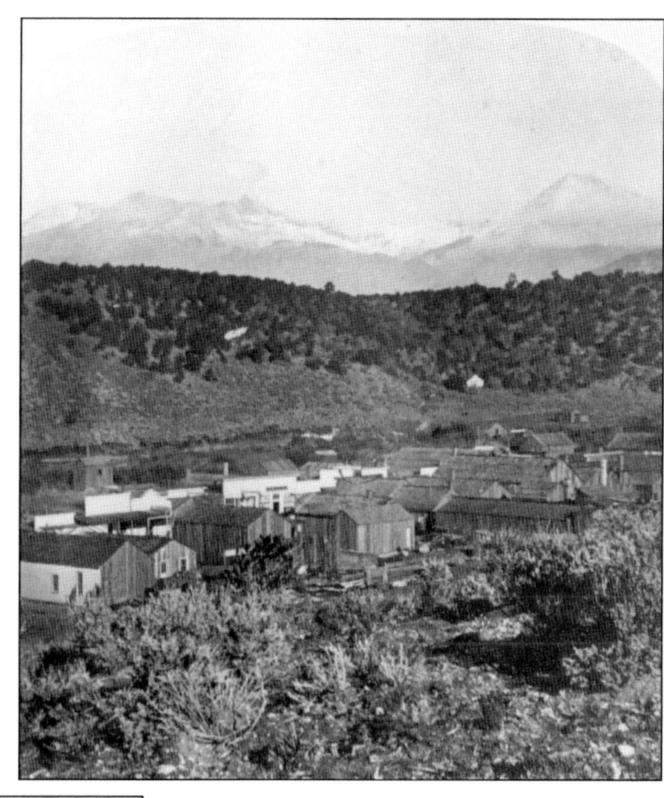

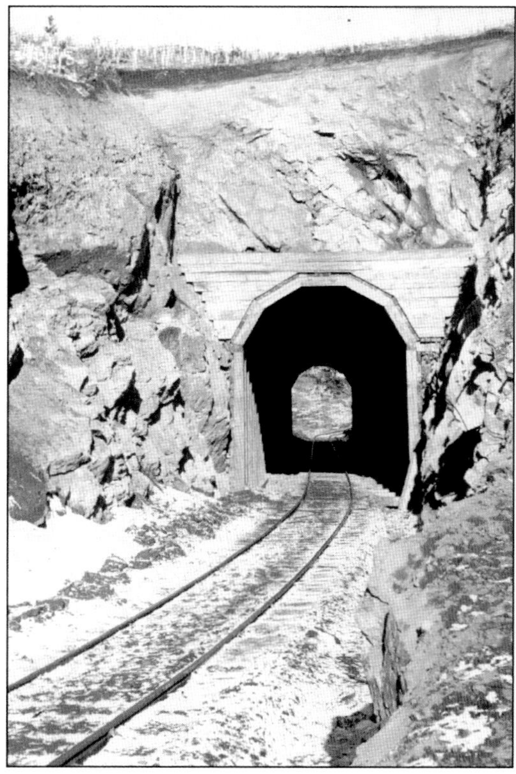

D&RG Railroad Tunnel. Standard-gauge service over South La Veta Pass was both lower in elevation and more gradual than the narrow-gauge tracks had been. The new course avoided the dangerous climb around Mule Shoe Curve and shaved a mile off the old route. (MVHS/O.T. Davis Collection.)

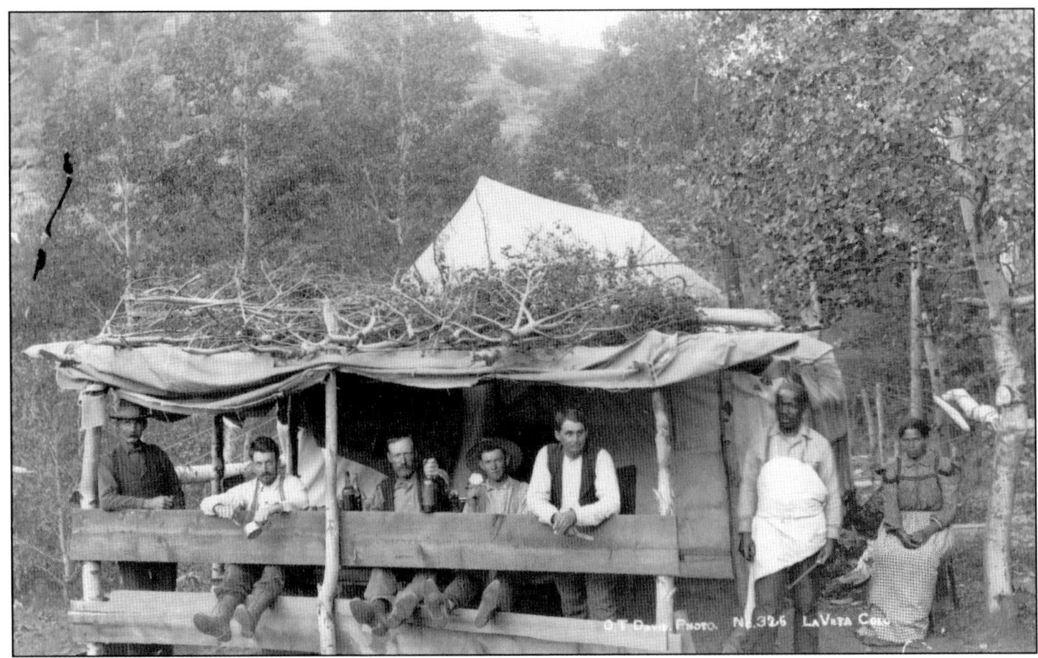

D&RG Construction Camp, 1899. During the construction of the standard-gauge track through the Huerfano and San Luis Valleys, these workers endured hard living conditions. They spent their short nights on folding cots inside canvas tents and their 16-hour days at the grueling task of pounding six-inch-long iron spikes into wooden railroad ties with a sledgehammer. (MVHS/O.T. Davis Collection.)

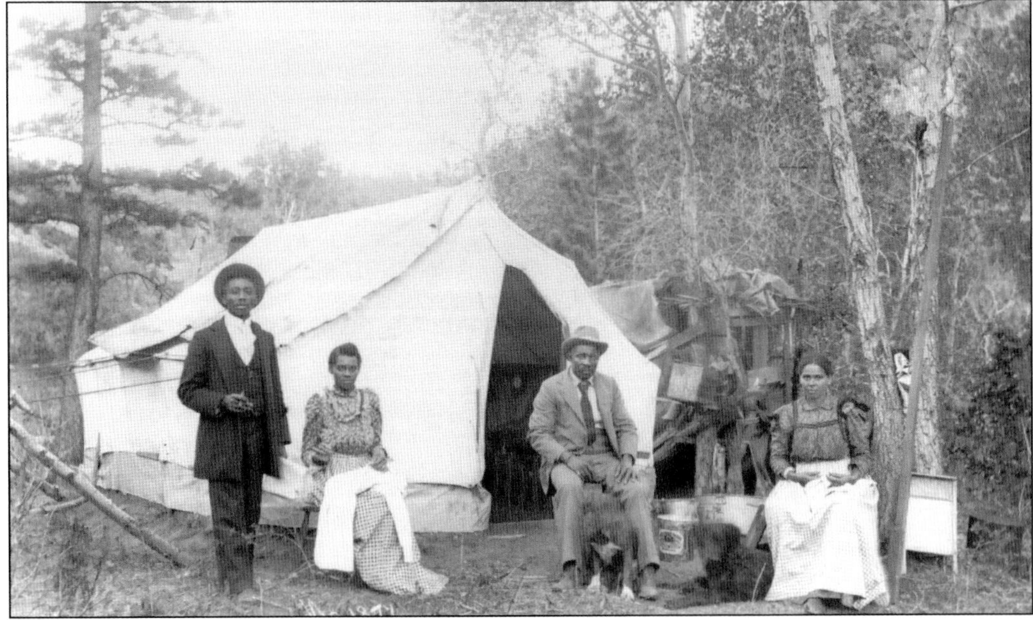

All Dressed Up, 1899. These employees posed for their picture in front of their tent living quarters on the new La Veta Pass D&RG Railway. The two women were probably hired as cooks and laundresses. Note the washtub and corrugated washboard near the woman who sits beneath the quaking aspen. (MVHS/O.T. Davis Collection.)

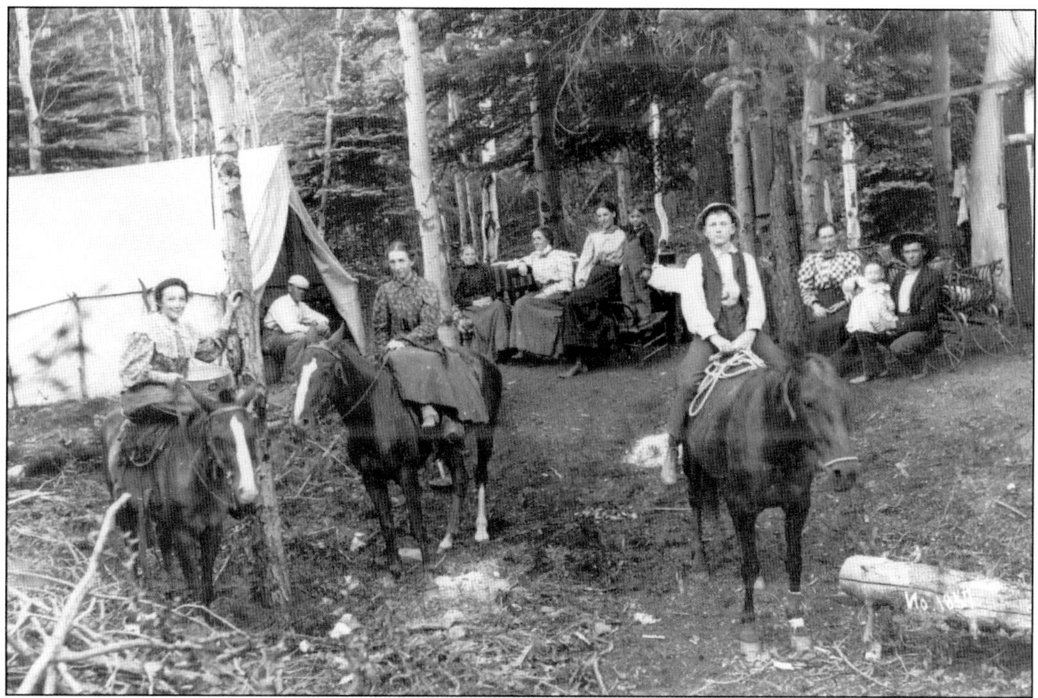

OUTING WITH FAMILIES, 1899. D&RG workers enjoyed visiting with their families during rare moments of leisure. Narrow-gauge track had been laid around Mule Shoe Curve in the 1870s, but standard-gauge construction from Walsenburg to Alamosa was not completed until 1899. The old route over La Veta Pass eventually became a gravel road. Sightseers can still drive over it and see the restored depot at the top. (MVHS/O.T. Davis Collection.)

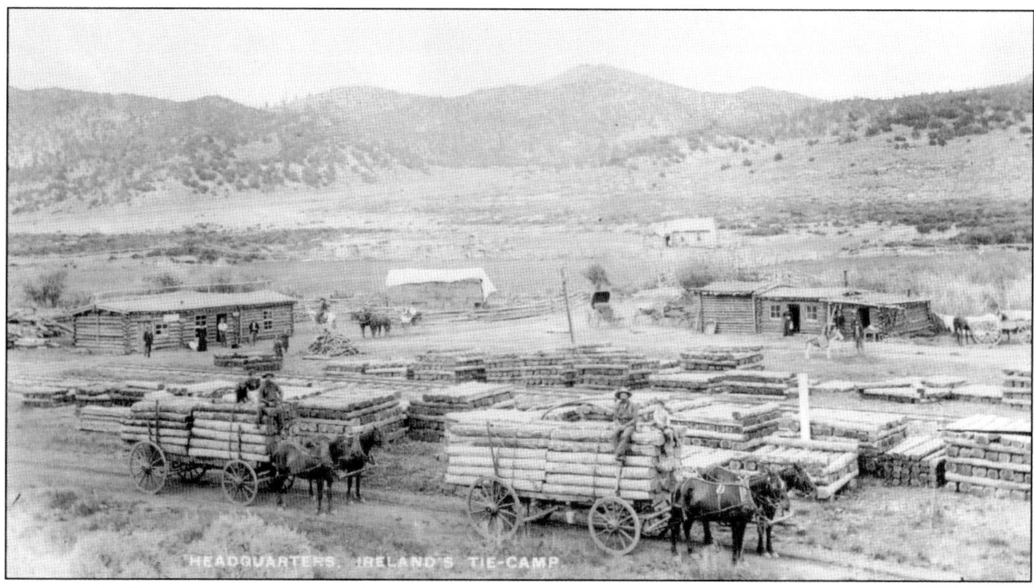

IRELAND'S TIE CAMP, C. 1910. Timber from a nearby forest was harvested for railroad ties and processed at this camp. The camp was near the former site of Garland City (six miles northeast of Fort Garland) in Costilla County. However, many Huerfano County pioneers also worked as railroad timber cutters during the last decades of the 19th century. (MVHS/O.T. Davis Collection.)

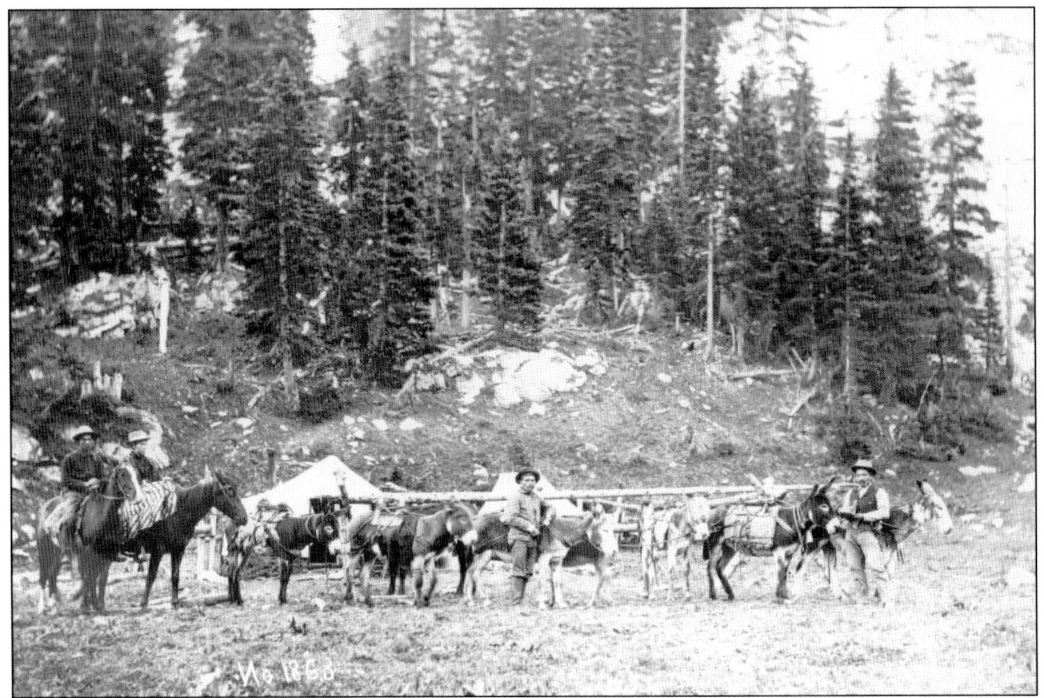

Martinez Pack Train, 1899. Pack burros brought supplies to Blanca Camp from Walsenburg while the standard-gauge line was being constructed. Perhaps the pack train followed the Baldy Scott Toll Road for part of the way, or maybe the freighters trekked up Middle Creek over Wagon Creek Pass. Light freight was also hauled across Indian Creek Pass to the south. (MVHS/O.T. Davis Collection.)

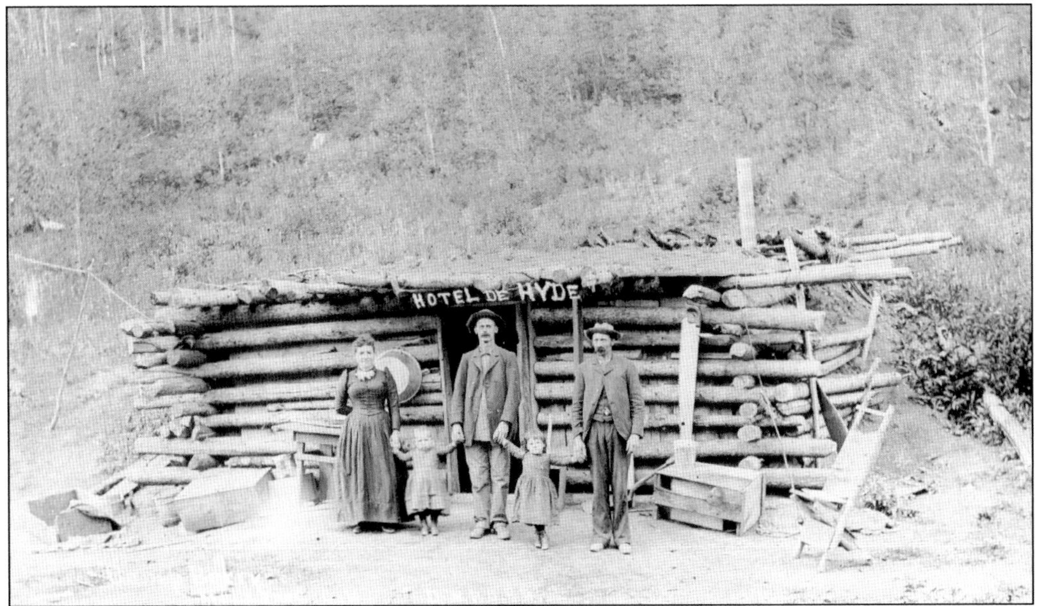

Hotel de Hyde, 1889. This rustic cabin, located at Camp Berry on Mule Shoe Curve, was not really a hostelry for railway passengers. The D&RG offered nonstop service from La Veta to Alamosa, a distance of 60 miles. (MVHS/O.T. Davis Collection.)

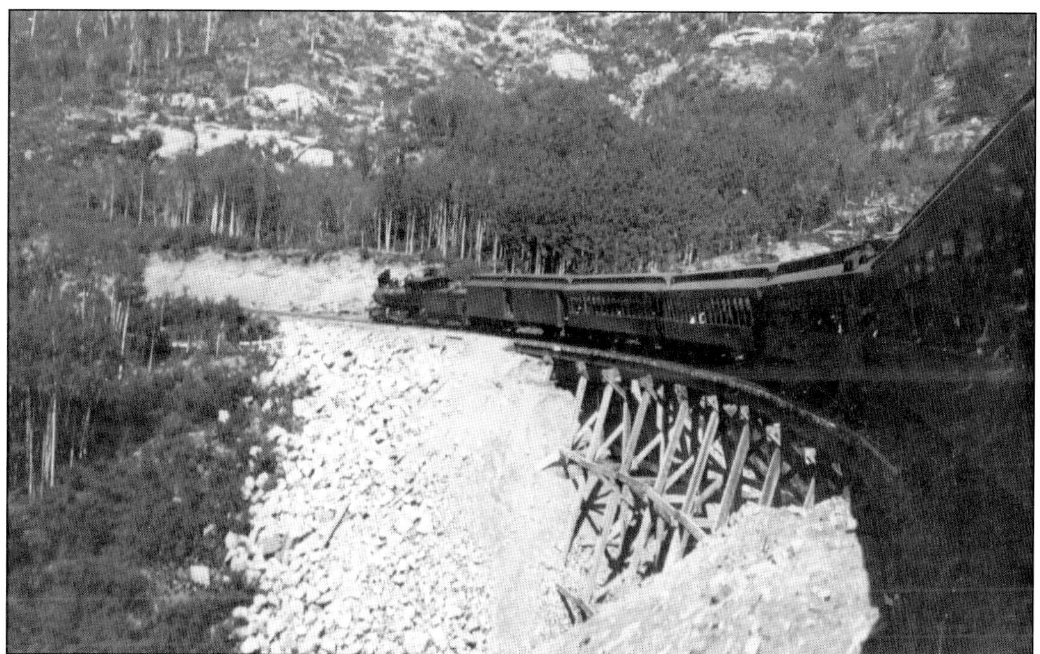

D&RG Passenger Train on the New La Veta Rail Line, c. 1900. Daytime passenger service was unusual on the standard-gauge route. Until February 1951, most of the passenger trains chugged over the pass at night. However, from December 1901 to May 1909, accommodation trains did run during daylight hours to serve local residents traveling between La Veta and Alamosa. (MVHS/O.T. Davis Collection.)

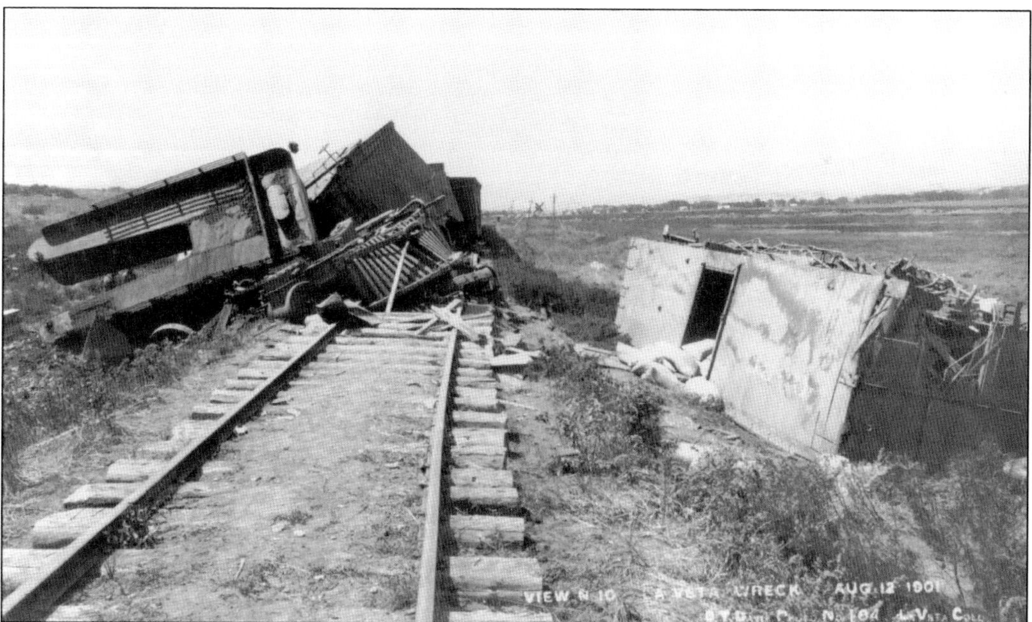

Train Wreck One Mile East of La Veta, August 12, 1901. This photograph shows the results of a wreck that happened when the boiler on the locomotive exploded. The battered cow catcher was twisted awry. An upended tender landed to the left of the cowcatcher. An overturned boxcar spilled its contents onto the ground. (MVHS/O.T. Davis Collection.)

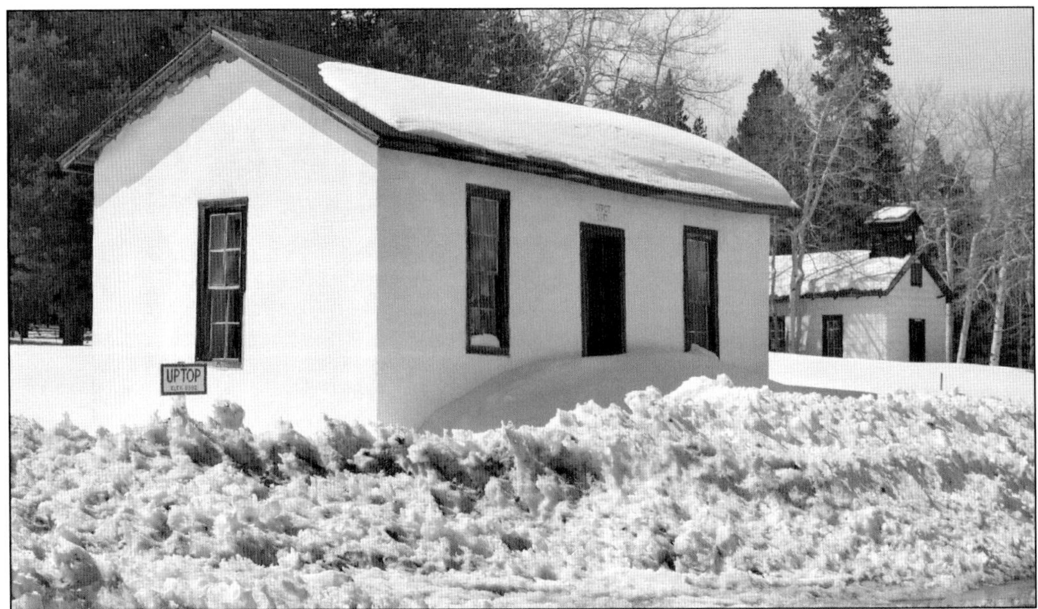

DEPOT ATOP OLD LA VETA PASS, 2015. This D&RG railroad depot was moved to its present location in 1877. It sits near the point where the summit of the narrow-gauge rail line and the crest of the Sangre de Cristo Pass Trail intersected. Winter storms in this area can be quite severe. On this sunny day in early spring, the snow still remained over three feet deep on the hillsides.

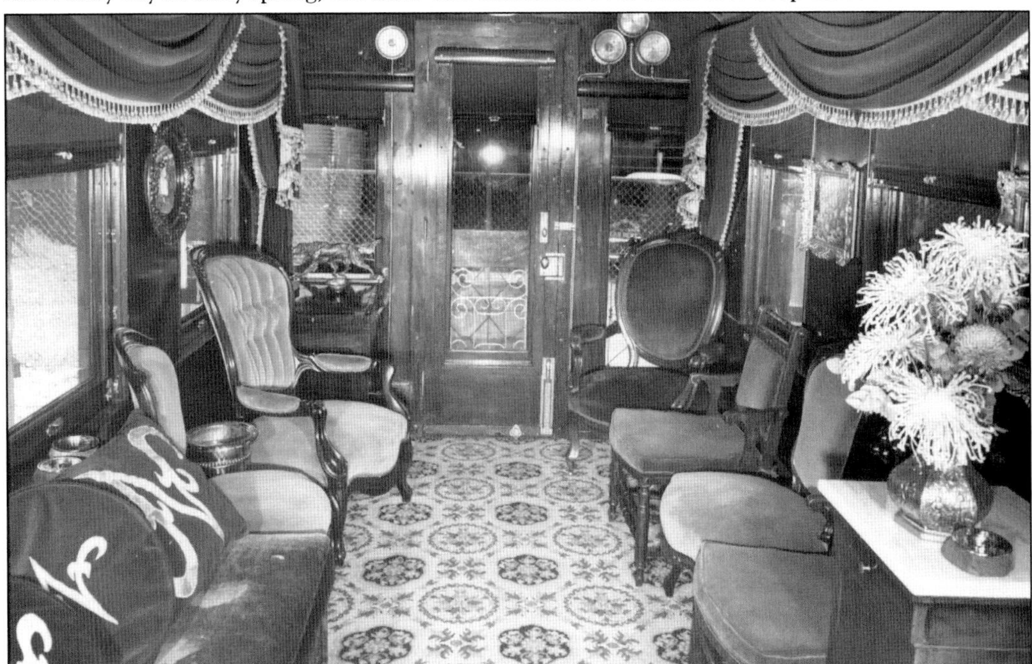

THE *Nomad*. As president of what became known as the Denver & Rio Grande Western (D&RGW), William Palmer often toured in this sleeper car. In 1901, he resigned his post and retired to his home in Colorado Springs. For the next 70 years, the D&RGW continued to be the main line through the Rockies. Today, this railroad is owned by the Union Pacific, with the exception of several branch lines that operate as heritage railways. (PCCLD, no. Ph-C-283-08_001.)

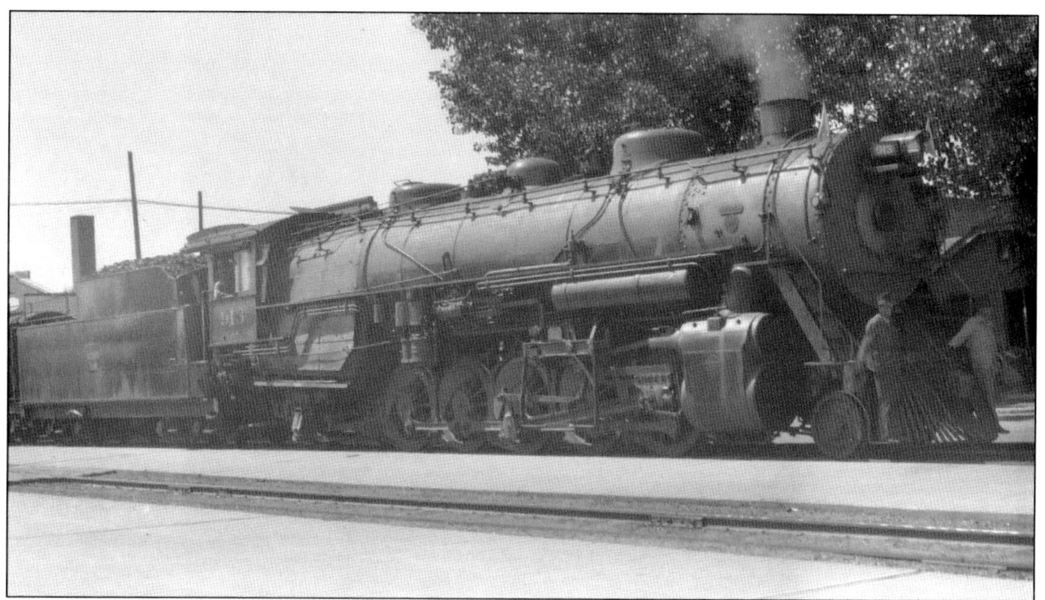

Colorado & Southern Locomotive, September 1, 1930. Colorado & Southern Railway (C&S) trains ran from Wendover, Wyoming, to Dallas, Texas, and back again. The C&S operated independently from 1898 to 1903, then as part of the Chicago, Burlington & Quincy Railroad until it was absorbed into the Burlington Northern Railroad in 1981. This three-quarter view of Engine 913 was photographed by Perry Otto in Walsenburg, Colorado. (DPL, no. OP-6751.)

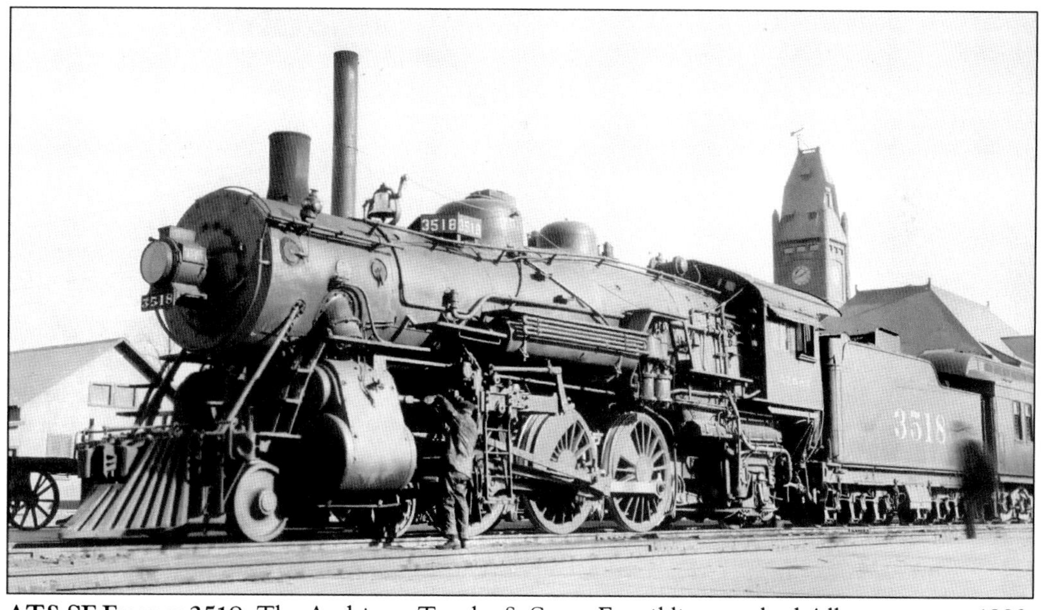

AT&SF Engine 3518. The Atchison, Topeka & Santa Fe rail line reached Albuquerque in 1880. In March 1881, this railroad connected with the Southern Pacific at Deming, New Mexico, forming the nation's second transcontinental rail route. Here, a worker inspects an AT&SF Baldwin steam locomotive at Union Depot in Pueblo, Colorado. Thomas Townsend Taber photographed the scene on January 12, 1933. (DPL, no. Z-5285.)

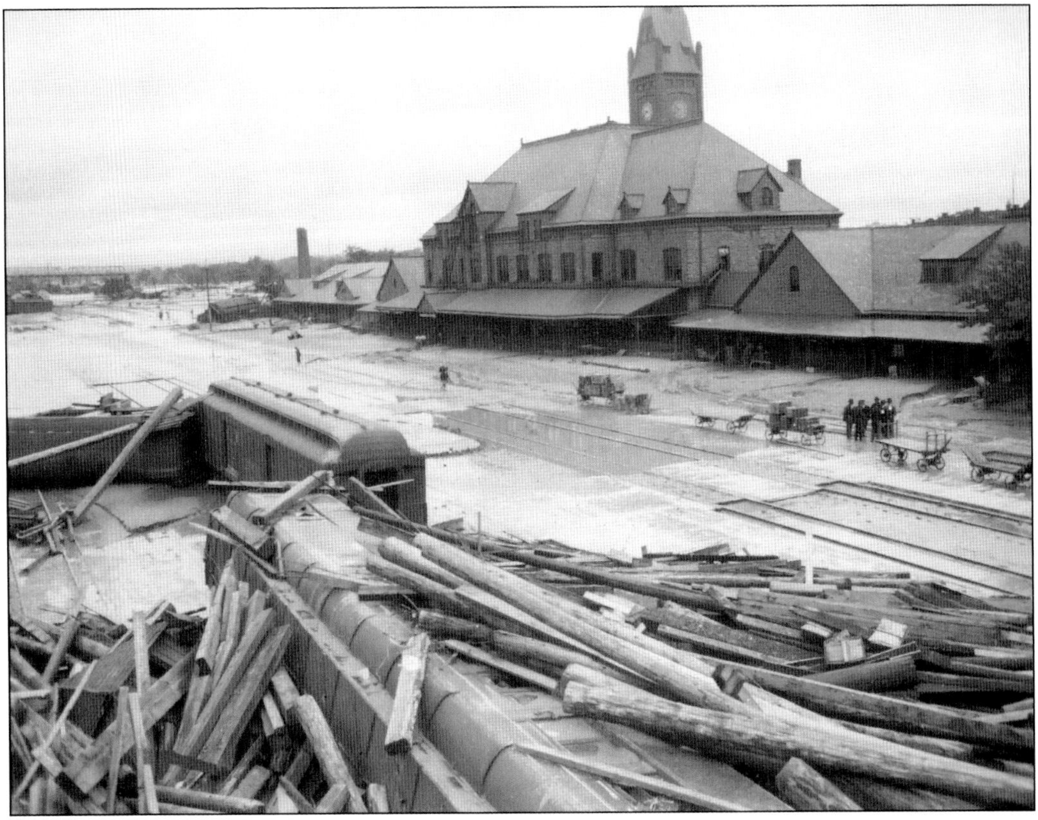

PUEBLO FLOOD, 1921. This photograph of the Pueblo Union Depot shows the aftermath of the 1921 flood. Piles of timber and beams are stacked against overturned railroad passenger cars. Mud and debris from the receded floodwaters extend all the way from the river to the railroad station platform. (DPL, no. X-10846.)

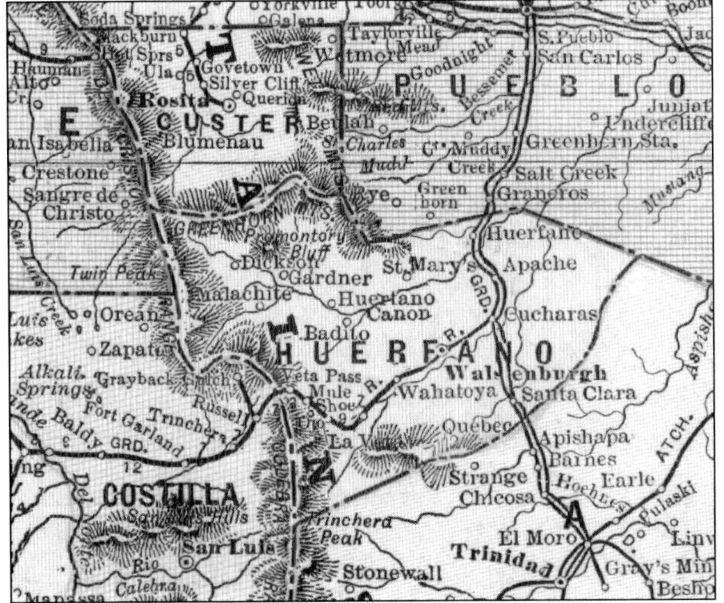

HUERFANO COUNTY ON COLORADO MAP, 1888. This railroad map shows the narrow-gauge route over old La Veta Pass through Fort Garland and beyond. It also displays many towns that existed in the 1880s but have disappeared from current maps. (DPL, Colorado Map 1888 CG4310 188a.C7.)

Five

Sheep and Cattle Ranchers

The D&RG had chosen to route through Walsenburg and La Veta instead of Badito and Gardner, thereby ignoring the ancient trail over Sangre de Cristo Pass. Settlements along the old trail immediately began to stagnate. However, livestock growers with good water rights managed to survive the change and even to prosper.

Milder weather made wintering cattle in southern Colorado a less risky business than raising cattle in Wyoming or Montana. During the disastrous winter of 1886–1887 that wiped out half the herds in the northwestern states, most southern Colorado ranchers actually made money.

Land along the lower Huerfano River became part of Pueblo County in 1865. Nevertheless, ranching continued to dominate the economy along southern Colorado's Front Range. One of the largest cattle operations in Pueblo County belonged to William Craig. His Hermosilla Estate encompassed more than a hundred square miles. Benjamin F. Butler, a prominent military figure and attorney from Massachusetts, purchased this ranch in 1882. Charles Goodnight, Annie Blake, and the Thatcher brothers also held large ranches near Pueblo in the 1870s.

Cattlemen on the upper Huerfano with herds large and small joined together to form the Cuerno Verde Livestock Association. In early June, after the snows had melted, these stockmen and their cowboys branded calves together and drove their herds onto Greenhorn Mountain. The cattle fattened on publicly owned mountain grasses all summer long. During the October roundup, breeding stock was driven back down the mountain to the home ranches, and the steers shipped off to market. The association's autumn roundups often included more than 10,000 cattle and took up to six weeks to complete.

Sheep ranching developed parallel to cattle ranching, except that the sheep men were not quite as vulnerable to boom-and-bust cycles because they had two products to sell: wool and meat on the hoof. Most of the *ganaderos de ovino* (sheep ranchers) had raised livestock in New Mexico and brought with them a long, systematic sheep raising tradition. Their expertise helped both Hispanic and Anglo ranching families make an effective, peaceful transition to mixed sheep and cattle operations sooner than occurred elsewhere in the West.

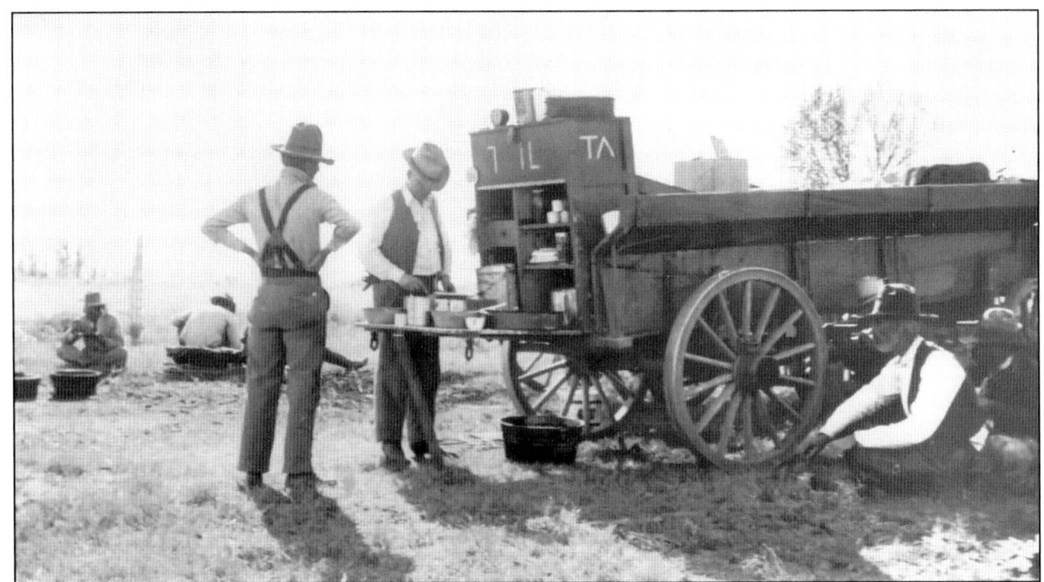

Thatcher Ranch. Jack Thatcher, the man in the vest standing beside the chuck wagon, was the grandson of John A. Thatcher, who, with his brother Mahlon D. Thatcher, carved a financial empire in the state beginning in the 1860s. Over a period of 50 years, the Thatcher brothers accumulated vast herds of cattle, controlling interest in several banks, various mercantile businesses, and a great deal of real estate in and around Pueblo. (PCHS.)

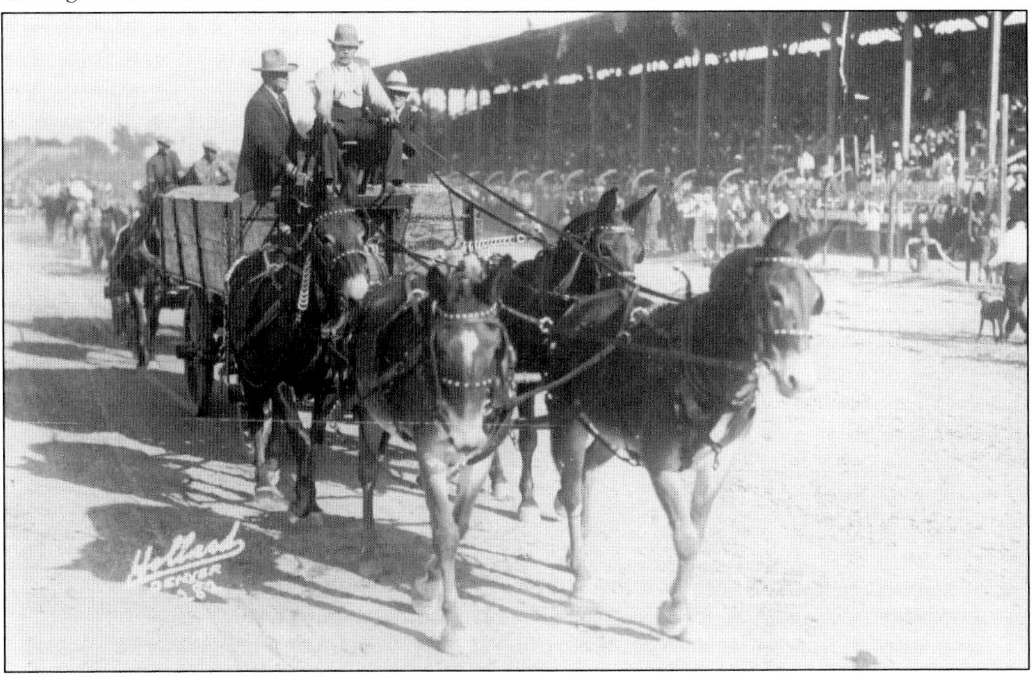

Jack's Mule Team. After his father died in 1928, John Henry "Jack" Thatcher took over operation of the 7IL Ranch north of Boone. This ranch included much of the 30,000 acres currently owned by the Association of American Railroads' Transportation Test Center plus acreage transformed into the Pueblo Army Depot. In this photograph, taken by Louis Hollard, Jack is dressed in black and sitting next to the mule driver. (PCHS.)

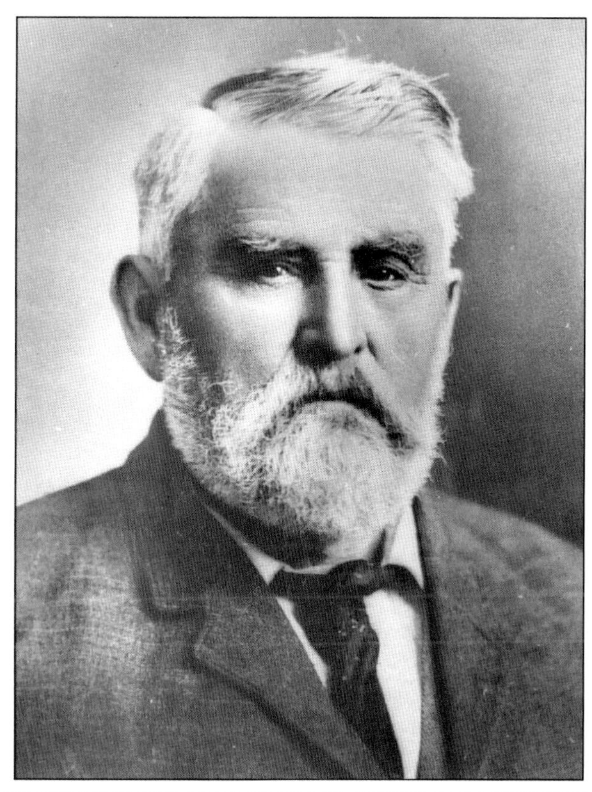

Charles Goodnight. Goodnight brought cattle herds across the Texas Panhandle into Colorado and Wyoming by way of both Raton Pass and Sangre de Cristo Pass. After his partner, Oliver Loving, was attacked and killed by a band of Comanche near Fort Sumner, New Mexico, Goodnight fulfilled a promise to bring the body back to Texas. Larry McMurtry's *Lonesome Dove* is based on this true story. (PCCLD, no. Ph-B-170-02_002.)

Goodnight Cattle Company Cowboys on Cattle Drive. Between 1869 and 1876, Goodnight headquartered near Pueblo, Colorado. Then, in 1876, he began to put together the John Adair Ranch in Palo Duro Canyon, Texas, a spread that eventually encompassed nearly a million acres and supported almost 100,000 cows. This photograph shows some of the men who worked for Goodnight and a chuck wagon built by James Hopkins. (PCHS.)

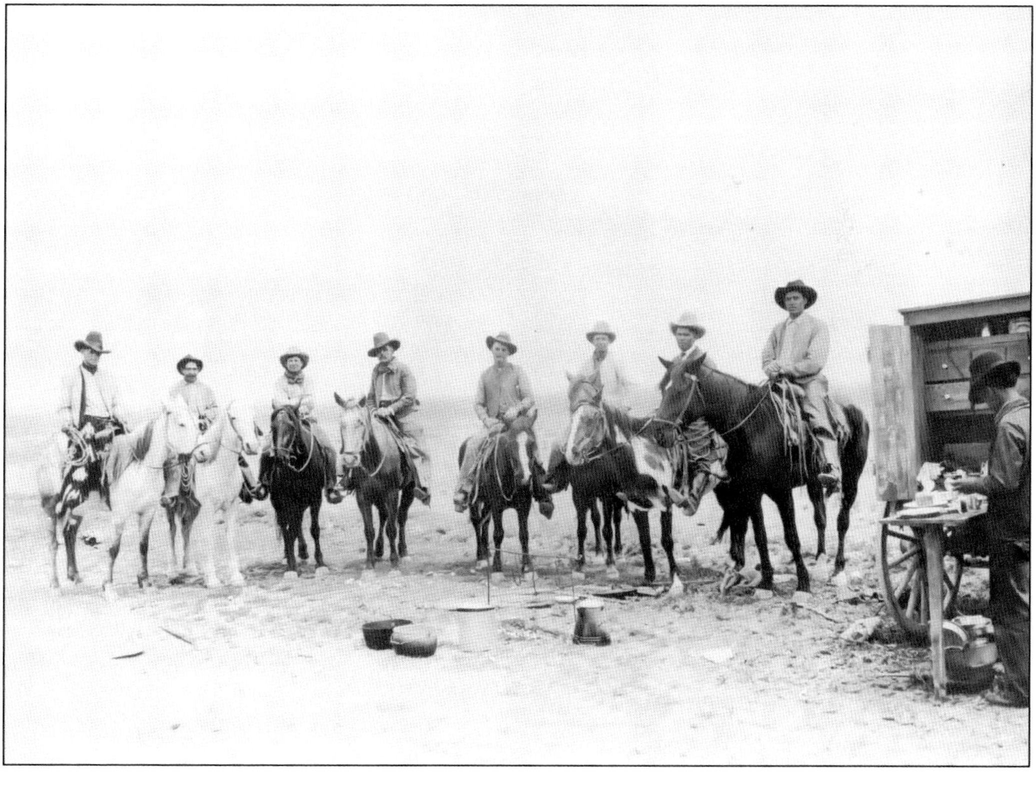

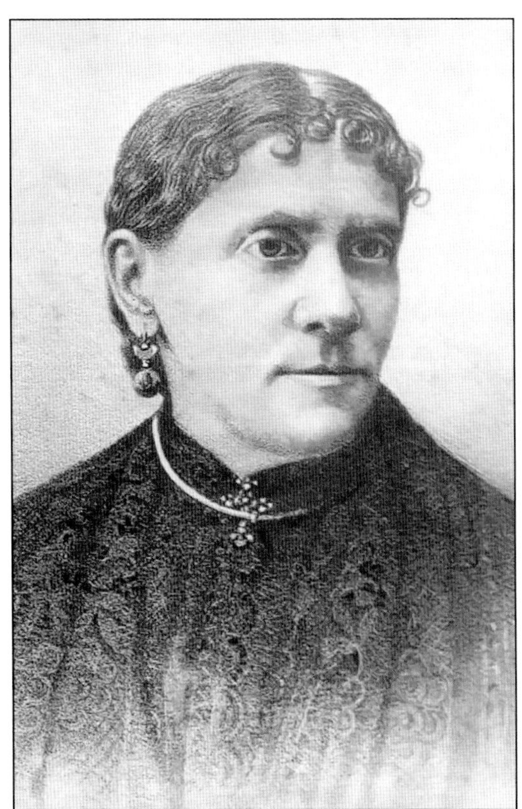

ANNIE BLAKE. Annie was both a ranch woman and a real estate agent. Her most famous transaction involved the purchase of the 48,000-acre Cervacio Nolan Land Grant for $10,000. She then sold one third of the grant to Charles Goodnight for $5,000 and another third to Peter Dotson for $5,000. A third she kept for herself and sold later for a handsome profit. (PCCLD, no. Ph-B-45-01_001.)

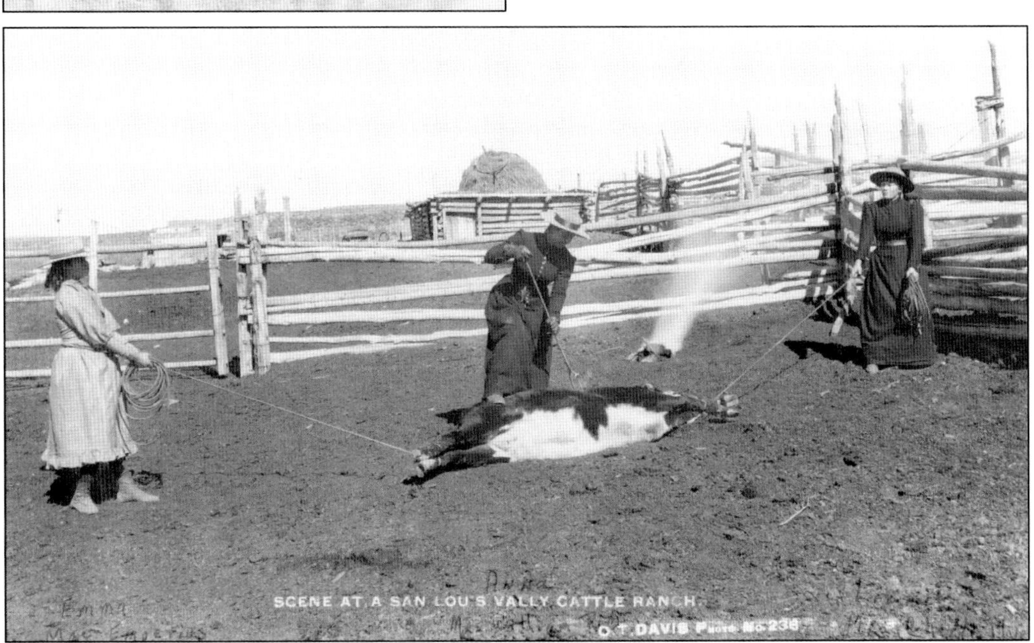

THE BECKER SISTERS. Livestock growers who did not have any sons sometimes encouraged their daughters to become cowgirls. Such was the case for Emma, Anna, and Lizzie Becker, who are pictured branding calves on the Harry Becker Ranch in the San Luis Valley in 1894. (MVHS/O.T. Davis Collection.)

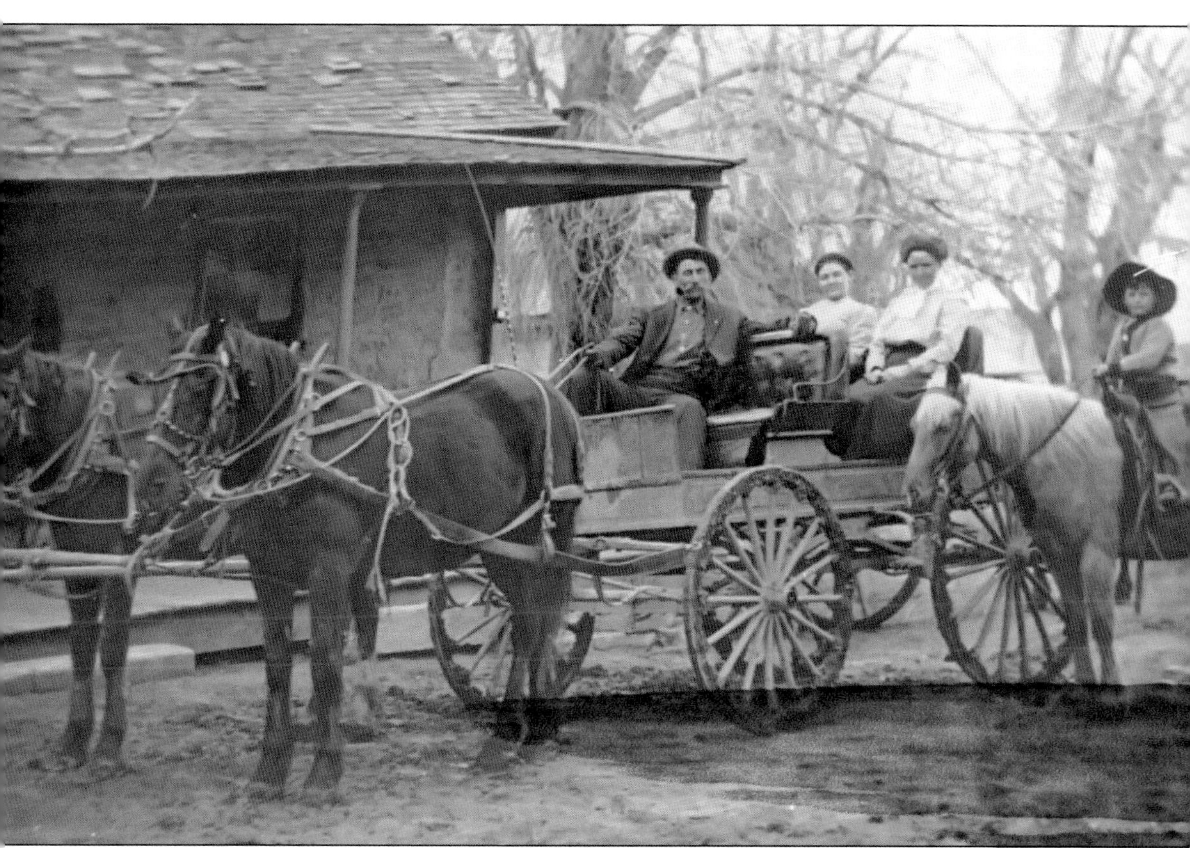

Joe Little Family. The four-million-acre Vigil–St. Vrain Land Grant was whittled down to 97,000 acres in the 1870s. William Craig, former land agent for Ceran St. Vrain, cornered nearly two thirds of the confirmed land tract. Craig named his ranch the Hermosilla (a Spanish word meaning "beautiful place"). In 1882, the ranch was sold at public auction to Benjamin F. Butler, a former member of the US House of Representatives and the 33rd governor of Massachusetts. The Butler family retained possession of the ranch for the next hundred years. Ranch headquarters consisted of five buildings, including the predominately adobe main house. The house is a one-story structure with a gable roof known to date from the 1880s. In this photograph, ranch manager Joe Little and his family are pictured in front of the main house. (PCCLD, no. Ph-P-486-04_001.)

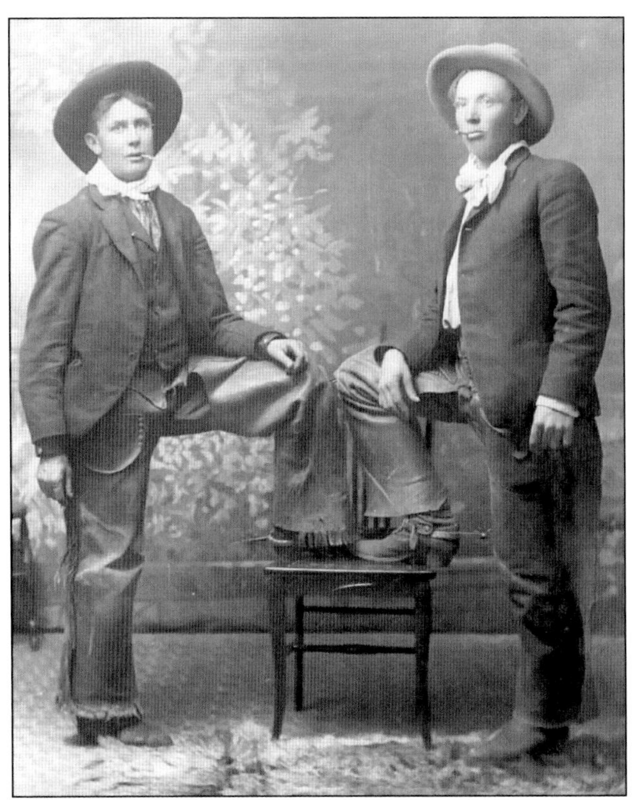

Two Cowboys: George Moyer and Hugh McQuarry. The cowboys who populated the ranches along the upper Huerfano were a tough breed. They worked long hours for low pay on outfits owned by men as tough as they were, men like Joshua Bains Hudson, Fred Diez, Albert Schmidt, and Felix St. Vrain. The St. Vrain family kept the ranch at Huerfano Butte until 1907. It is currently owned by Eric Sporleder and two of his sisters. (PCCLD, no. Ph-C-400-04_001.)

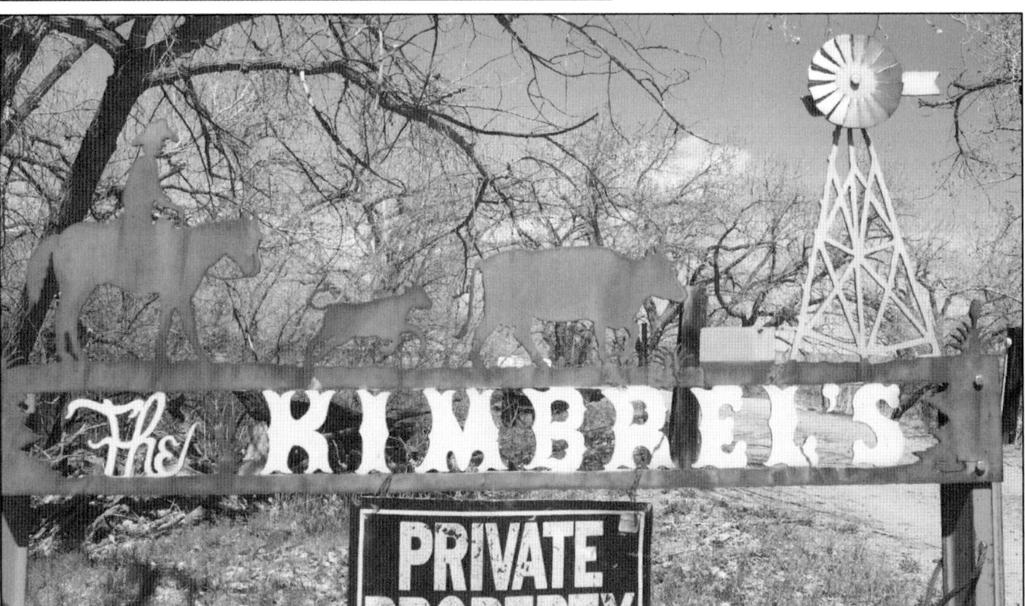

Kimbrel Ranch. Perry Thomas Kimbrel came west from Georgia in 1870 with a wagon train led by William Green Russell. Eventually he saved enough money to purchase land near the St. Mary's settlement. The Kimbrel Ranch earned the designation of a Colorado Centennial Farm in 1995. To qualify, a ranch must have been maintained as a working unit by members of the same family for at least 100 years.

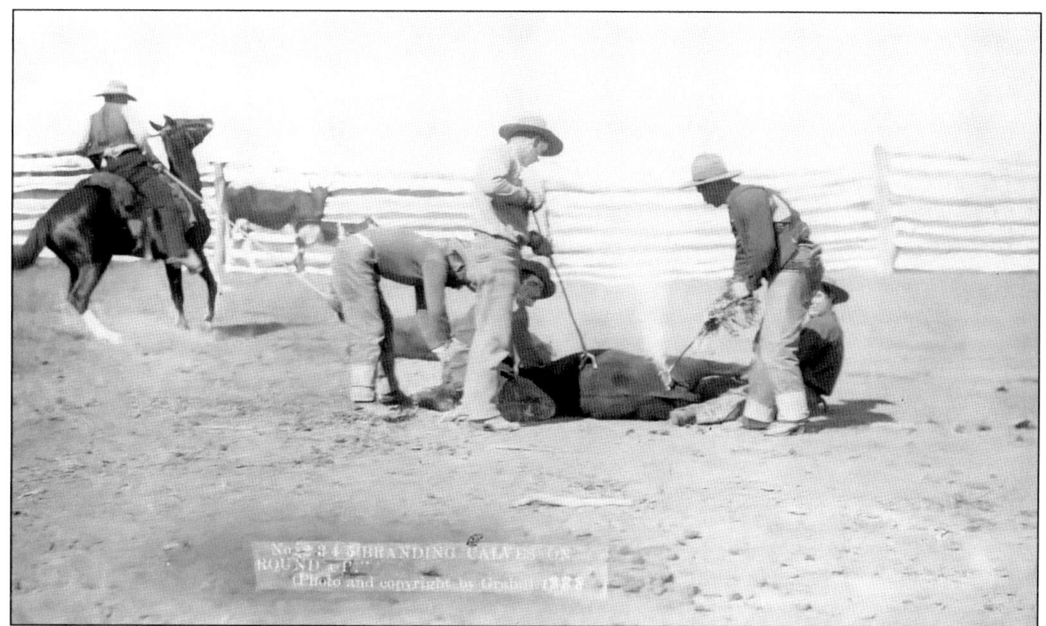

Branding Calves on Roundup, 1888. After the calves were branded at the spring roundup, cowboys herded the cattle up to the meadows on Greenhorn Mountain, where they stayed until October. A half-million miles of barbed wire was being produced annually in the United States by 1880, but much of Huerfano County remained open rangeland well into the 20th century. (LOC/John C.H. Grabill Collection.)

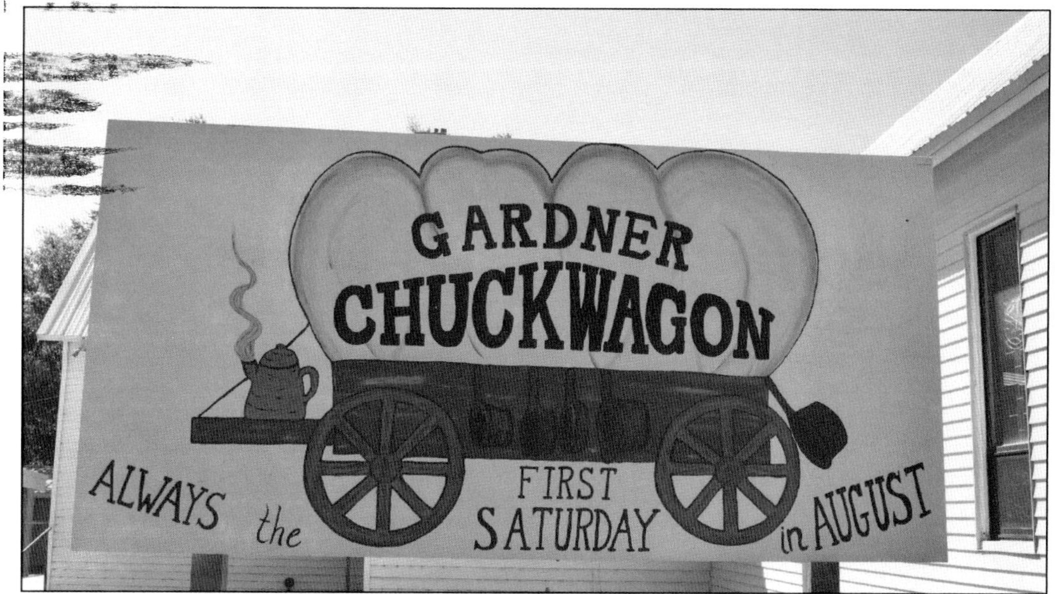

Chuck Wagon Dinner in Gardner. Ranchers on the upper Huerfano branded their calves together, herded their cattle to market together, and ate their meals from the same chuck wagon. The open-range roundups ended in the late 1930s. Then, in 1942, Gardner Methodist Church sponsored the first official Gardner Chuck Wagon Dinner as a fundraiser. Proceeds from the dinner currently pay for student scholarships and for capital improvements at the Gardner Community Center.

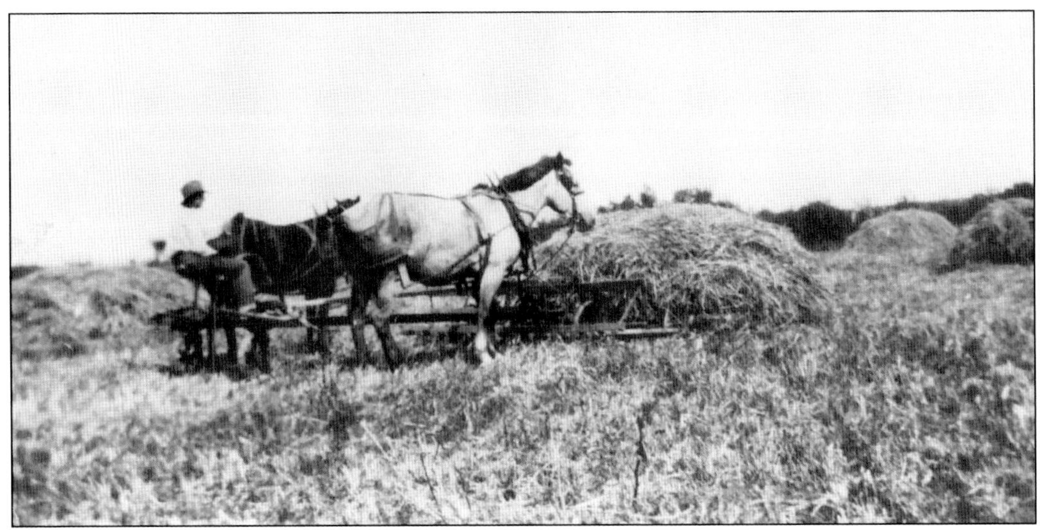

Horse-Powered Hay Rake. The main crop produced in the upper Huerfano Valley was hay for livestock. Ranch families grew vegetable gardens and fruit orchards but only enough for themselves. On the plains east of Walsenburg, winter wheat was also a popular commodity. In 1912, for example, more than 5,000 acres of wheat were grown within the county. (PCCLD, no. Ph-P-486-04_004.)

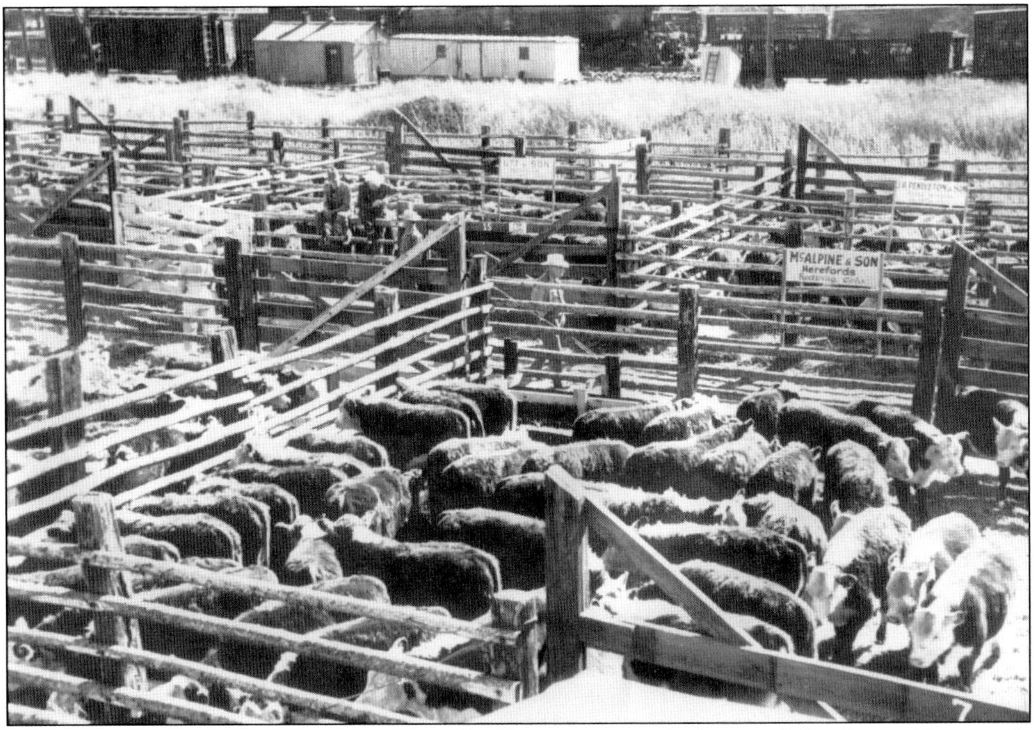

Walsenburg Stockyard. The ranch families living near Malachite and Gardner seldom made trips into Walsenburg, because travel by wagon was a three-day round-trip—more time than it took to send cows by rail from Walsenburg to Kansas City. For the convenience of ranchers on the upper Huerfano, an additional railroad stockyard was built near the Tioga Mine Camp a few miles northwest of Walsenburg. (PCCLD, no. Ph-C-400-03_001.)

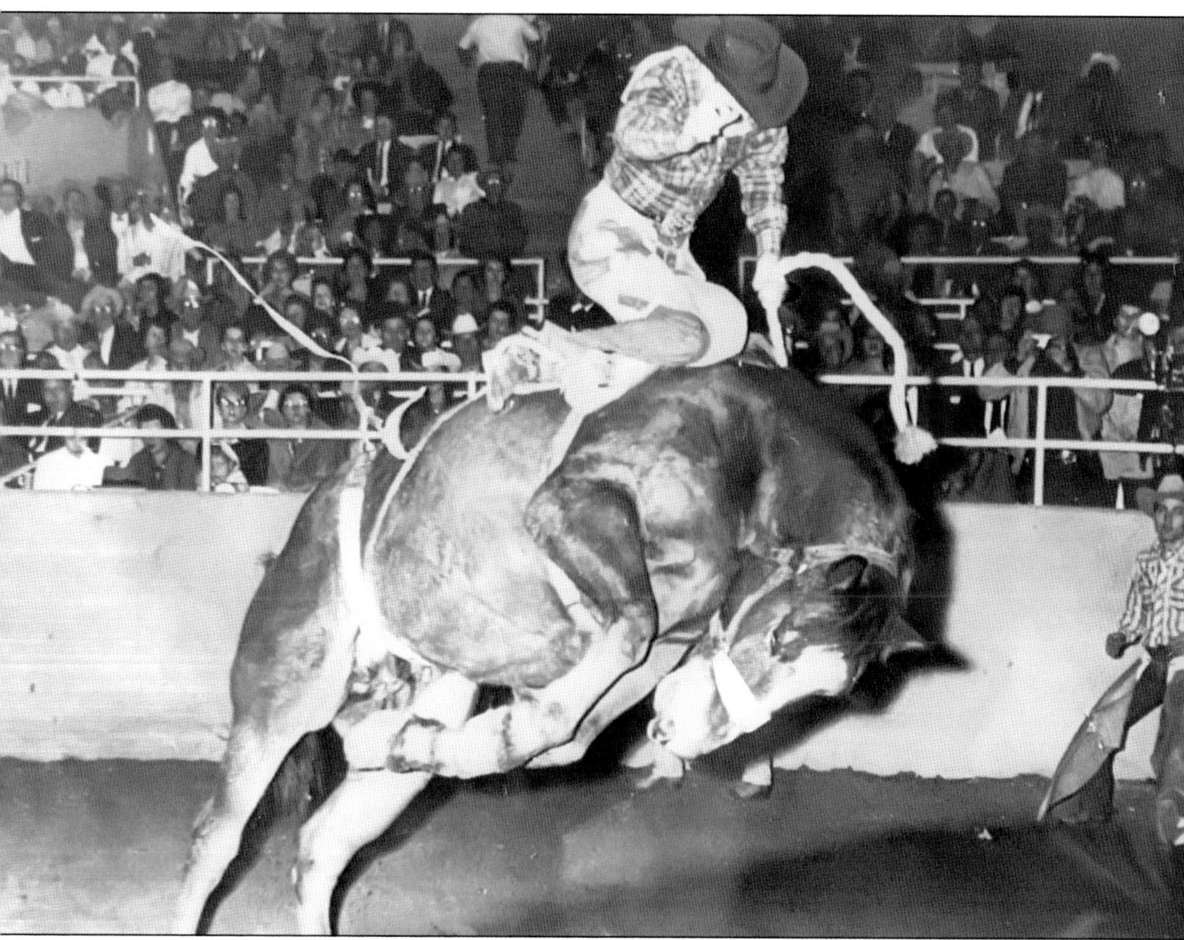

Bareback Bronc Rider. Casey Tibbs, a Huerfano County cowboy, tries to stay on his horse for at least eight seconds and to put on a show that will earn him a winning score. Tibbs made the cover of *Time* magazine in 1951 as World All-Around Rodeo Champion. Most rodeo events were based on the real-life tasks required on cattle ranches. (PCCLD, no. Ph-C-400-09_005.)

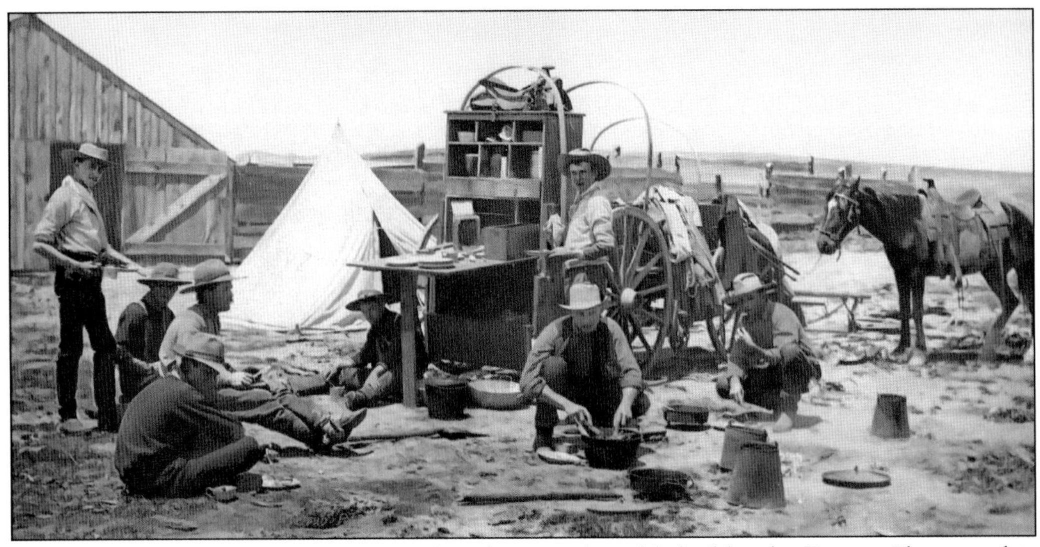

The Roundup "Grub Pile," 1898. This photograph, published by the Detroit Photographic Company, shows a large cattle ranch similar to the one owned by John Adam Meyer. Meyer served as the leader of many roundups and as an officer in the Cuerno Verde Cattlemen's Association. He owned a large ranch northwest of Gardner. Today, much of this land belongs to the 55,000-acre Wolf Springs Ranch. (LOC.)

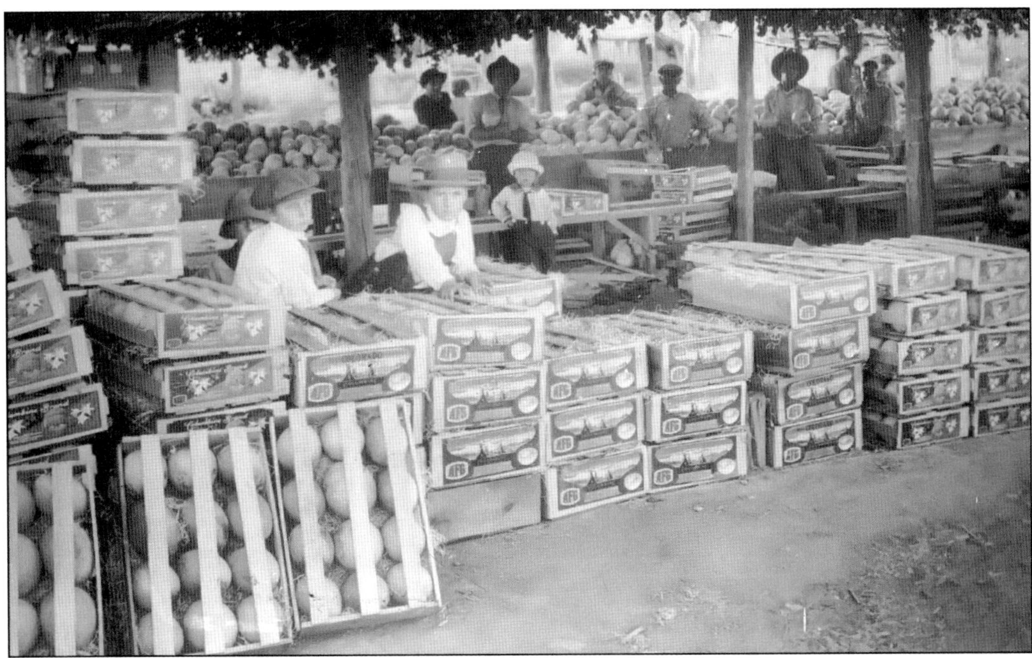

Packing Cantaloupes at Rocky Ford. Herbert Gardner started ranching in the upper Huerfano Valley in 1872, near the town that now bears his name. However, he is best known for his gift of melon seeds to George W. Swink, who developed the watermelon and cantaloupe industry in Rocky Ford, Colorado. Swink also invented the cantaloupe crate, which replaced the wooden barrels formerly used for shipping fruit to market. (DPL, no. Z-2973.)

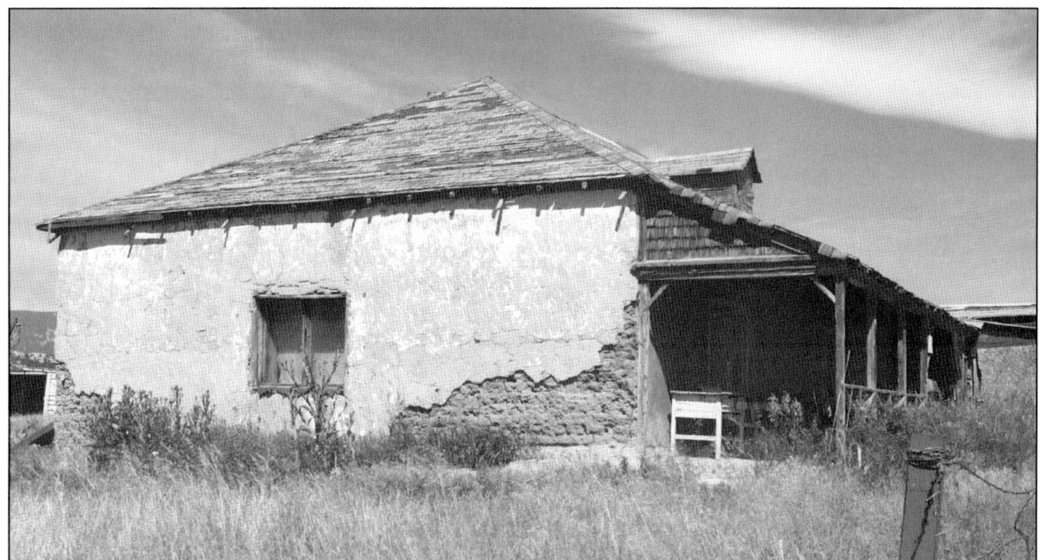

Montoya Ranch. Listed in the National Register of Historic Places on July 3, 2012, the Montoya Ranch dates to the 1860s, when hundreds of Hispanic settlers migrated north from New Mexico. The property features a home with a functional adobe basement, historic sheep pens, an irrigation ditch, an underground icehouse, and many examples of Spanish Colonial and territorial adobe styles of architecture.

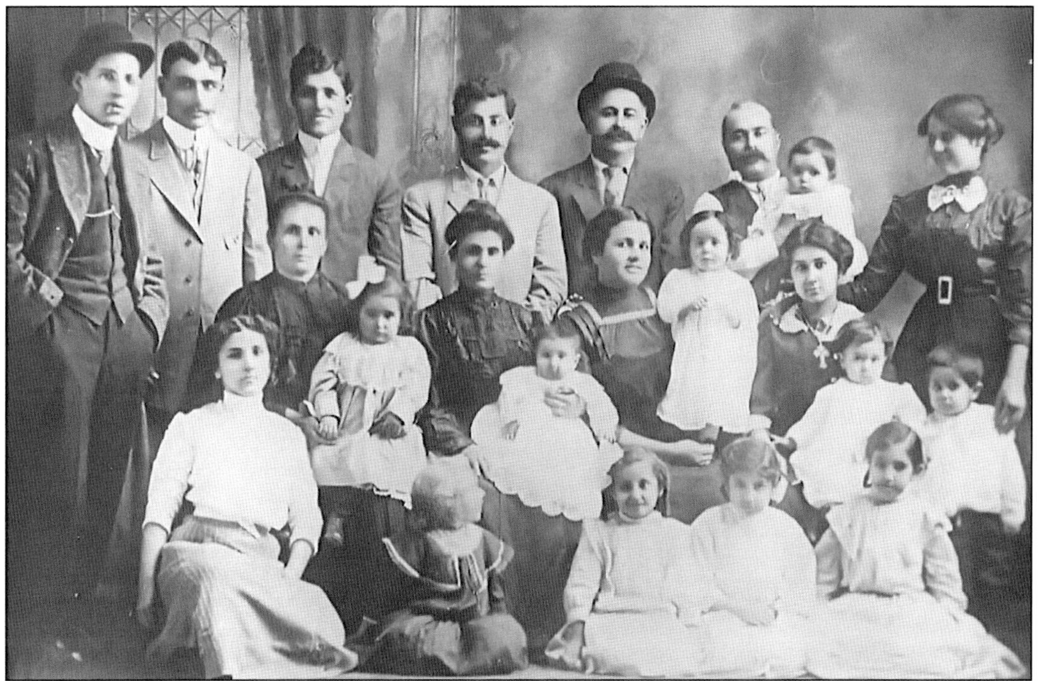

Saliba Family, c. 1911. Victor and Juliana Montoya lived at the Montoya Ranch from 1874 to 1910. Then Lebanese immigrants Asperidon Faris and Louise Saliba Faris occupied the premises. In addition to operating a general store, they raised sheep and grew fresh produce to sell in their store. Louise and her daughter Jeanette are pictured in this Saliba family photograph (middle row, third pair from the left).

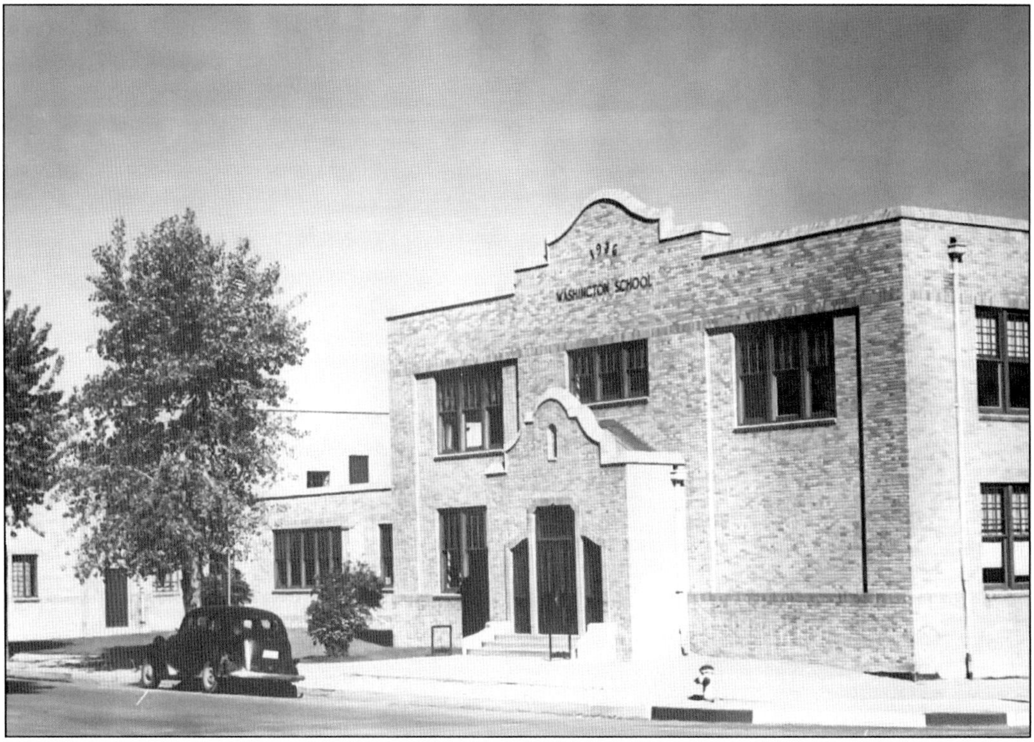

Washington School. Alton Tirey was a descendant of Huerfano Valley pioneers. His maternal grandfather settled near Malachite in 1874. Tirey left an endowment to the Huerfano County Historical Society that made possible the creation of the Alton M. Tirey Local History Center, housed here in Washington School until early 2016. It is now on West Sixth Street and undergoing a name change to the Huerfano Heritage Center. (PCCLD, no. Ph-C-400-04_003.)

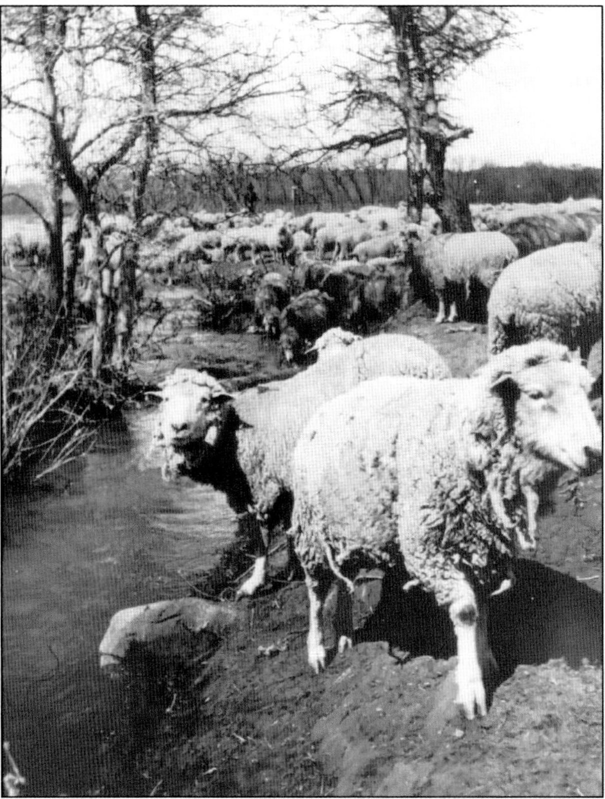

Sheep on Pasture near Avondale. According to Alton Tirey, there were no range wars in the Huerfano Valley. Tirey himself raised both cattle and sheep. In an interview he granted to a representative of the *La Veta Signature* shortly before his death in 2005, Tirey estimated that as many as 20,000 sheep were pasturing on land along the Huerfano in the early 20th century. (PCHS.)

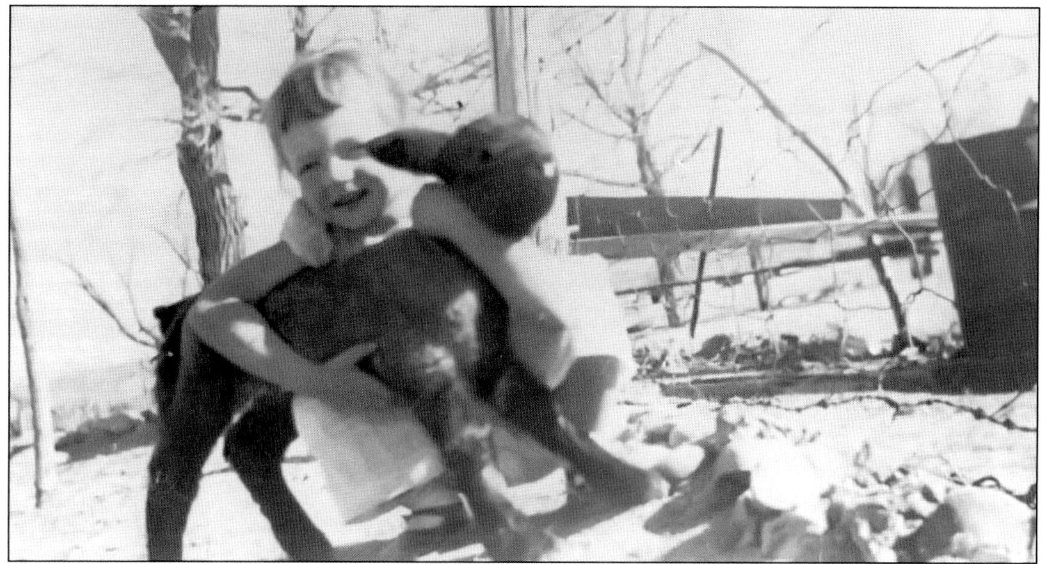

Bummer Lamb, 1955. Orphaned baby lambs were often turned over to ranch children to bottle feed twice a day. This photograph shows five-year-old Kay Beth Faris, who became quite attached to one of these lambs.

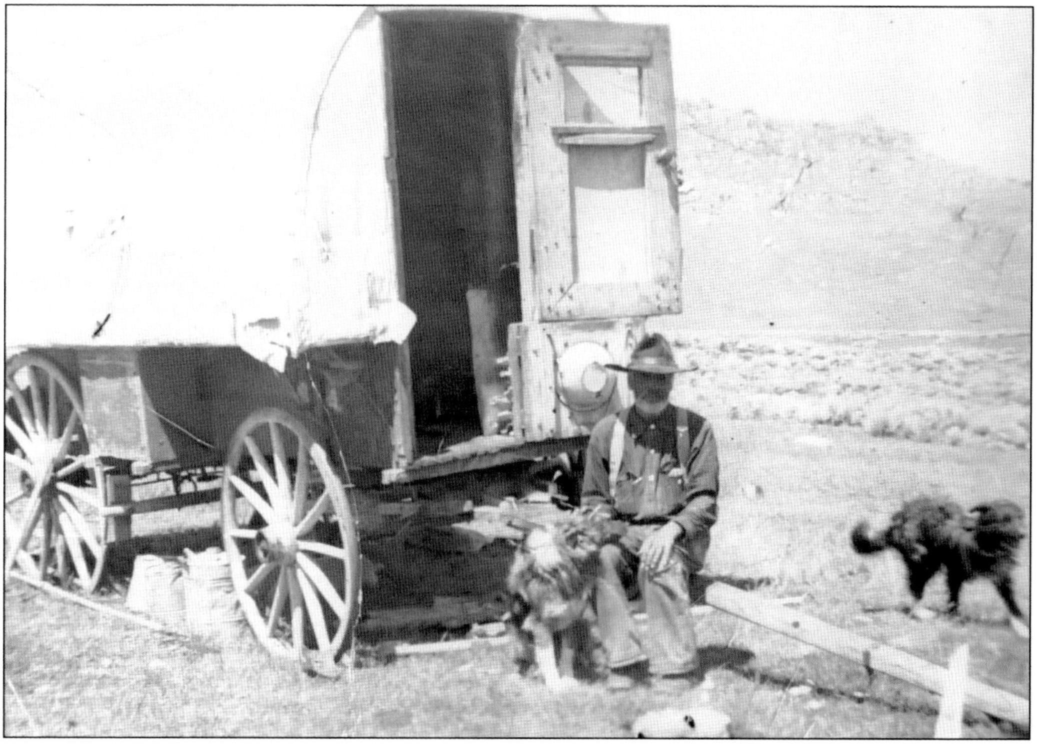

Sheepherder Jose Manuel Cordova and His House on Wheels. The sheep wintered in protected fields at the home ranches for seven months of the year and summered in the national forest atop Greenhorn Mountain. Margaret Archuleta Garcia remembers her family raising 1,000 head near Apache Canyon. Her grandfather Jose Benigno Archuleta had to ride up the mountain several times each summer to take supplies to his sheepherders. (HCHS/ATC.)

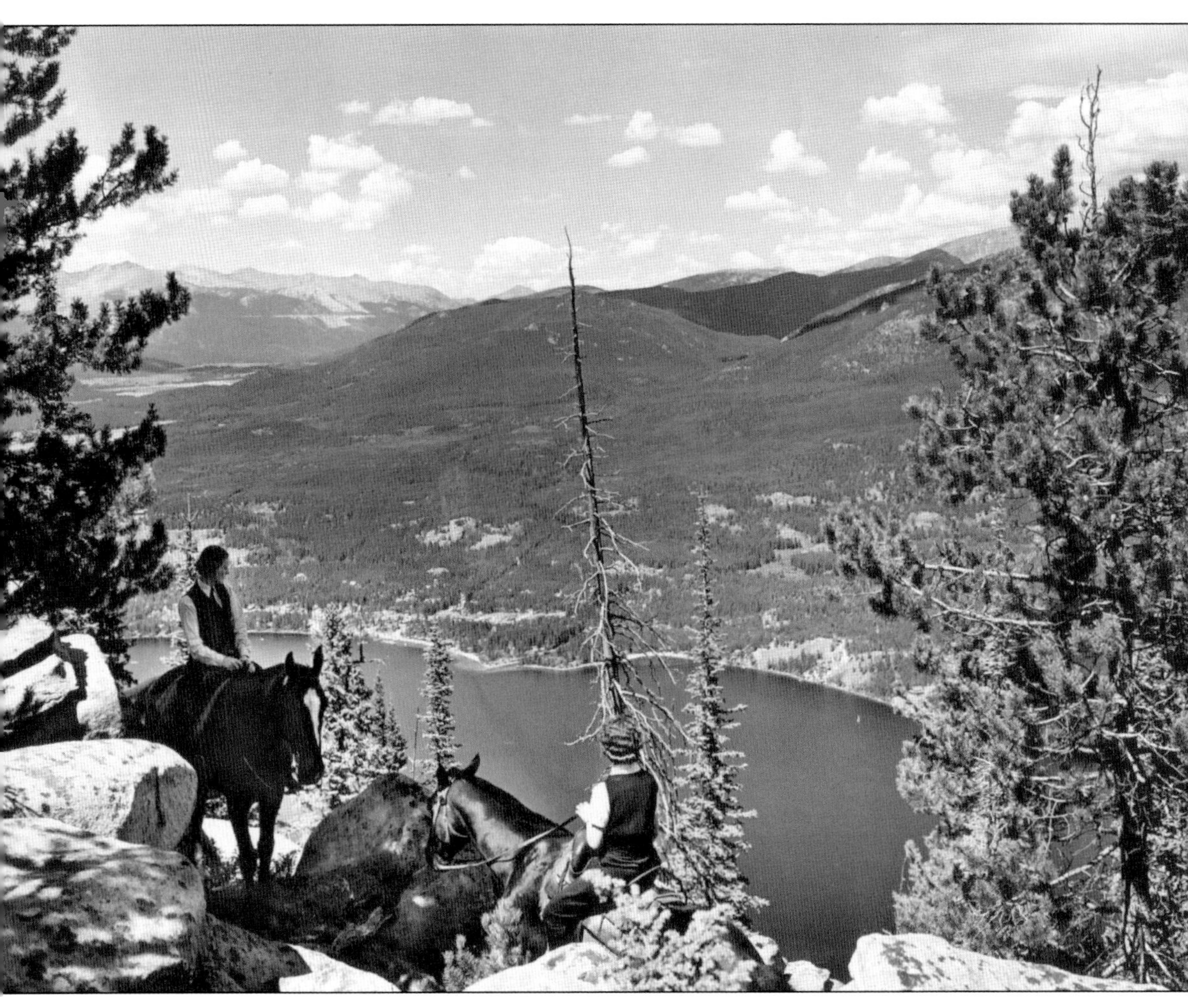

Lake in San Isabel National Forest. The absence of gunplay did not mean there was total harmony between cattle ranchers and sheep growers. After all, each stockman was in competition with his neighbors for summer pasturage. Perhaps the big winners were the conservationists. In order to protect some of the West's most beautiful public lands from overgrazing, Pres. Theodore Roosevelt set aside millions of acres as forest reserves. The land set aside in south central Colorado in 1902 was called the Las Animas Forest Preserve and was renamed the San Isabel National Forest in 1907. From 1907 until 1945, the forest reserve grew steadily in size as more acreage was integrated into it. Today, the San Isabel National Forest contains land in the Sawatch Range, Collegiate Peaks, and Sangre de Cristos. It has a total area of 1,117,131 acres stretched over 11 counties. (PCCLD, no. Ph-P-444-06_001.)

Six

Miners and Steelmakers

Commercial coal mining in Huerfano County began one mile west of Walsenburg at the Walsen Mine in March 1876. Initially, the Southern Colorado Coal and Town Company used wagons to haul its 16-tons-per-day output east to Cucharas (also called Cuchara Junction). After the D&RG laid track seven miles west to the Walsen Mine tipple later that year, coal production increased to 300 tons a day.

Railroad magnate William J. Palmer leased the mine from Fred Walsen in 1876 and then purchased it in 1879. In 1892, Palmer's Colorado Coal and Iron merged with the Colorado Fuel Company to form the Colorado Fuel and Iron Company (CF&I). John Cleveland Osgood served as president of the new enterprise until 1903, when a financial crisis forced Osgood to sell CF&I to Jay Gould and John D. Rockefeller. By then, the mines in Huerfano County were producing over a million tons of coal annually. Coal production increased steadily throughout the 1920s. In 1926, Huerfano County generated one fifth of Colorado's coal, a total of 1,965,912 tons, worth $6,405,000.

Some of that coal was sold to railroads to power locomotive boilers. Some was used for home heating. Much of the best bituminous coal was converted to coke and freighted into Pueblo to be utilized in the largest steel manufacturing plant west of the Mississippi. Colorado Fuel and Iron began to make steel at the Pueblo mill in 1881 using molten pig iron produced in a blast furnace. Products created through this method included railroad rails, iron plates, steel bars, cut nails, and spikes.

For more than 100 years, the steel mill was Pueblo's main industry. However, the steel market crash of 1982 forced the company into a series of bankruptcies. Colorado Fuel and Iron was acquired by Oregon Steel Mills and the name changed to Rocky Mountain Steel Mills in 1993. Evraz, a Russian steel corporation, purchased Oregon Steel's holdings in 2007 for $2.3 billion. In the past decade, multimillion-dollar upgrades have produced the state-of-the-art Product Technology Center and extra-long, premium-quality rails competitive on the world market.

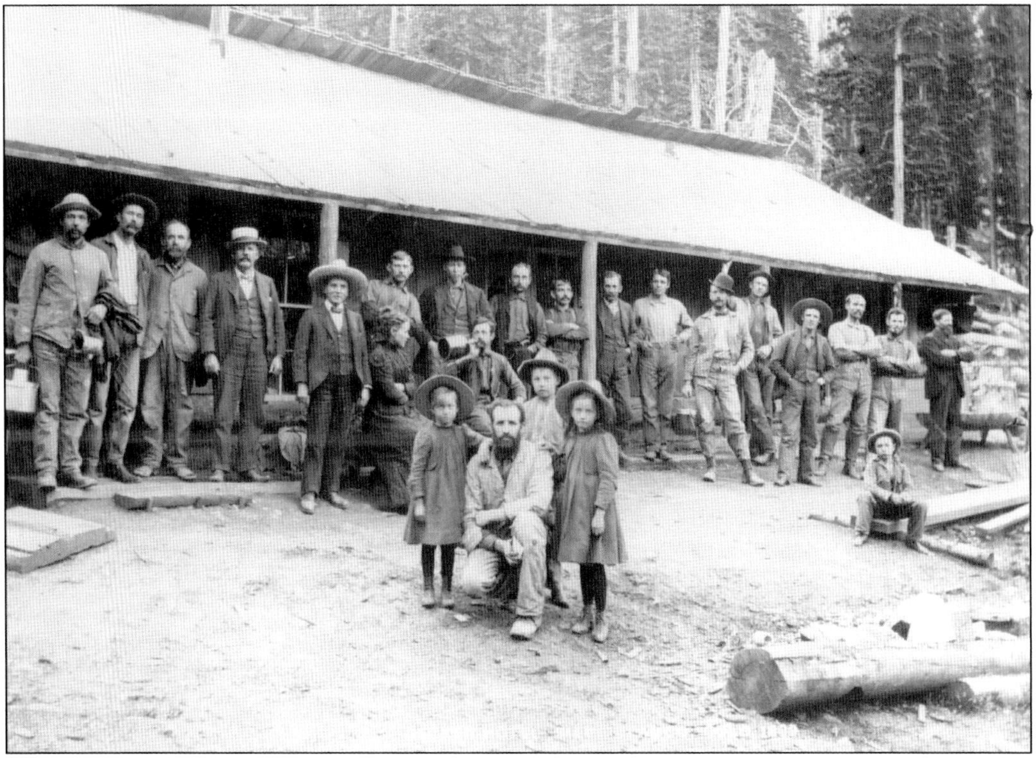

Decker Hotel, Sierra Blanco, 1899. Located on the lower slopes of Mount Blanca, the Decker Hotel accommodated tourists and miners dredging for gold at nearby mines. Gold was being sought at the McMillan Mine close to the headwaters of the Huerfano River and at the placer pits on the west side of La Veta Pass, near the town of Russell. (MVHS/O.T. Davis Collection.)

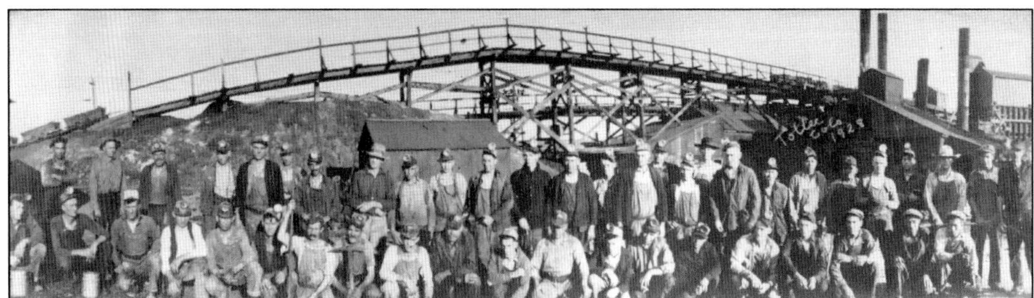

Toltec Mine. During its 50 years in operation, this mine changed hands several times. It was probably opened by CF&I in 1894 as an extension of the Pictou. Other owners included the Northern Coal Company (1899–1916), Aztec Coal Company (1916–1941), and Benassi family (1941–1944). For much of the 50-year period, families at the Toltec Mine Camp sent their children to the Kebler School at Pictou. (PCCLD, no. Ph-C-400-11_007.)

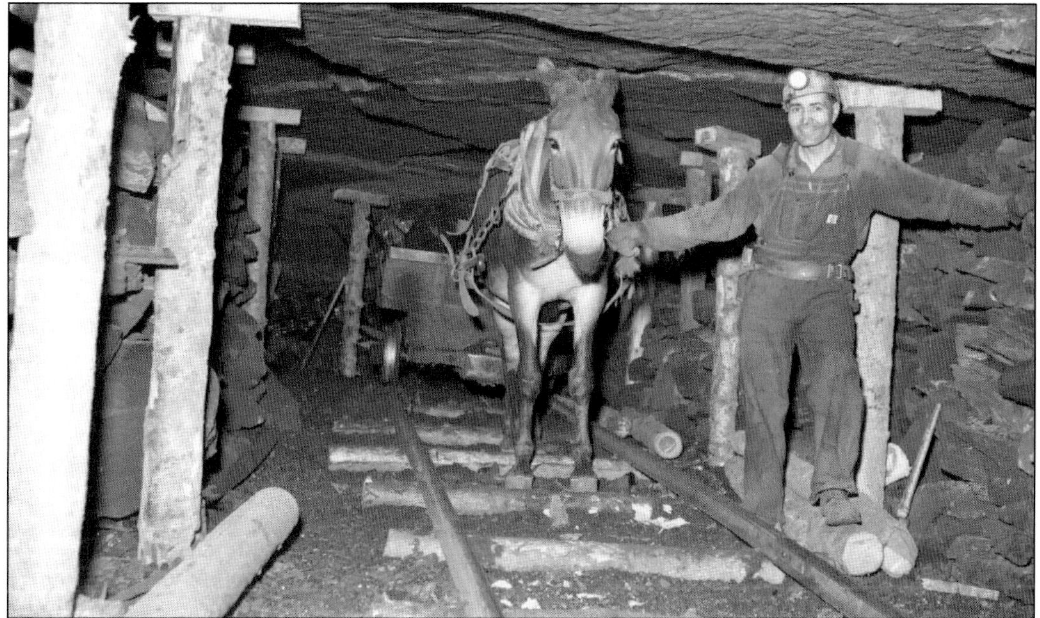

Miner Guiding a Mule. From 1883 through 1946, the Cameron Mine produced nearly four million tons of coal. The mine employed 250 men during its busiest years and shipped 1,600 tons of coal per day. Since 1946, the wooden buildings have been shipped away or demolished, but many of the cement foundations remain, including the steps to nowhere that mark the site of the old YMCA. (Steelworks.)

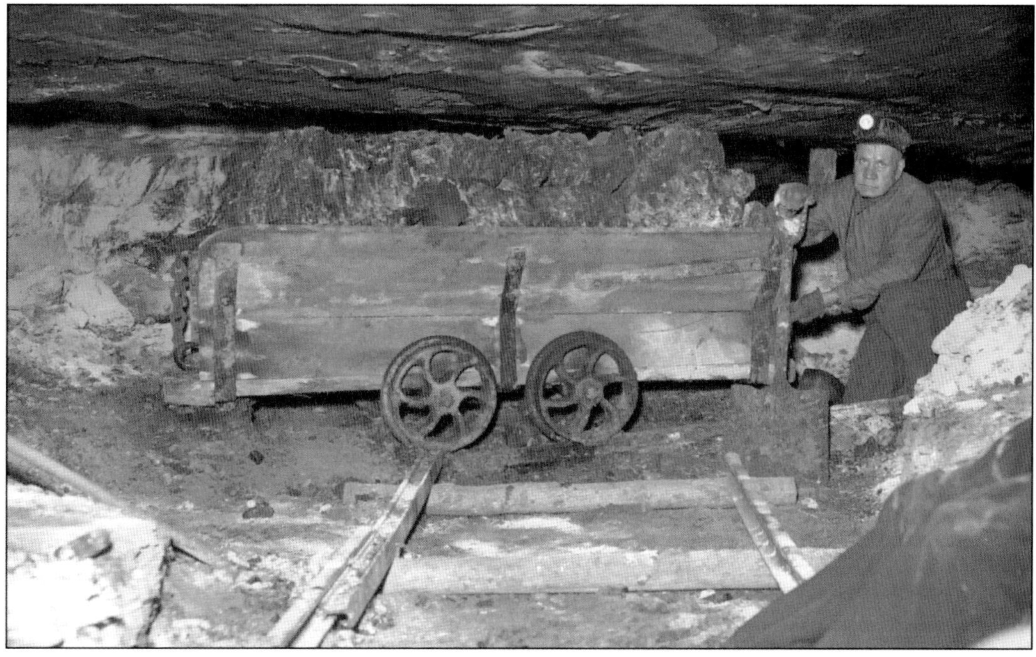

Miner and Cart in Cameron Mine, 1944. Workmen opening a new coal seam happened upon a loaded pit car sitting in an old section of tunnel. Although the wooden coal car and its load had been abandoned since 1889, they were in remarkably good condition, considering they had been walled up inside a tunnel for more than 50 years. (Steelworks.)

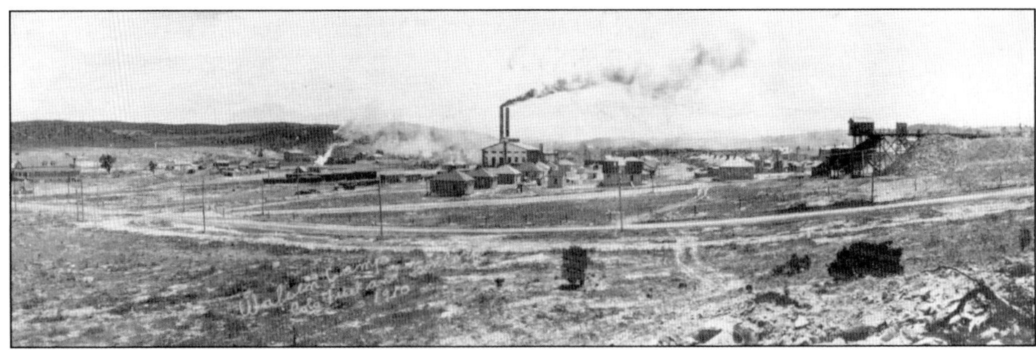

Walsen Housing and Power Plant. By 1904, output at the Walsen Mine had increased to 1,000 tons per day. The electric power plants, built in 1898 and 1911, helped to bring about improved productivity. The camp offered three-, four-, and five-room houses with an electrical outlet in each room and a water hydrant on each street. However, indoor plumbing was not part of the housing package. (PCCLD, no. Ph-C-400-06_001.)

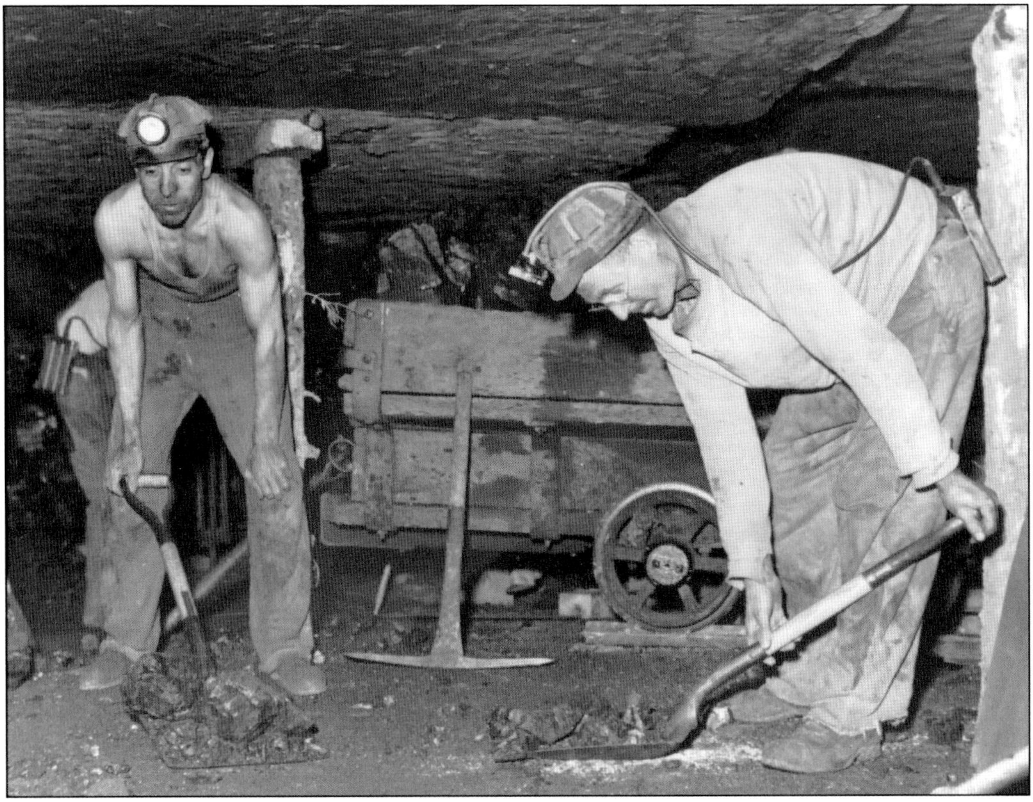

Miners Shoveling Coal into a Cart. By 1931, tunnels similar to this one were under water at the Walsen Mine. Some 2,500 gallons of water were being pumped out of the mine every 24 hours, an expensive operation forcing closure of the mine. However, the Cameron remained open through World War II. (PCHS.)

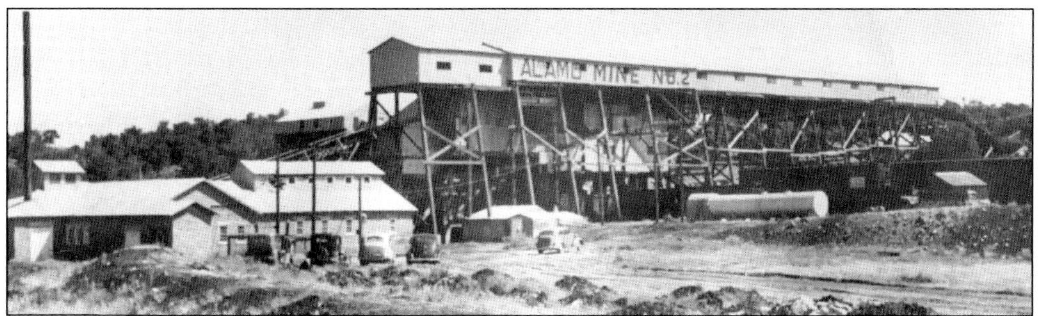

Alamo Mine. The Oakdale Coal Company began development of the Alamo Mine in 1922. A neighboring slope, Alamo No. 2, was opened in 1926. For several years, the Alamo Mines had one of the few competitive soccer teams in Huerfano County. The original Alamo Mine was dismantled in 1941, but the Dick brothers operated Alamo No. 2 as the Butte Valley Mine from 1937 to 1952. (HCHS/WMM.)

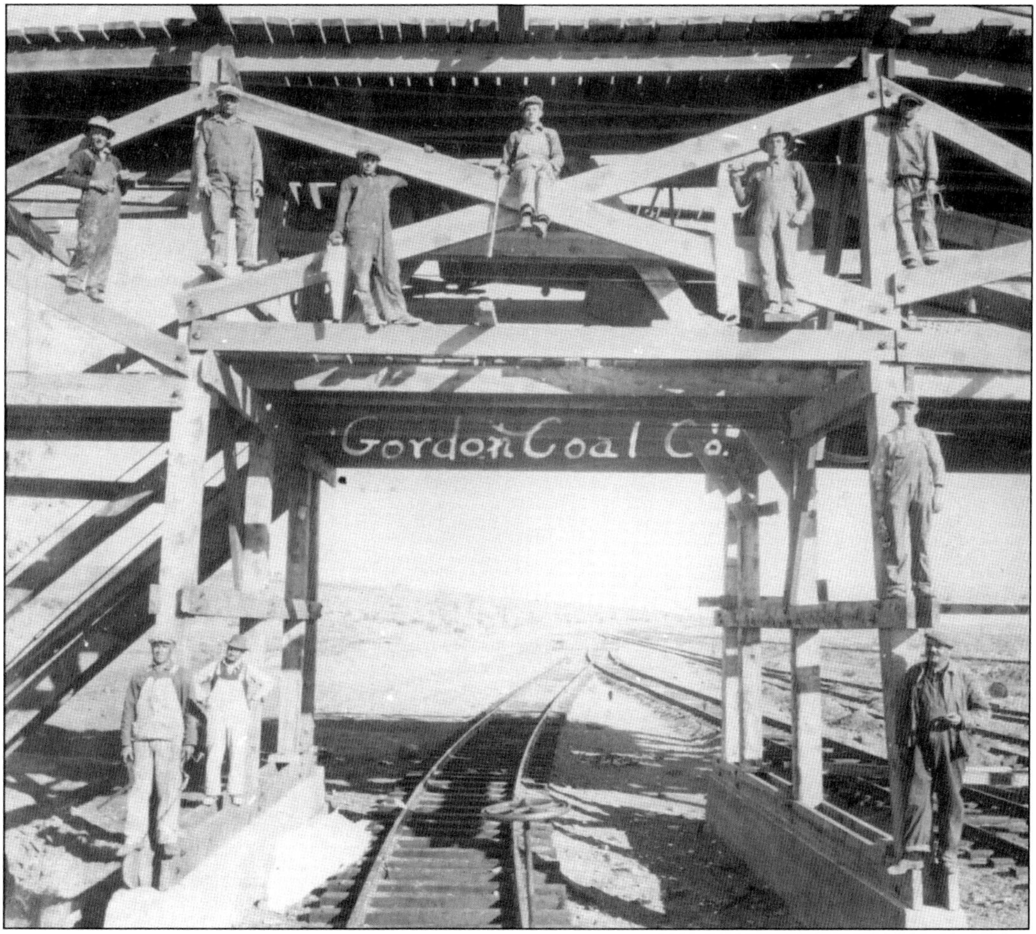

Gordon Mine. Lying northwest of Walsenburg near Highway 69, the Gordon opened in 1907 and closed in 1965 after producing more than two million tons of coal. This photograph, taken by the *Huerfano World* staff, includes, from left to right, Mike Sudar, Tony Vercelli, unidentified, Frank Slevec (seated), and two Sudar brothers. Standing at bottom left are Gonzales and Moñtano Ghione. The men at bottom right are unidentified. (PCCLD, no. Ph-C-400-11_009.)

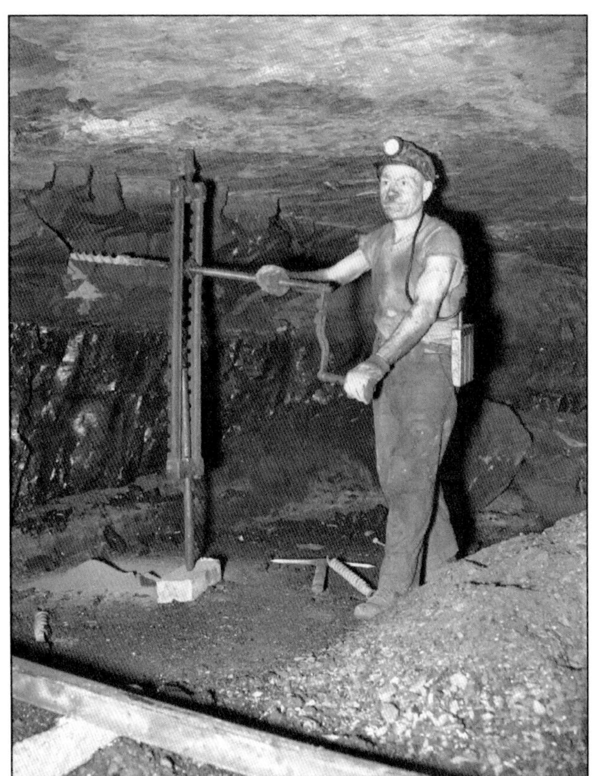

Man Using Hand Drill. In order to blast the coal free, holes had to be bored into the coal vein and explosives poked into the holes. In the early years of coal mining, "shooting" or "blasting" the coal was accomplished with black powder. By the 1940s, safer procedures were in place. (Steelworks.)

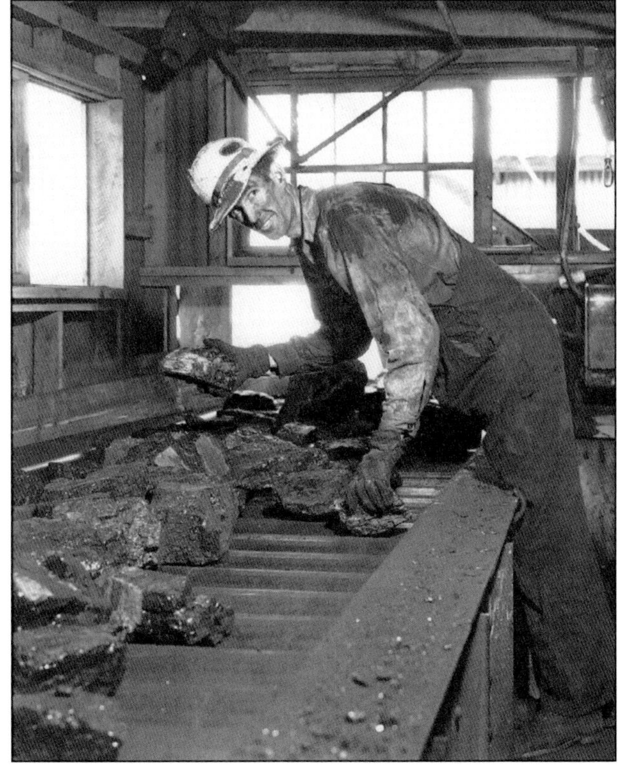

Worker at the Nut Picking Table, Kebler Mine. CF&I produced at least three grades of coal: large chunks called stove coal, mid-sized or nut coal, and pea-sized chunks called pea coal. The nut coal was discharged onto a conveyor belt, where workers culled out the slate and allowed the nut coal to continue toward loading boxcars. (Steelworks.)

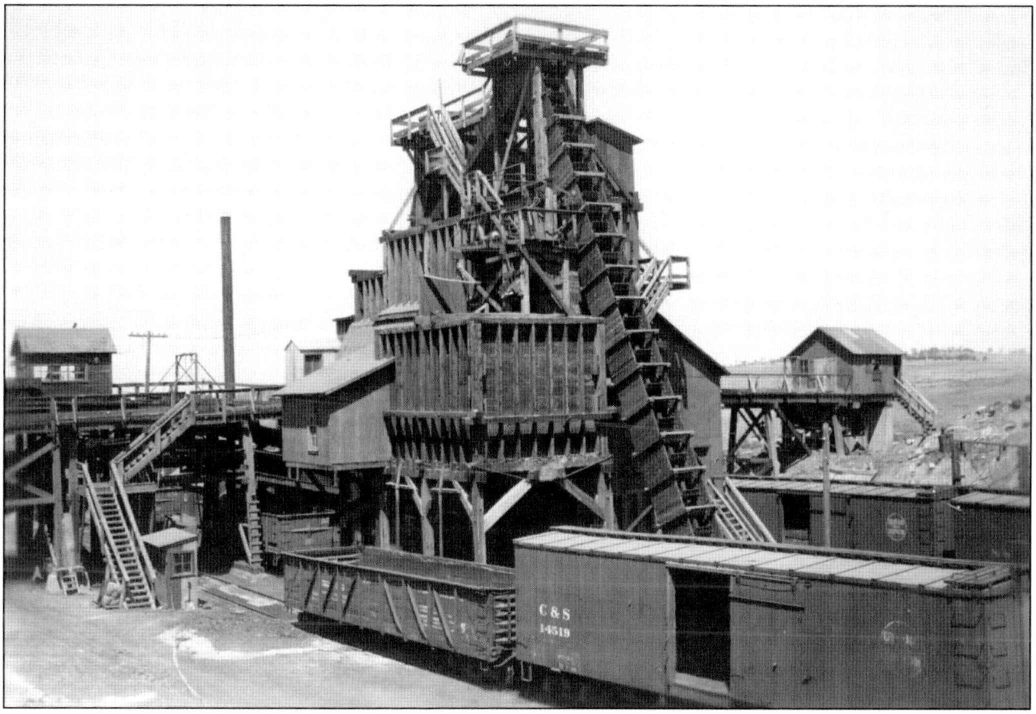

WASHERY AT THE CAMERON MINE. A coal preparation plant or wash plant washed soil and rock off the coal, crushed the coal, sorted it into graded sizes, and prepared it for shipment. The coal could then be stockpiled by grade or loaded onto railcars for immediate transport to market. The more efficient the wash plant was at removing waste material, the lower the transportation costs and the greater the coal's market value. (Steelworks.)

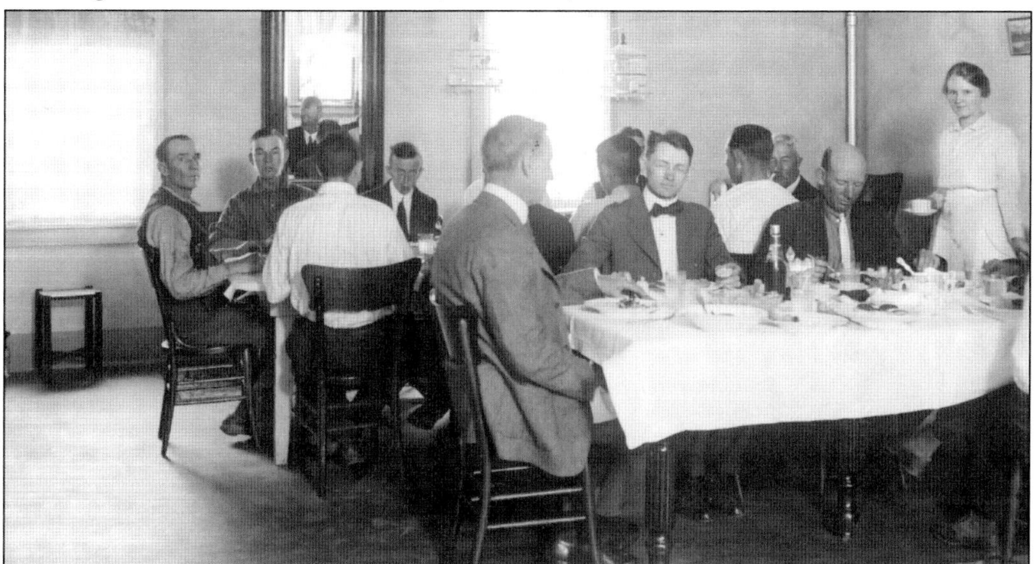

MEN EATING A MEAL INSIDE A ROUSE BOARDINGHOUSE, 1915. In the most crowded coal camps, single men were forced to share a room or even a bed. The quality of the boardinghouses varied from camp to camp. There were company-owned boardinghouses and privately run boardinghouses. Meals, laundry, and cleaning services were usually included in the weekly boarding fee. (Steelworks.)

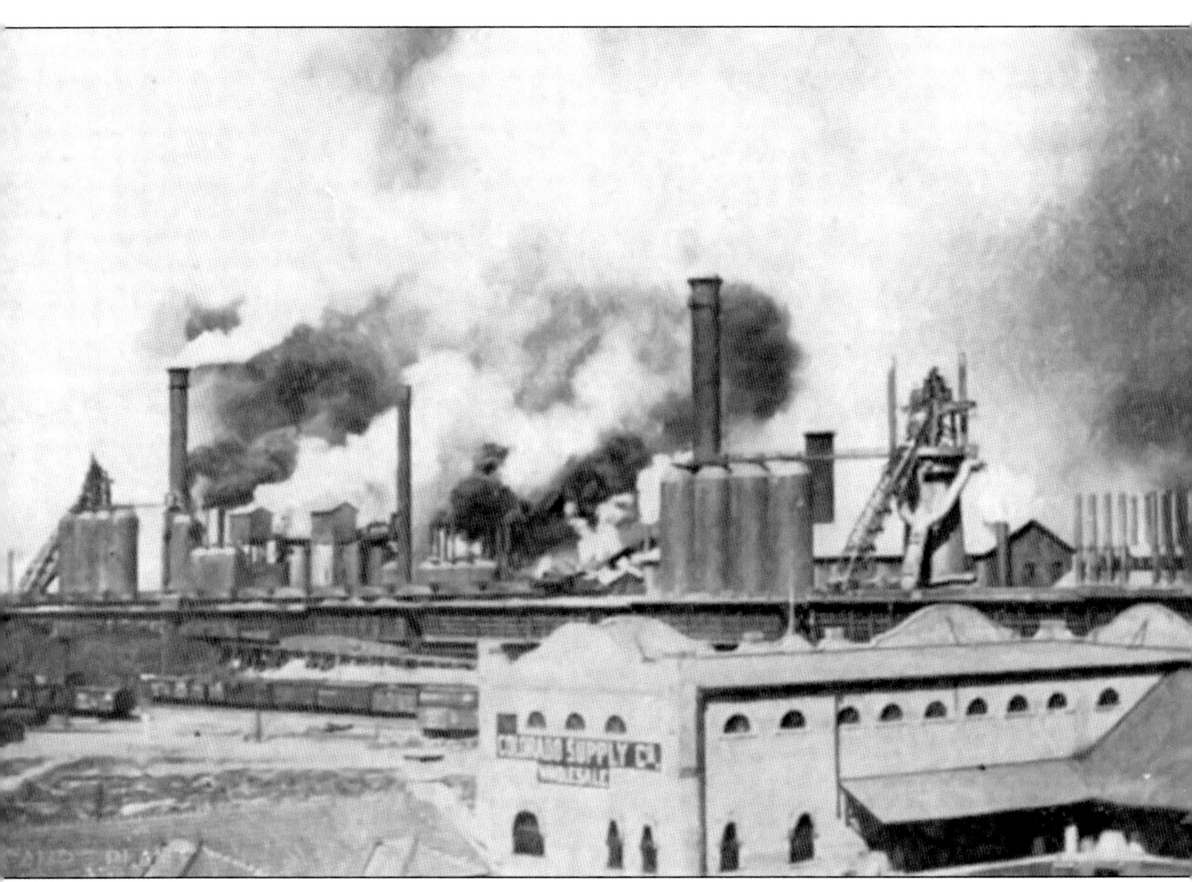

Colorado Fuel and Iron Company Steel Mill, Pueblo. In 1903, this steel manufacturing plant was modernized with improvements that included an expensive Bessemer converter for transforming pig iron into steel, several blast furnaces, and a large rolling mill. Most of these structures were torn down in 1989, but due to their asbestos content, the blast furnace stoves were

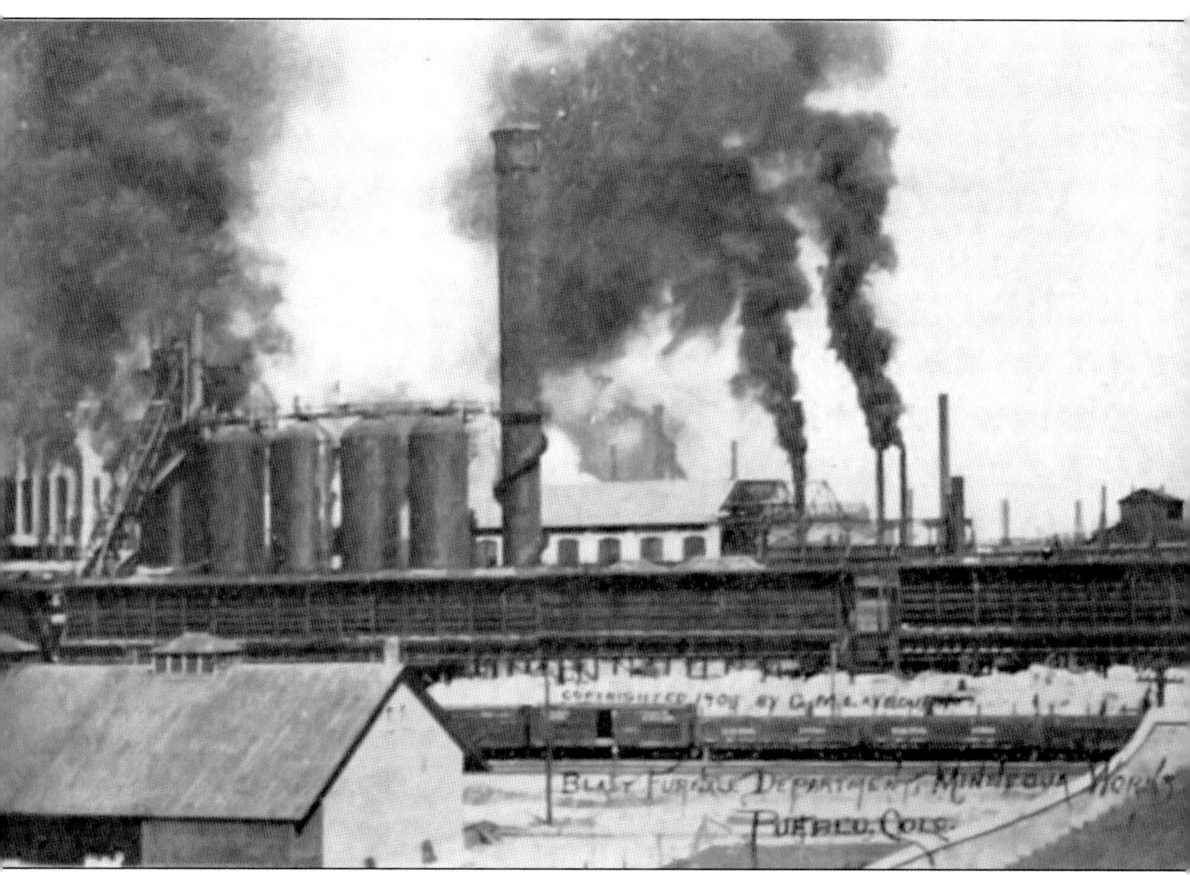

left standing. These stoves can be seen from Interstate 25, which runs parallel to the plant's west boundary. The Bessemer Historical Society purchased the mill's main office building, dispensary, and tunnel gatehouse to create the Steelworks Center of the West. This center includes both a museum and the Colorado Fuel and Iron Archives. (Steelworks.)

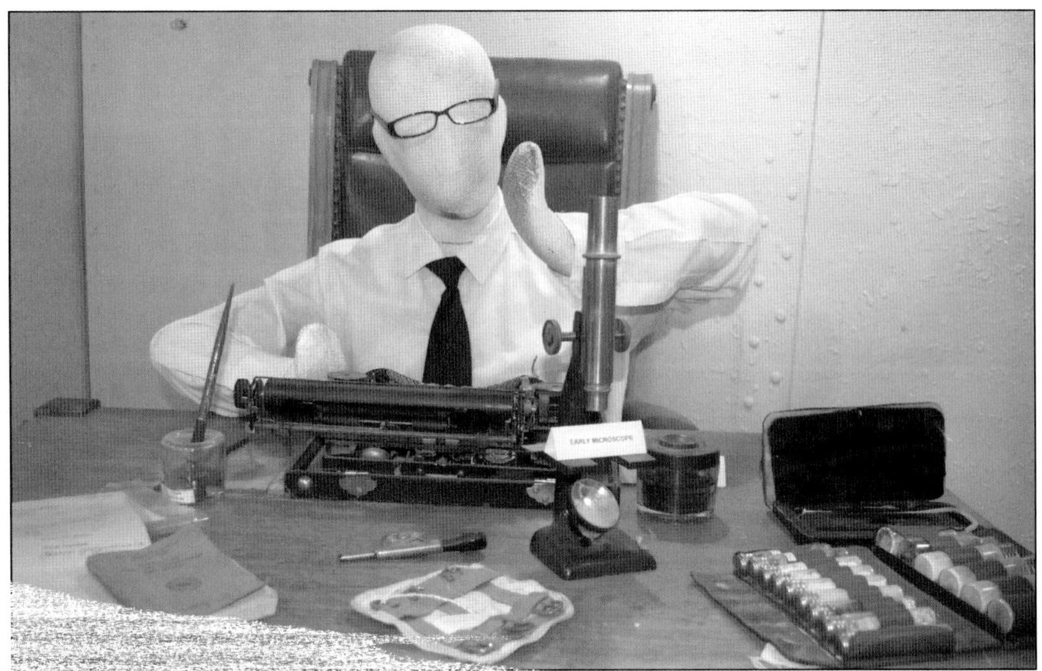

Early-20th-Century Physician's Office at Walsenburg Mining Museum. In 1898, CF&I hired Dr. Walter S. Chapman to work as the company physician at the Rouse Mine Camp. In 1922, he moved into Walsenburg and set up a private practice with two other physicians. In 1948, Dr. Chapman received a special award from the Walsenburg Chamber of Commerce to acknowledge his 50 years of service to the local community.

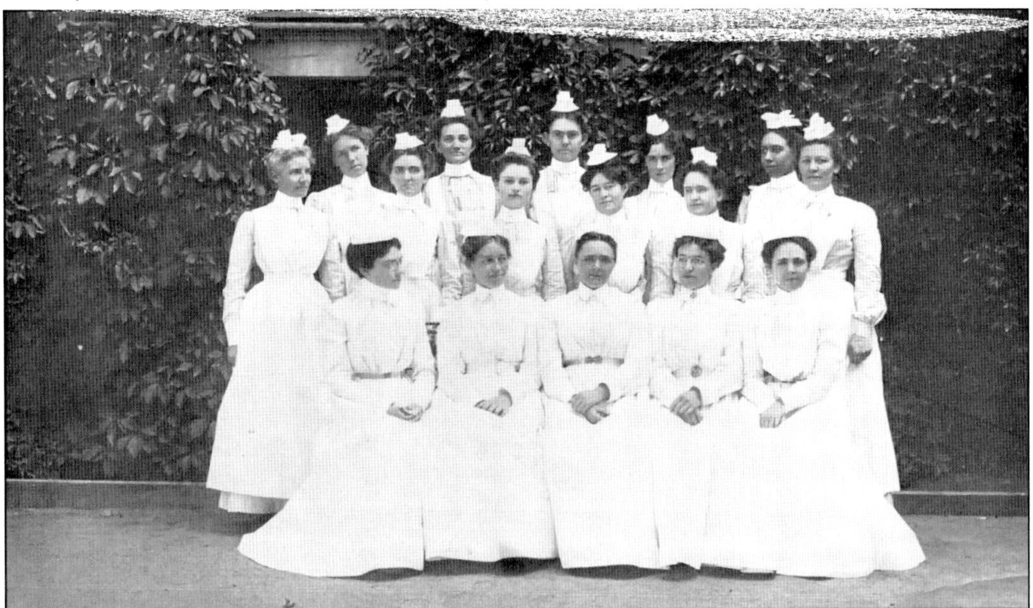

Nurses of Minnequa Hospital, 1902. This image includes student nurses, graduate nurses in charge of wards, and Jennie S. Cottle. Cottle had been appointed lead nurse and superintendent of the hospital's training school for nurses. Her nurses served in the 200-bed Minnequa Hospital, owned by CF&I and designed by the company's chief surgeon, Dr. Richard W. Corwin. (Steelworks.)

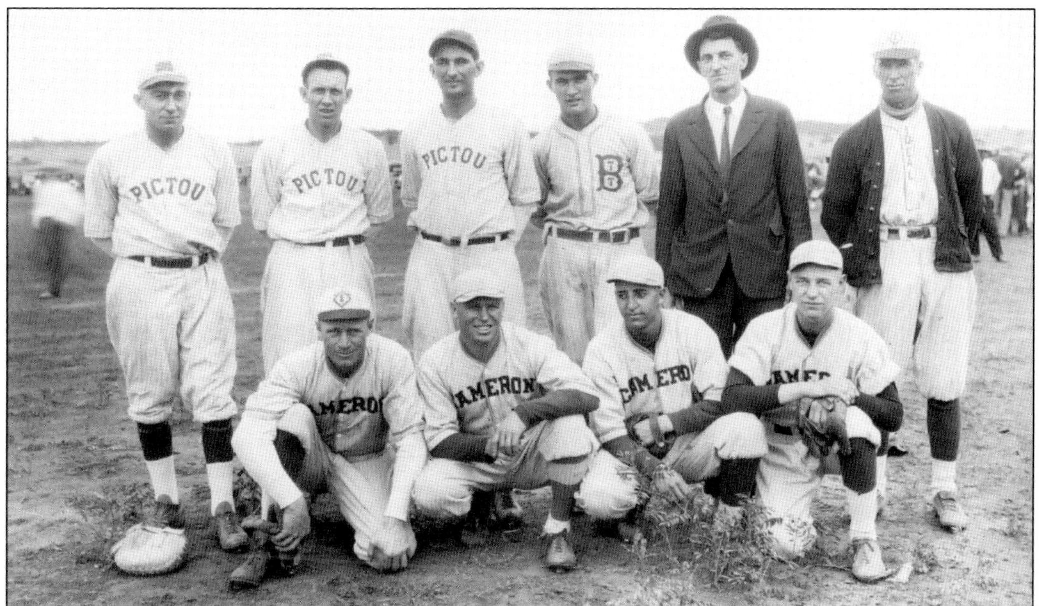

Nine Baseball Players from Pictou, Cameron, and Ideal Teams, 1926. Nearly every mine camp had its own baseball team. The season started early in the spring and lasted late into the fall. Many camps were connected by railroad. Others were within walking distance of neighboring camps. It was not unusual for a team to walk seven or eight miles, play a game, and then walk all the way home again. (Steelworks.)

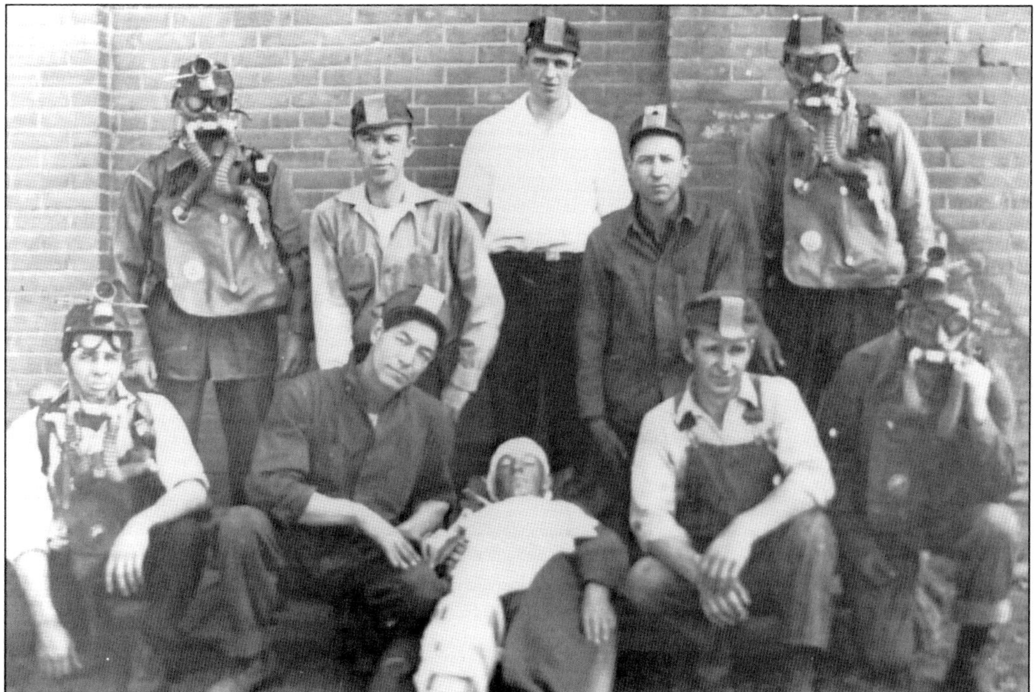

Huerfano County First Aid Team. In addition to skilled baseball players, the coal camps also produced competitive first aid teams. The teams from Huerfano County usually did well, often competing in the Denver playoffs against miners from the northern fields and Wyoming. (PCHS.)

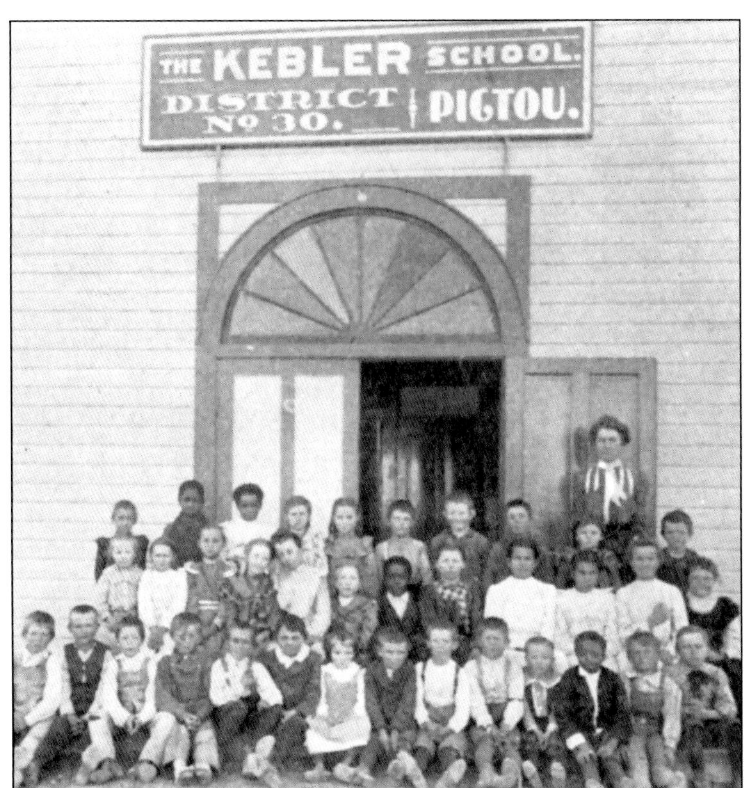

KEBLER SCHOOL AT PICTOU, 1902. Miss Blickhahn's second-through-fifth-grade class poses for its annual class picture. The building had four rooms plus a central hall, entry, and cloak room. The school remained open until 1951. At that time, School District No. 30 was dissolved, and all students remaining in the vicinity were bussed into Walsenburg. (Steelworks.)

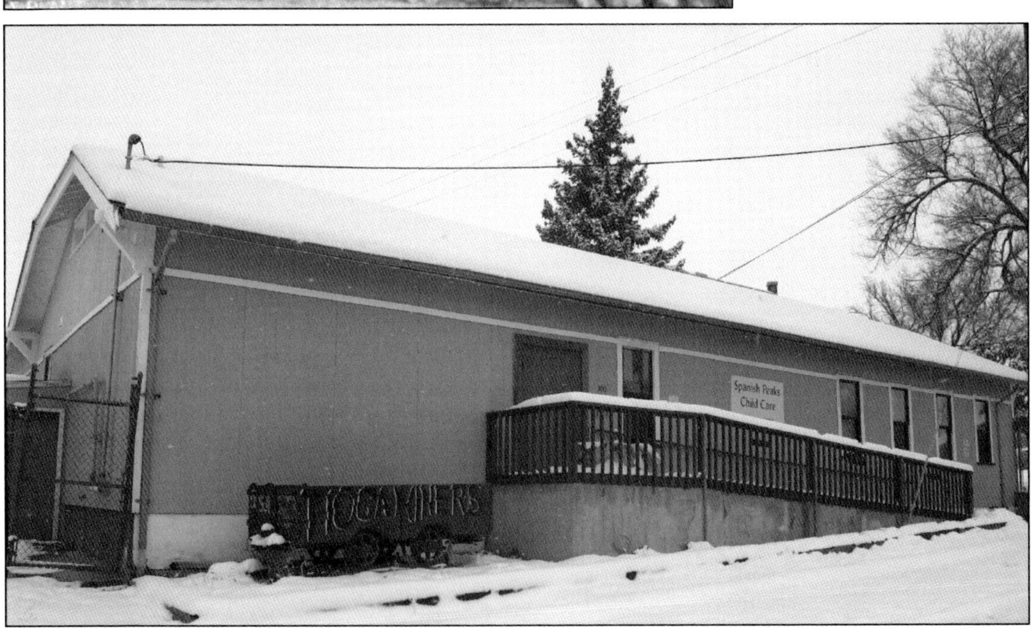

TIOGA SCHOOL. This building was erected in 1931 to accommodate the children living in the Tioga (Kebler No. 2) Mine Camp. When the mine closed in 1953, the school was moved into Walsenburg. During the 63 years it has been situated in Walsenburg, this sturdy three-room structure has served as a high school music department, school cafeteria, alternative high school, and day care center for young children.

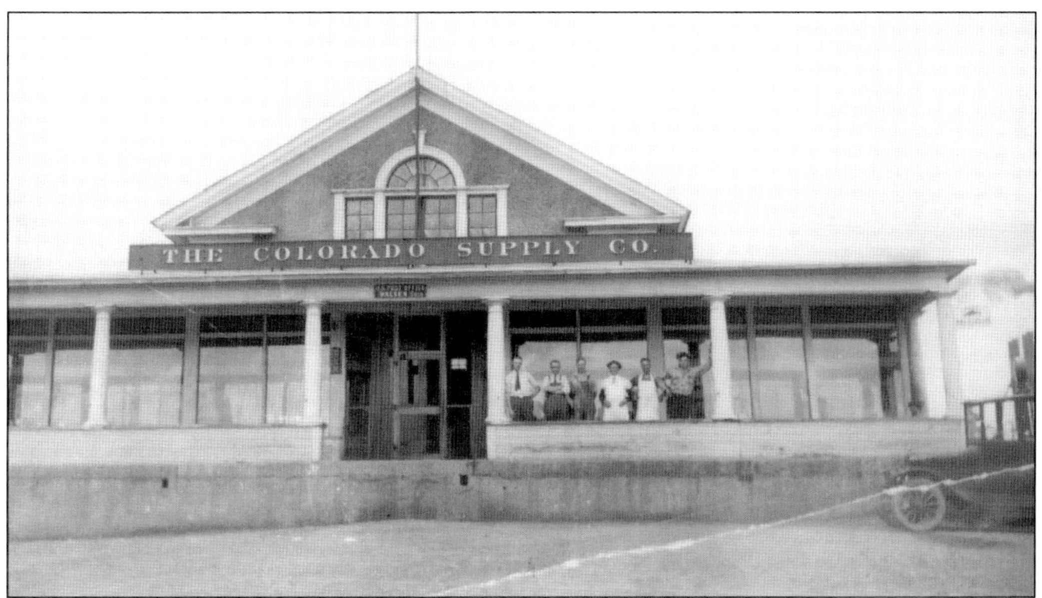

COLORADO SUPPLY COMPANY STORE IN WALSEN CAMP. The Colorado Supply Company was an affiliate of Colorado Fuel and Iron organized in 1888 to bring general stores into the mine camps. These stores offered product variety, but prices were higher in company-owned stores than they were in competitive markets. To force miners to trade at company-owned businesses, mine owners paid in scrip until 1914. (HCHS/WMM.)

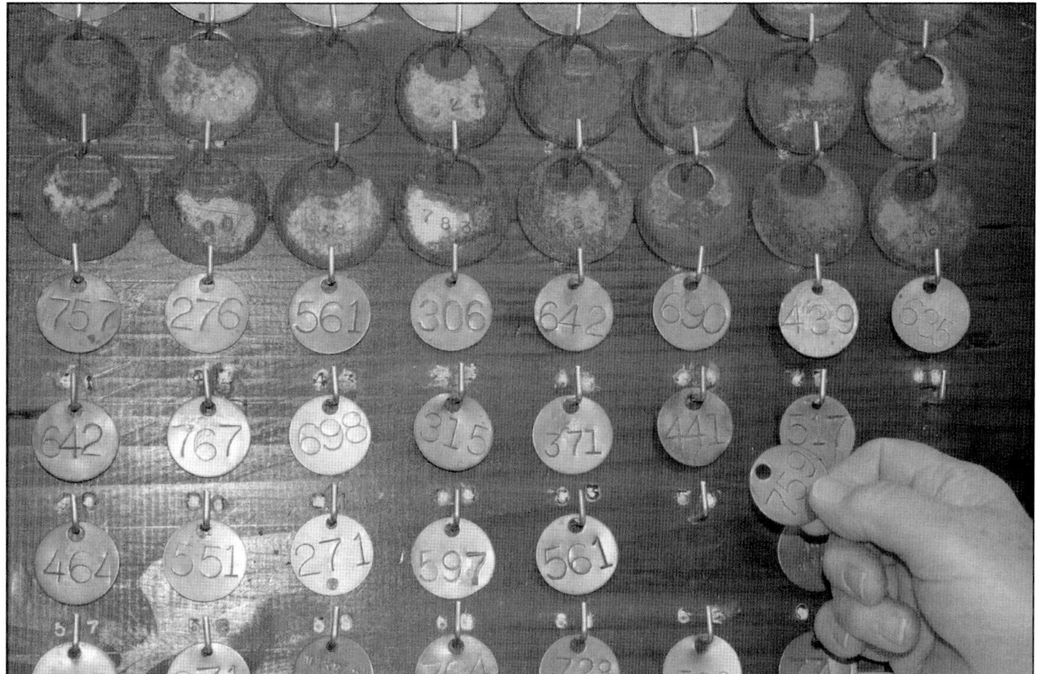

TAG IN/OUT BOARD AT THE WALSENBURG MINING MUSEUM. Each miner was assigned a brass tag with a unique number on it. The metal tag was taken off the board by the miner as he entered the mine and placed back on the board when he finished his shift. This system allowed supervisors to quickly see who was underground at any given time.

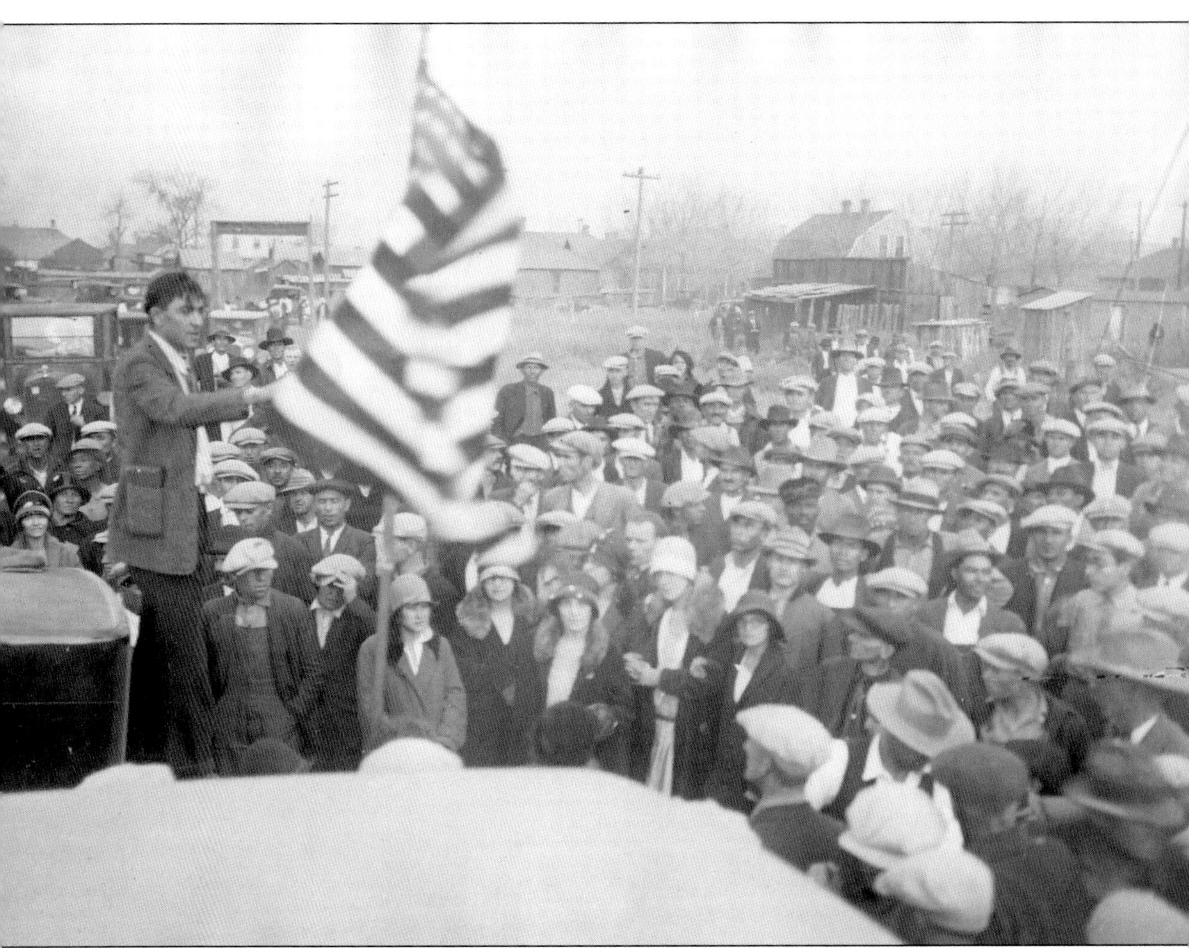

Workers Gather Outside at the Walsen Mine. Over the course of its history, the CF&I had numerous disputes with labor unions. Southern Colorado coal miners struck in 1884, 1894, 1903, 1913, and 1927, each time striving for better pay, better living conditions, and recognition of their union. The most famous walkout occurred on September 23, 1913. Seven months later, on April 20, 1914, Colorado National Guardsmen and CF&I camp guards attacked a tent colony composed of out-of-work miners and their families living near the Ludlow train station. The battle raged for hours. During the fighting, the tents caught fire. Eleven children and two women trapped beneath one of the tents died from smoke inhalation. Thus began a series of deadly conflicts as bands of miners retaliated by attacking coal company facilities along a 40-mile front from Trinidad to Walsenburg. Pres. Woodrow Wilson eventually sent in federal troops to disarm both sides. (Steelworks.)

Seven

Town Planners and Builders

By 1900, Huerfano County boasted 18 post offices, 37 school districts, 19 coal mines, and a population of 8,395. Over the next 10 years, the county's population grew to 13,320 residents, many of them living in coal camps. Rouse alone counted 1,000 denizens with another 250 in nearby Pryor.

During the Roaring Twenties, when Pres. Calvin Coolidge bragged that "the business of America is business," the coal industry, railroads, agriculture, and tourism gave employment and a living wage to nearly anyone who wanted to work. However, the Great Depression and prolonged drought brought hard times to Huerfano County in the 1930s. Entire herds of cattle had to be slaughtered because there was no feed and no money to buy it. From 1935 to 1942, the Works Progress Administration (WPA) employed thousands of men to construct roads, bridges, a water filtration system, post offices, schools, and other government buildings.

Of course, the biggest changes to the region during the 1940s were caused by World War II, including intense patriotism, the tragic deaths of young heroes, savings bond drives to help finance the war, and rationing of every valuable commodity from butter to rubber tires. Goat herds in the county expanded production of one item on the critical shortage list, as La Veta's cheese factory shipped goat cheese all over the nation.

The number of residents in Huerfano County shrank from 17,062 in 1930 to 10,549 by 1950. Much of this decrease was attributable to the closing of coal mines and the depopulation of family farms as returning veterans chose to move to big cities with higher-paying jobs. Also in the 1950s, the Walsenburg Utilities Board and La Veta's San Isabel Electric extended power lines through rural electrification projects. Gone were the days of houses lighted with kerosene lamps. The world was ushering in a new age of fast cars, jet airplanes, men walking on the moon, transistor radios, color television sets, cassette decks, electric dishwashers, and shopping malls.

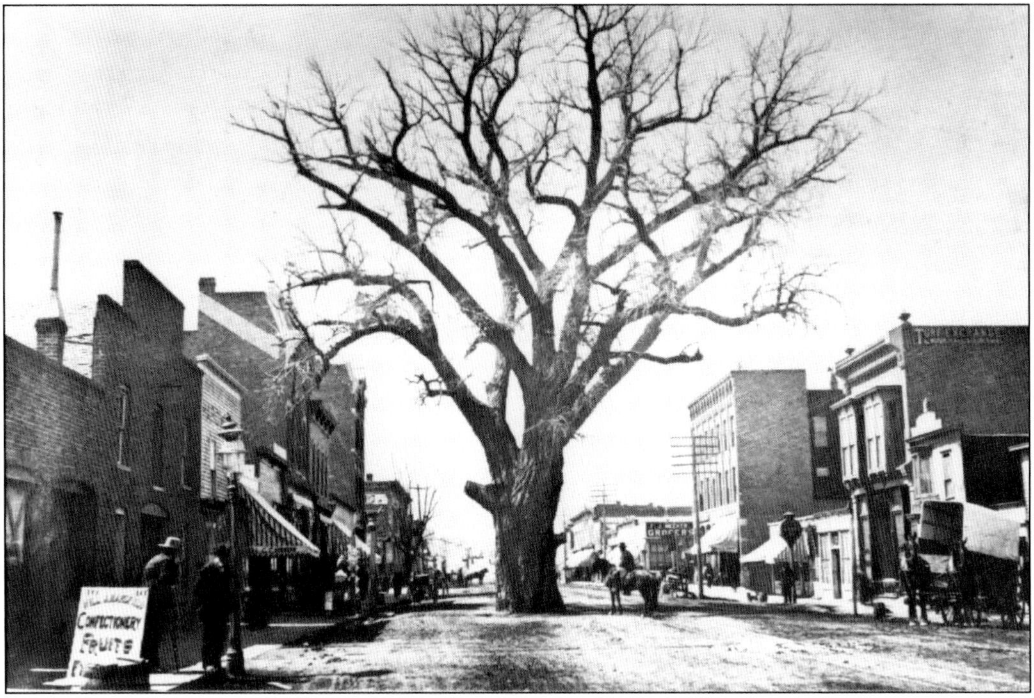

PUEBLO, 1880. Between 1861 and 1865, Huerfano County encompassed all of present-day Huerfano County plus Las Animas, Baca, Bent, Otero, Prowers, Crowley, the west half of Kiowa, and the southern part of Pueblo Counties. After 1865, Huerfano County's northern boundary lay 30 miles south of downtown Pueblo. This image includes Old Monarch, a stately cottonwood that stood in the middle of Pueblo's Union Avenue until 1883. (PCHS.)

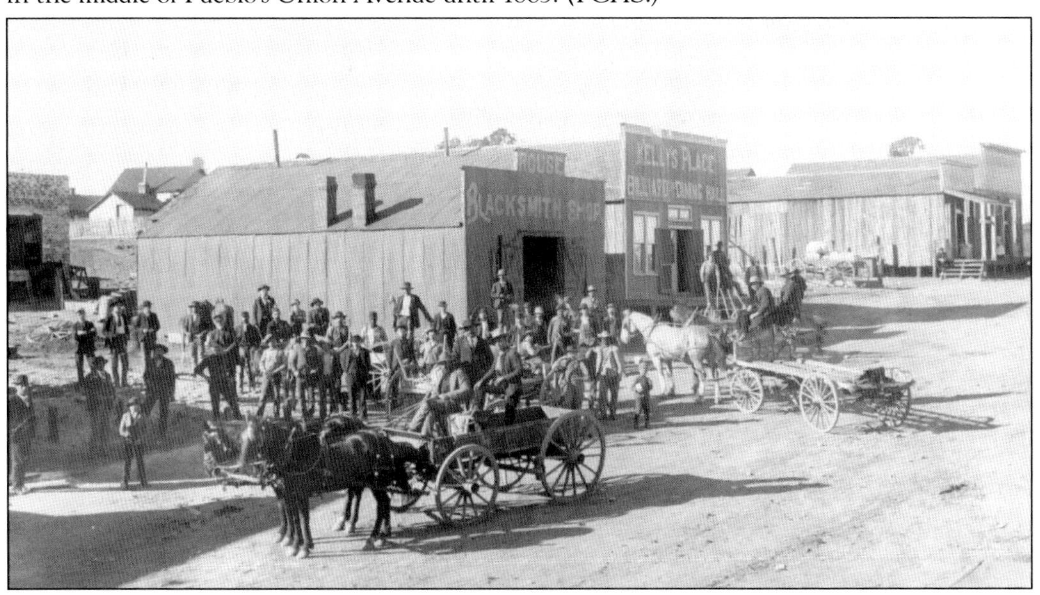

A TOWN CALLED ROUSE, C. 1896. Rouse was situated about 20 miles south of the Huerfano River. In 1896, it looked very much like the other large settlements in Huerfano County, including Gardner, La Veta, and Walsenburg. In fact, some historians have erroneously labeled this photograph as a street scene in Walsenburg. (MVHS/O.T. Davis Collection.)

Twelve Apostles. When this photograph was taken around 1875, the 12 men pictured here were leading citizens in and around the young town of Walsenburg. From left to right are (seated) A.R. Campbell, Charles Mazzone, Isaac Dailey, Henry Strange, Frank Duhme, John H. Brown, and August Sporleder; (standing) Capt. James Thompson, John Chapell, John Albert, Fred Walsen, and T.L. Creesy. (HCHS/ATC.)

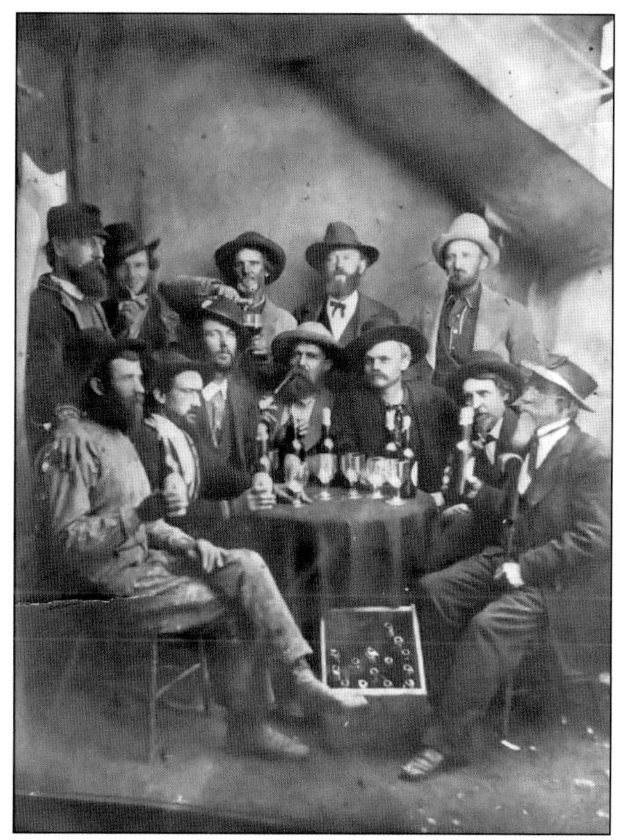

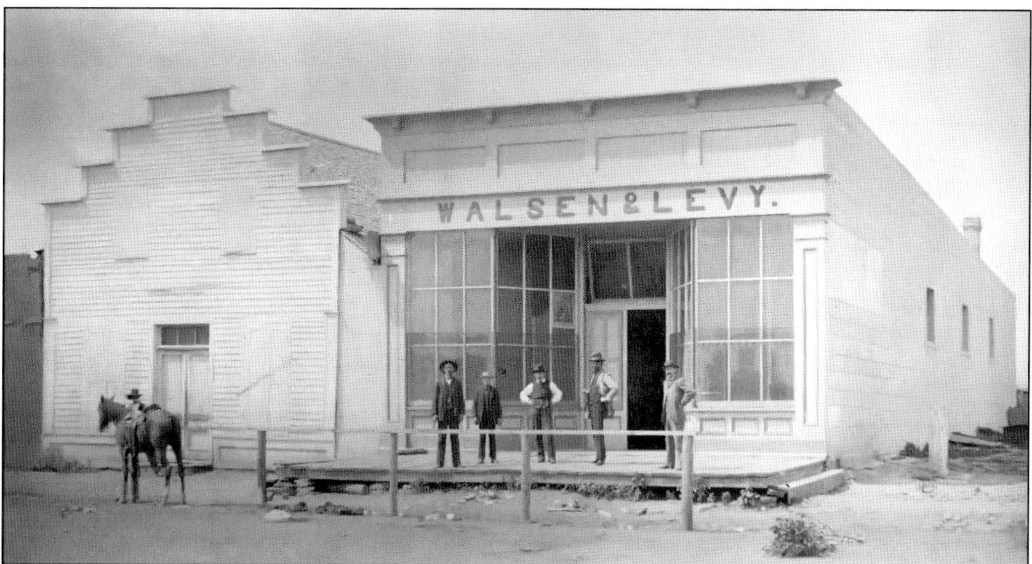

Walsen and Levy Store, Walsenburg. Photographed sometime between 1880 and 1890, this building attested to a mercantile partnership that furthered the business interests of both Fred Walsen and Alexander Levy. The two were also brothers-in-law married to Emilie and Lillie Sporleder, daughters of August Sporleder. The adjacent building with the stepped false front served as the town's first Masonic hall. (DPL, no. X-14007.)

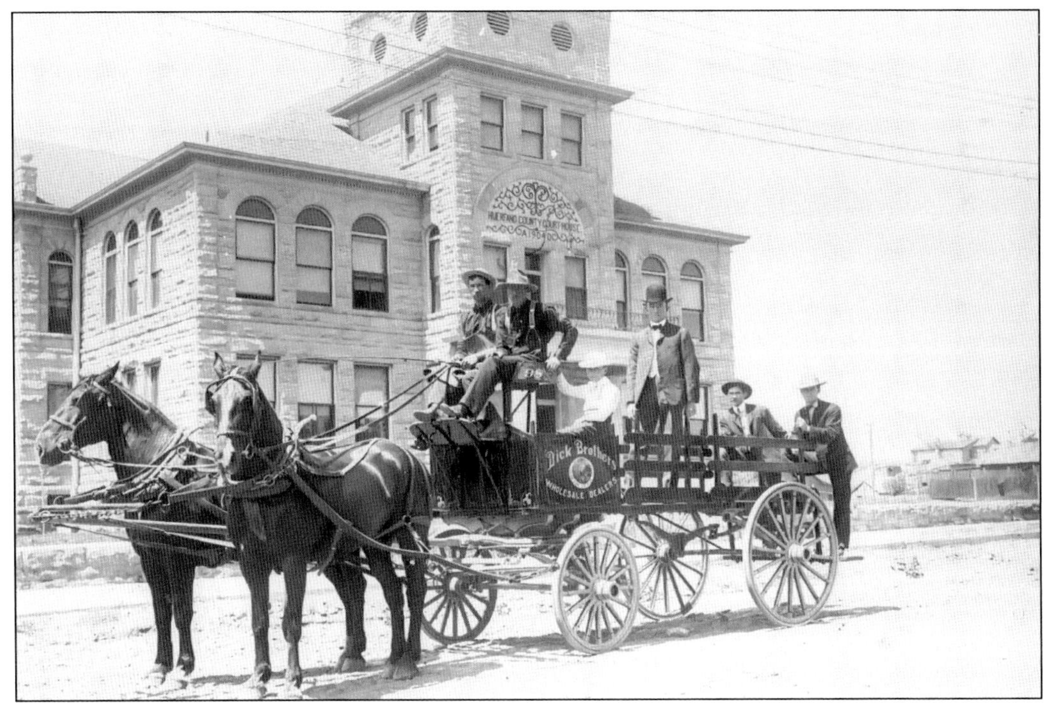

DICK BROTHERS, 1905. William, George, and James B. Dick owned ranches, coal mines, various town businesses, and a license to sell wholesale liquors. Here they pose atop their delivery wagon, which is parked in front of the Huerfano County Courthouse. The courthouse, designed by C.A. Henderson of Pueblo, was built from local sandstone and completed in 1904. (HCHS/ATC.)

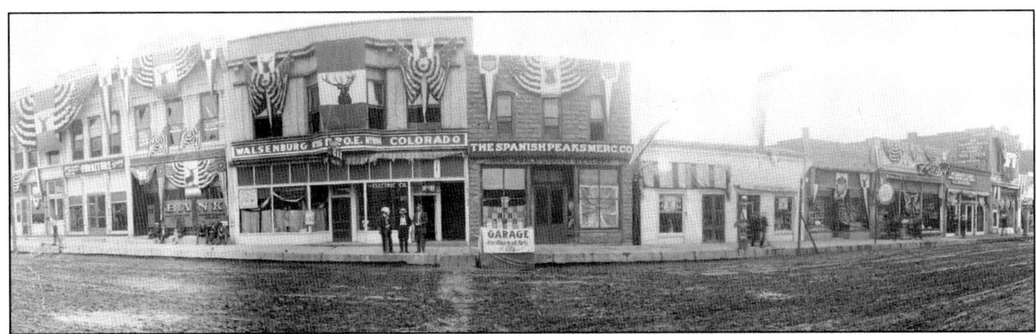

ELKS CONVENTION, WALSENBURG. This wide-angle view of Main Street shows stone commercial buildings draped in bunting and US flags. It was photographed by Lours Studio in 1913. From left to right, the signs on the first five buildings read: "Agnes/Kalmes Wholesale & Retail Furniture Store," "The Independent, The Paper with a Backbone," "Walsenburg B.P.O.E. No 1086 Colorado," "The Spanish Peaks Merc Co.," and "Braun's Bakery." (DPL, no. X-15099.)

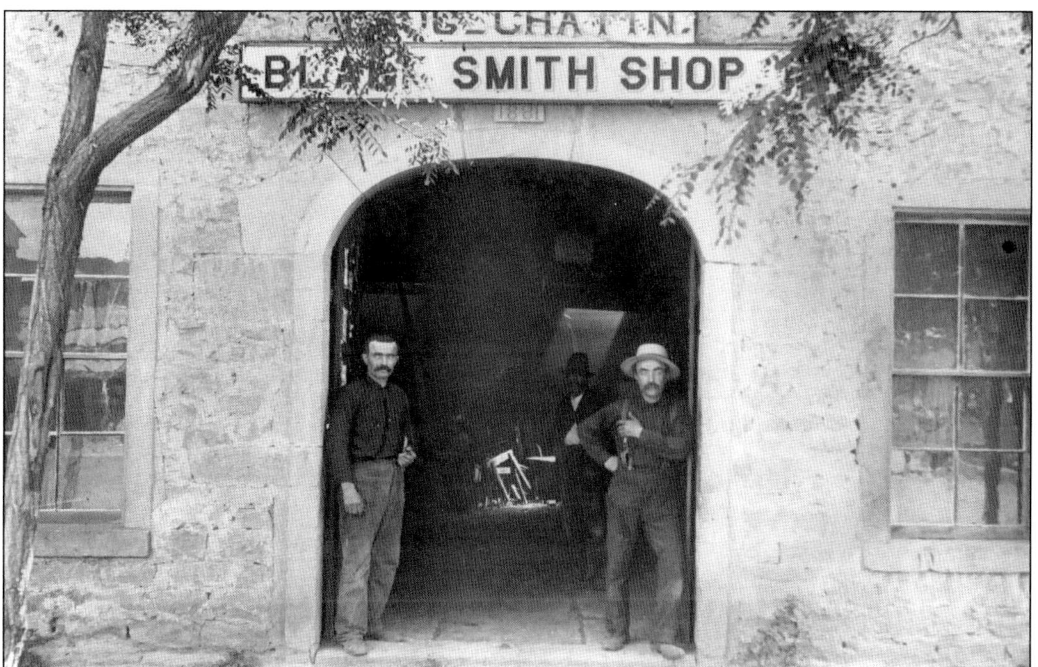

CHATIN BLACKSMITH SHOP, WALSENBURG. This building, constructed in 1891, was situated on the east side of Main Street, between Sixth and Seventh Streets. The owners lived behind the shop on the rear portion of the town lot. (PCCLD, no. Ph-C-400-05_002.)

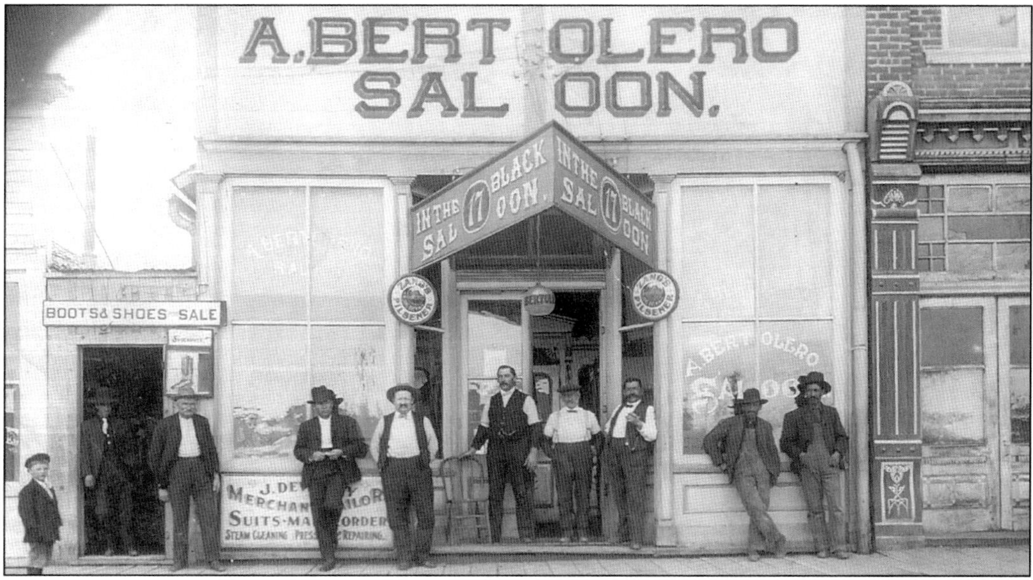

ANTONIO BERTOLERO SALOON. By 1910, Walsenburg supported 15 saloons, two newspapers, two undertakers, three drugstores, 10 physicians, 24 grocery and dry goods stores, and various other businesses. In 1902, Walsenburg contained three churches, three town schools, and 44 licensed businesses, including several saloons. In this year, Antonio "Tony" Bertolero sold his establishment on South Main Street and moved elsewhere. The most famous saloon keeper to set up shop in Walsenburg was Robert Ford, the infamous killer of Jesse James, who operated a saloon and gambling house on Seventh Street from 1889 to 1892. (HCHS/ATC.)

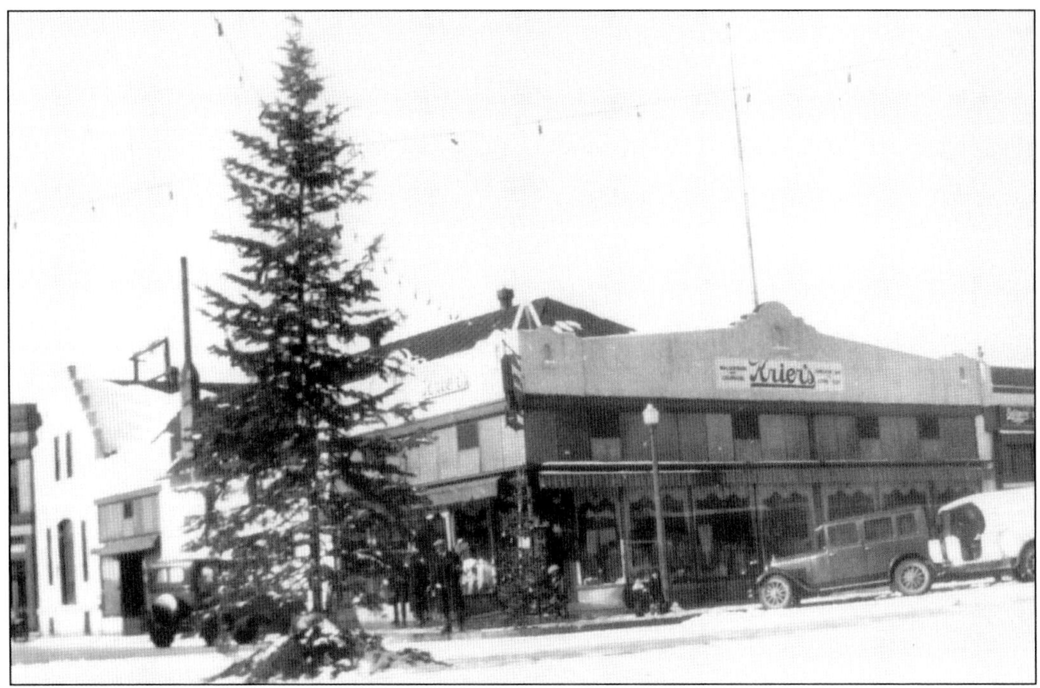

KRIER'S IN WALSENBURG. Peter Krier owned this store at the northwest corner of Sixth and Main Streets, the current location of April's Attic. Because it was in the center of town, it was a perfect site for the town Christmas tree. Like other merchants in the area, Krier maintained store hours of 7:30 a.m. to 8:00 p.m., Monday through Saturday, plus a half-day on Sunday. (HCHS/ATC/Gordon Kelly Collection.)

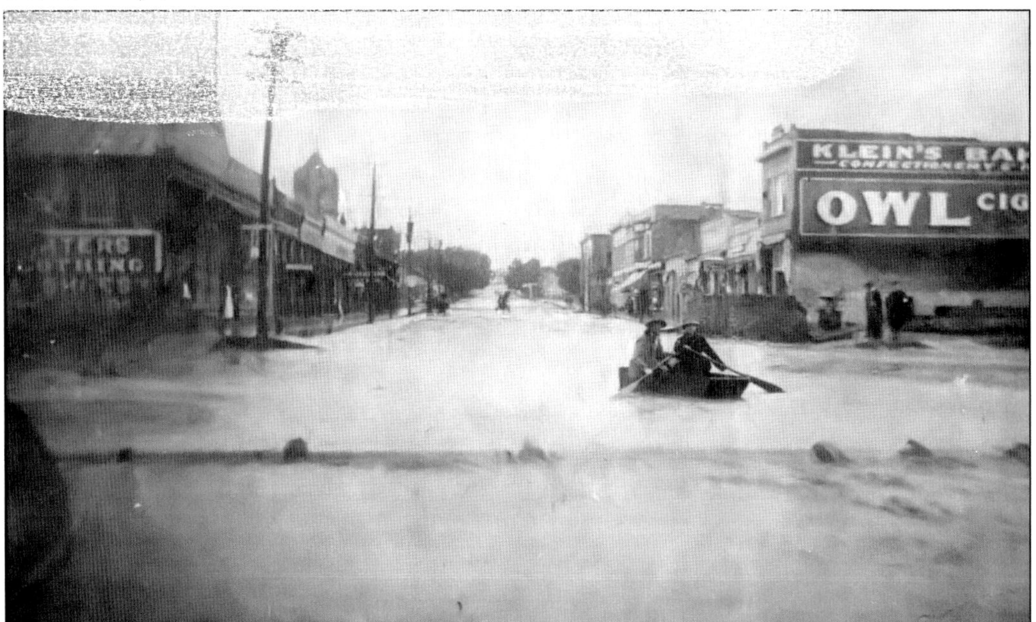

WALSENBURG, 1907. Heavy snowfalls and turbulent rainstorms could produce dangerous conditions in the days before sophisticated flood control measures tamed the rivers in the Huerfano Valley. This is a view of downtown Walsenburg during the 1907 Cucharas River flood. (DPL, no. X-13998.)

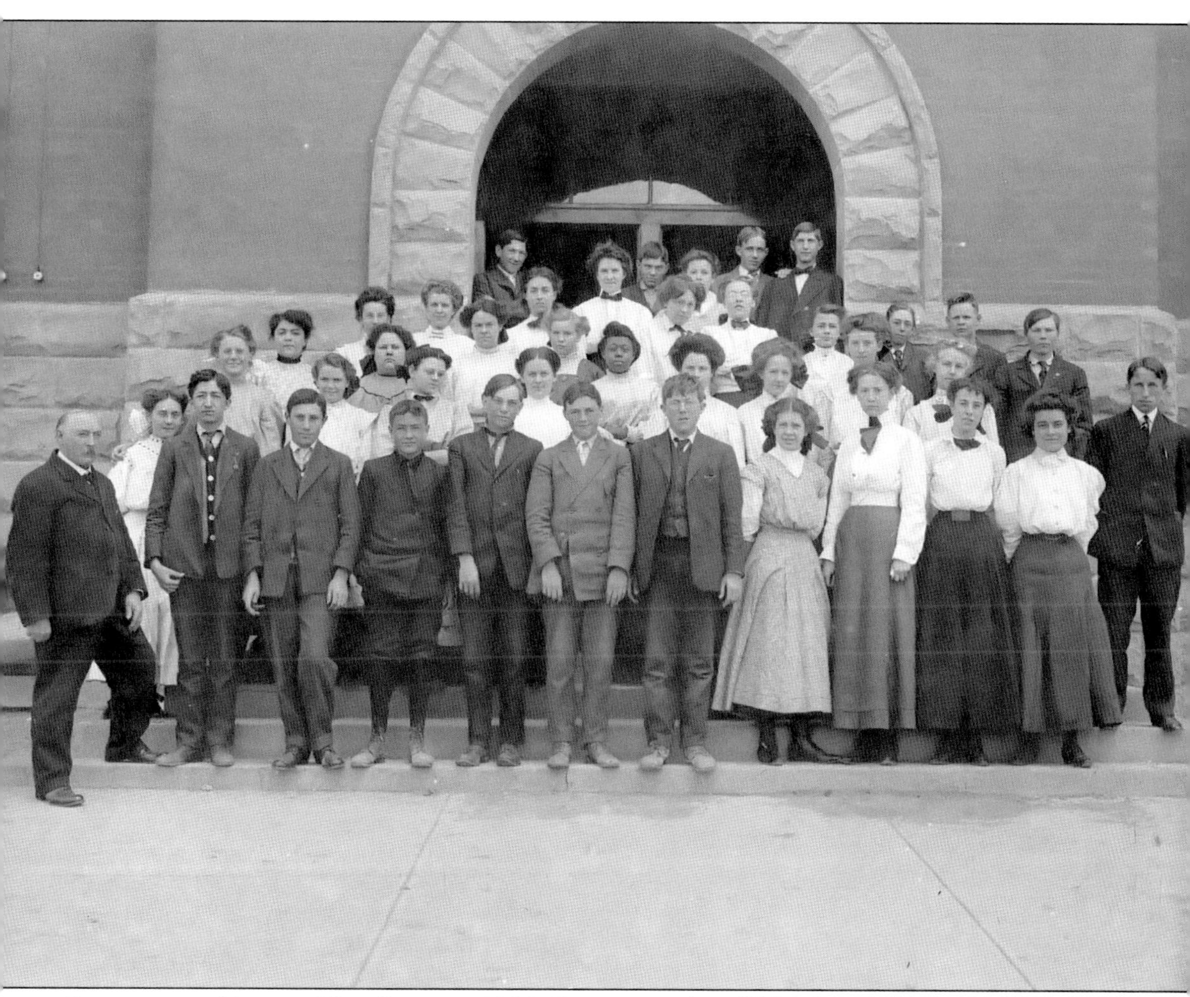

Students at Capitol Hill School, 1908. Six years earlier, Walsenburg's three schools had a total enrollment of 470 students. The nine instructors teaching these students earned an average salary of $60 per month. From 1913 to 1916, the Walsenburg National Guard Armory housed high school classes because there was a classroom shortage within the town. The brick, three-story Huerfano County High School on Walsen Avenue designed by the architectural firm Rapp and Rapp wasn't completed until 1921. Then the building on Capitol Hill became an elementary school. Today it is a private residence. (HCHS/ATC.)

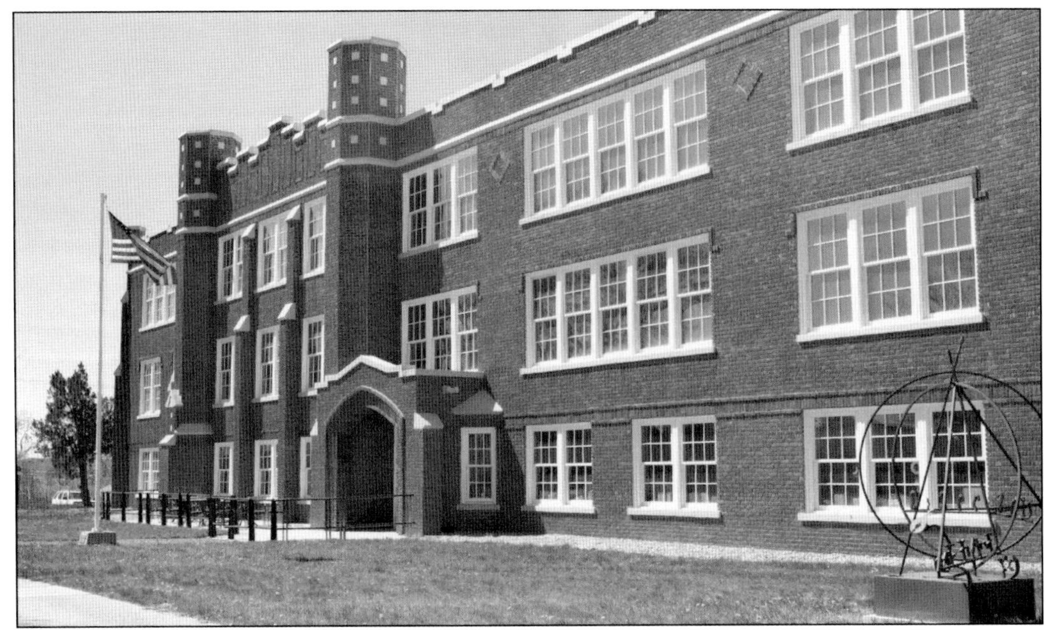

Huerfano County High School. From 1921 to 1959, this building served as the county high school. The name was changed to Walsenburg High School in 1959. After John Mall High School was completed on Pine Street in 1976, this older structure became known as Walsenburg Middle School. It was listed in the National Register of Historic Places in 2005 and currently houses the Spanish Peaks Library.

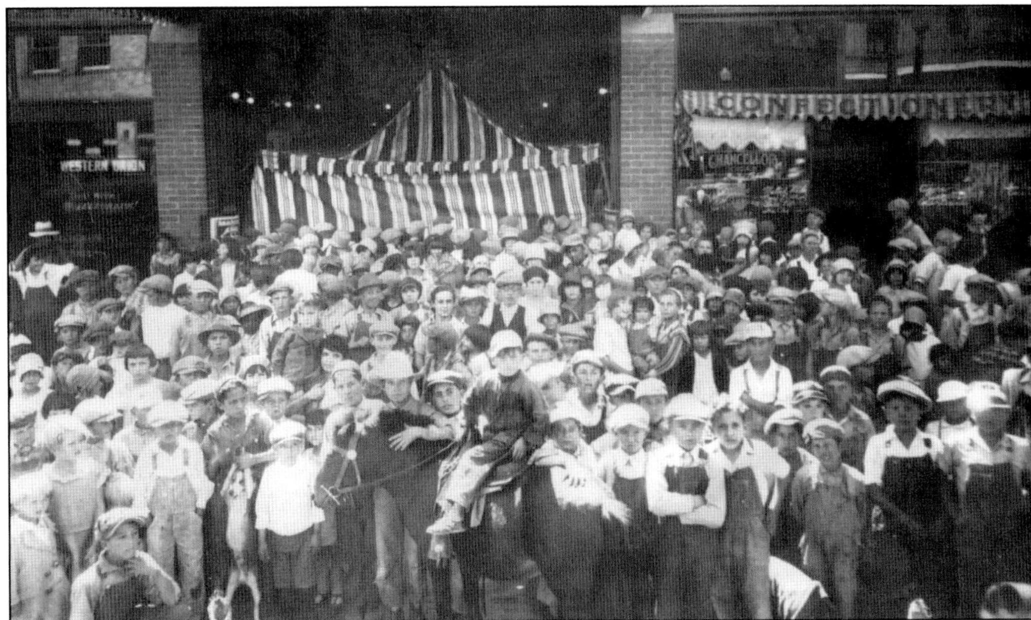

Kids Day at the Movies, c. 1930. Many children who grew up in the Great Depression and had a dime to spend experienced the joy of Saturday afternoons at the neighborhood motion picture theater. Entertainment included a double feature and a short cartoon sandwiched between the two shows. This photograph was taken in front of the Star Theatre at Walsenburg. (PCCLD, no. Ph-C-400-08_009.)

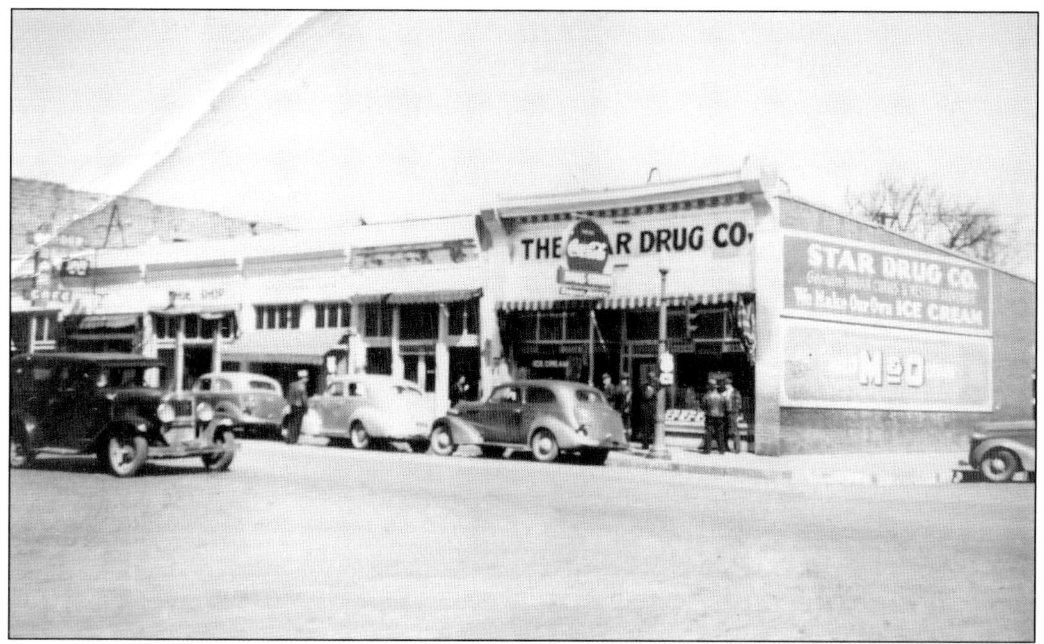

Star Drug, 1947. The pharmacy at the northeast corner of Main and Seventh Streets in Walsenburg has been in operation for more than 100 years. It was started by brothers Ed and Andy Merritt in September 1914. It was the town's first corner drugstore and for many years housed a soda fountain and a Western Union office. (HCHS/ATC.)

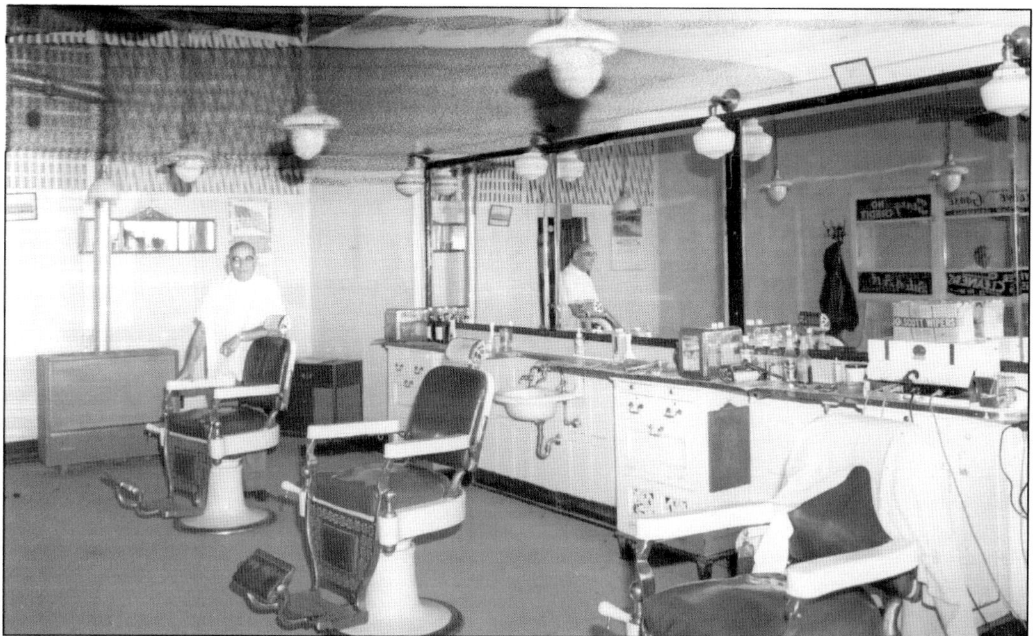

A Neighborhood Barbershop. Charlie Fertitta established his barbershop next door to Star Drug in Walsenburg. He remained in business for 47 years. In the early 1950s, when he opened his shop, a local miner earned $2,500–$3,000 per year, if he could find work. Huerfano County High School set $2,400 as the base salary for beginning teachers, and auto mechanics in Walsenburg earned $45–$65 per month. (HCHS/ATC/Gordon Kelly Collection.)

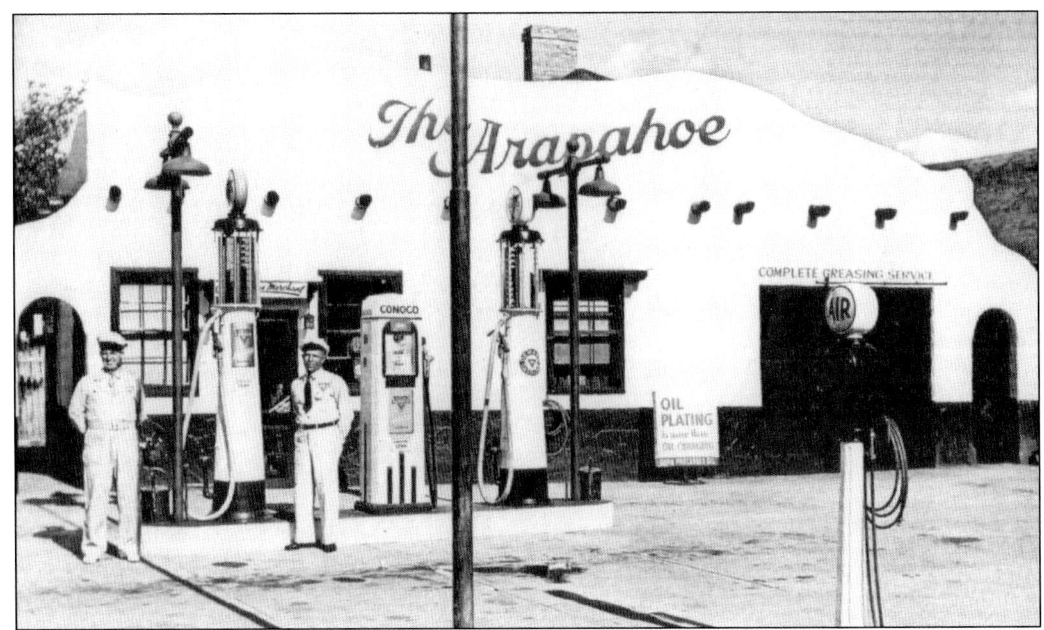

Arapaho Station on South Main Street, Walsenburg. S.F. Bowser in 1905 converted a kerosene pump into a machine for dispensing gasoline directly into an automobile tank. The first "drive-in" filling station opened to motorists in 1913. By the mid-20th century, almost every town in America had at least one filling station. This station, owned by the Lenzini family, was operated by a Mr. Johnson (left) and Al Feiccabrino (right). (HCHS/ATC.)

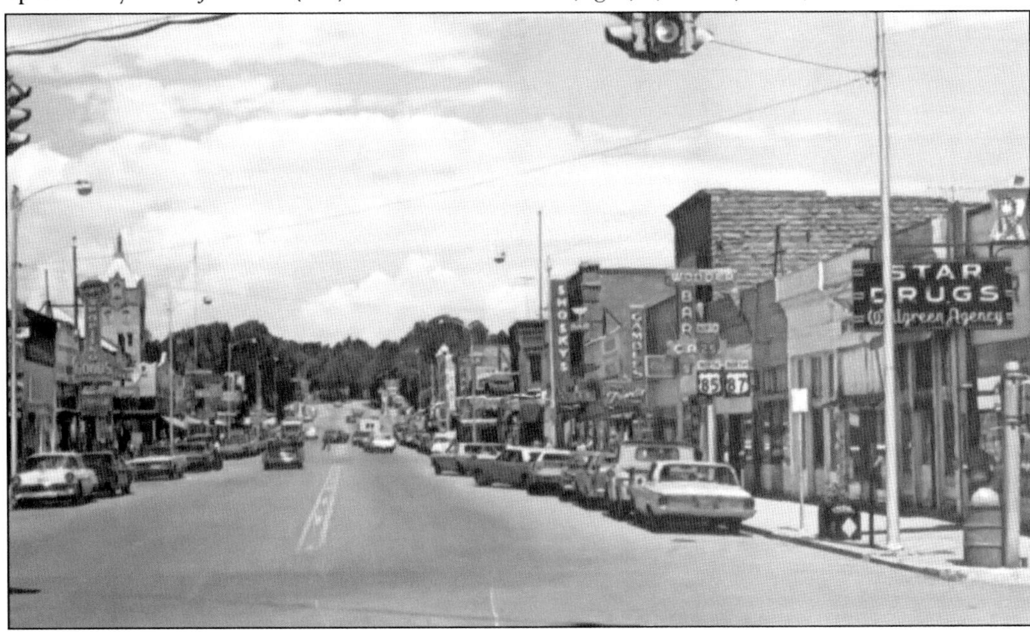

Main Street in Walsenburg. Over a period of nine decades, hand-painted placards, wooden boardwalks, dusty streets, buggies, and buckboards gave way to new contrivances such as neon signs, electric stoplights, cement sidewalks, sealed asphalt, Ford Fairlanes, and Chevy pickups. This postcard was created in the early 1960s to highlight the bustling modernity of Huerfano County's biggest population center. (John Carlson.)

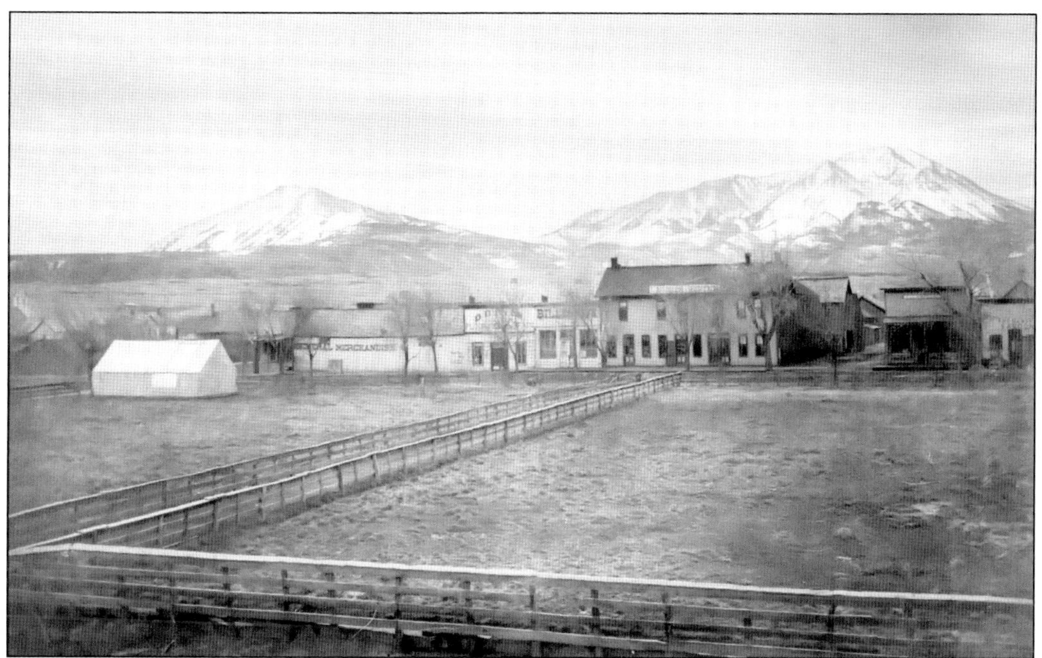

Ryus Street in La Veta, c. 1895. Note the scenic Spanish Peaks in the background and the neat and tidy fences in the foreground. The buildings, from left to right, include D.D. Ryus's General Merchandise, a billiards hall, the La Veta Hotel, C.A. Martins's store, and the Denver Saloon. (MVHS/O.T. Davis Collection.)

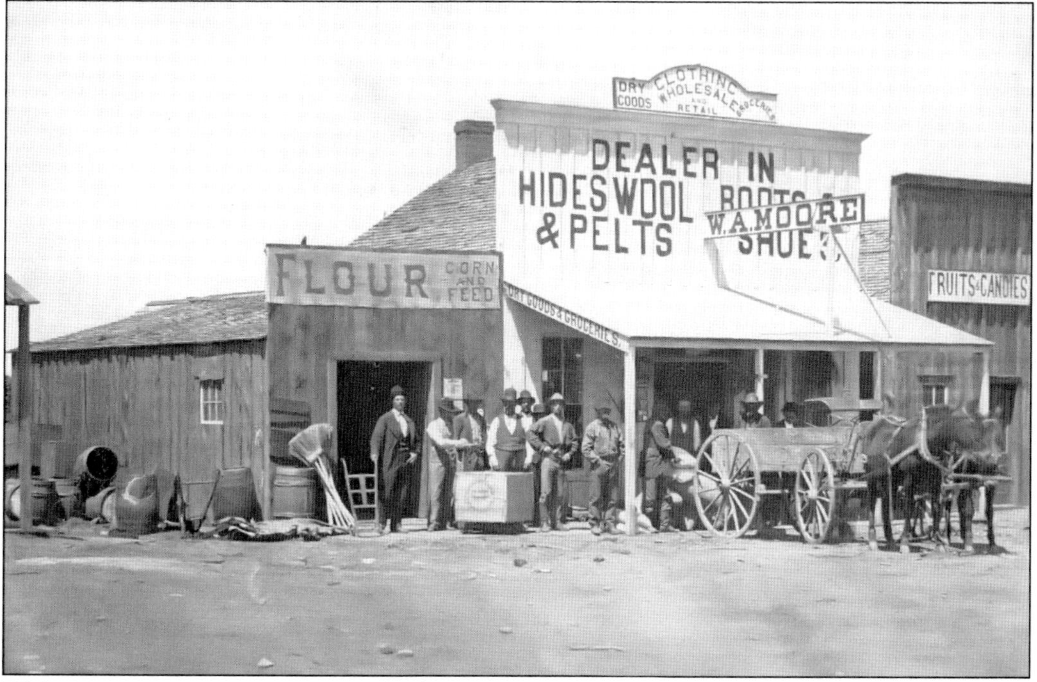

W.A. Moore Mercantile. Moore had a store in La Veta in 1876 that stocked liquor, groceries, hides, wool, dry goods, and medicines. His general store also carried corn and feed, shoes, boots, fruits, and candies. In 1877, he served on the town board. (HCHS/FFM.)

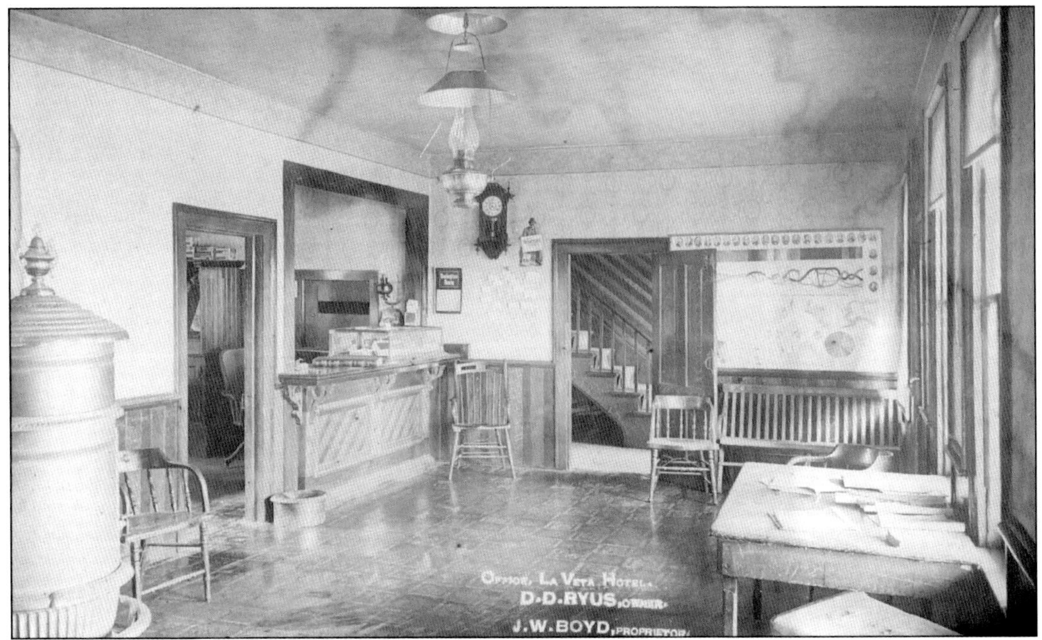

LA VETA HOTEL LOBBY, C. 1907. Known also as the Alamo and the Spanish Peaks Hotel, the La Veta Hotel was built in 1876. It was destroyed by fire in May 1944. At the time this picture was taken, the building had 22 guest rooms, gas lights, an elegant parlor, and one indoor bathroom with hot and cold running water. (HCHS/FFM.)

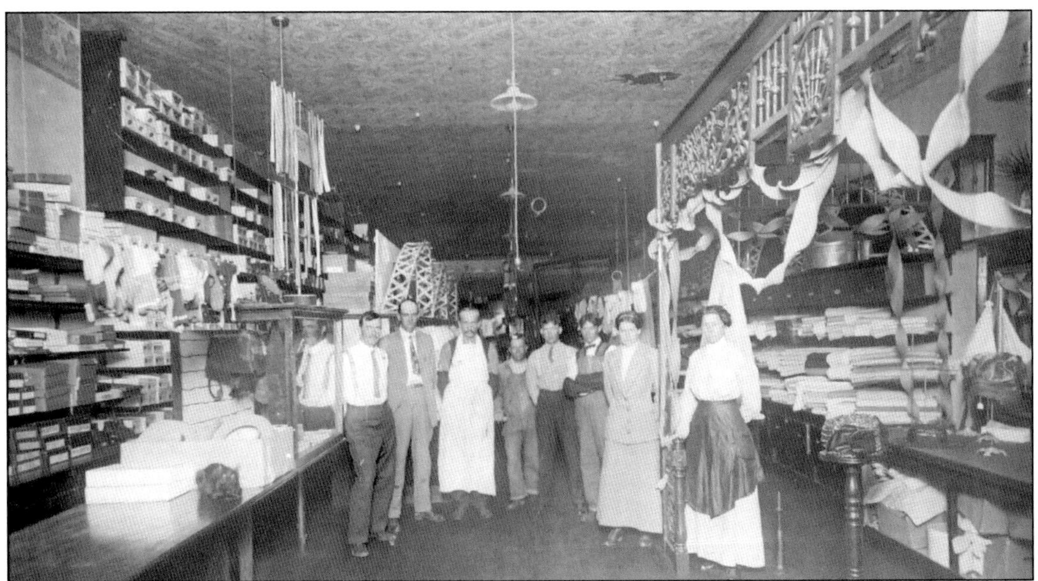

CISNEY AND SPARKS STORE, LA VETA. Store personnel pictured here include, from left to right, Joe Cisney, Abe Sparks, Poley Erwin, Rich Wagener, two unidentified clerks, Hettie Sparks, and Maggie Cisney. Note the embossed tin ceiling, the hanging lamps, the many shelves crammed full of dry goods, and the furnishings so typical of the early decades of the 20th century. (HCHS/FFM.)

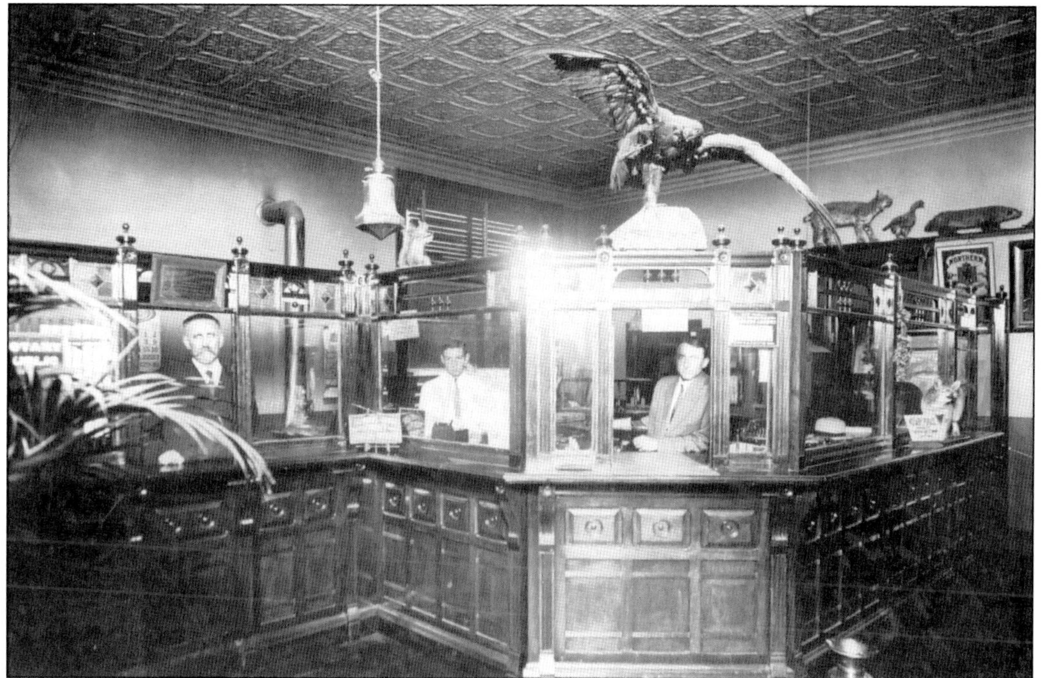

La Veta State Bank. Photographed between 1912 and 1913, three men stand behind windows in the ornate teller's cage. A taxidermied owl was mounted above one of the teller cage windows. In addition to the usual financial transactions, this bank offered the services of a notary public. (HCHS/FFM.)

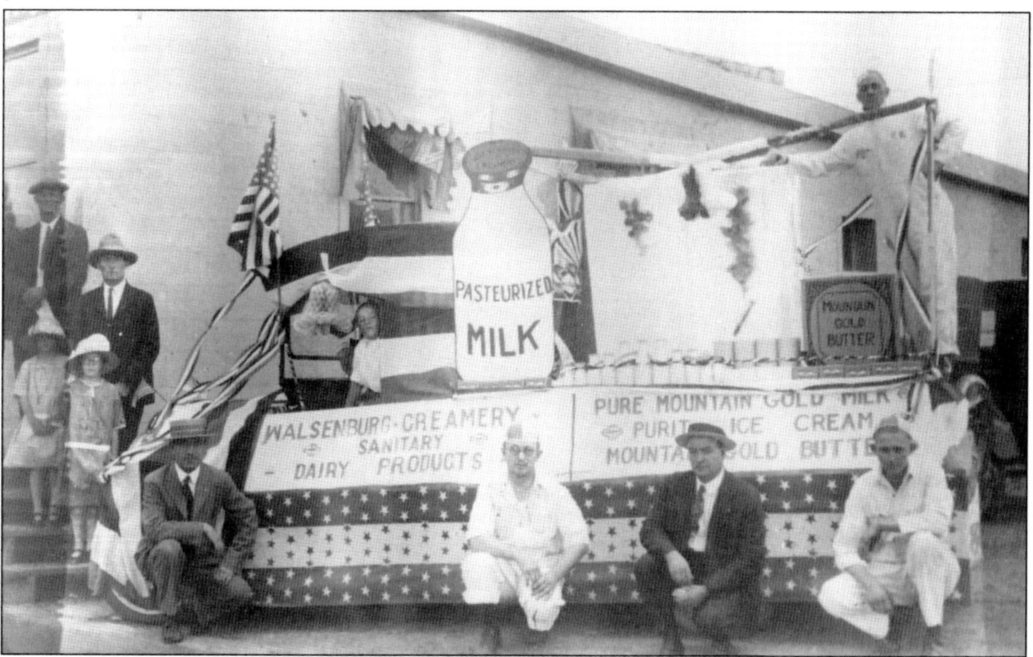

Walsenburg Creamery. The Colorado Cheese Company of La Veta shipped goat cheese throughout the United States. The Walsenburg Creamery was more localized, but it specialized in many dairy products, including milk, ice cream, and butter. (PCCLD, no. Ph-C-400-02_004.)

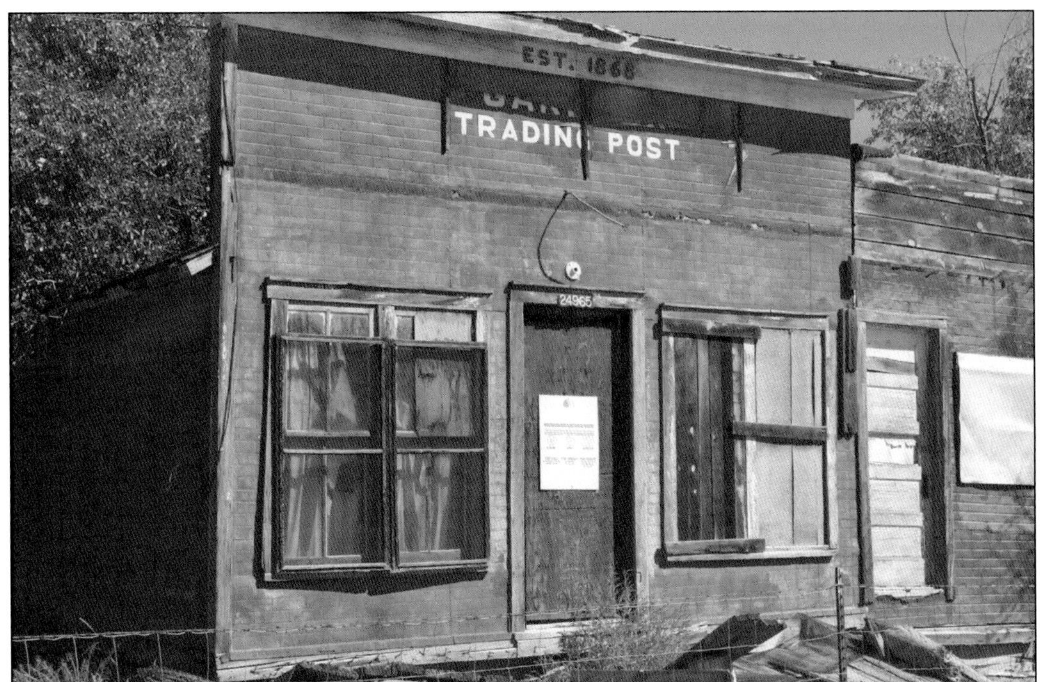

Gardner Trading Post. Gardner is situated 25 miles west of Walsenburg along Highway 69. The town lies halfway between the Wet Mountains and the Sangre de Cristos on an old stage line that extended from Walsenburg to Westcliffe/Silver Cliff when Silver Cliff was a boom town enriched by silver mines. This old trading post on the east side of Gardner could have been built as early as 1868.

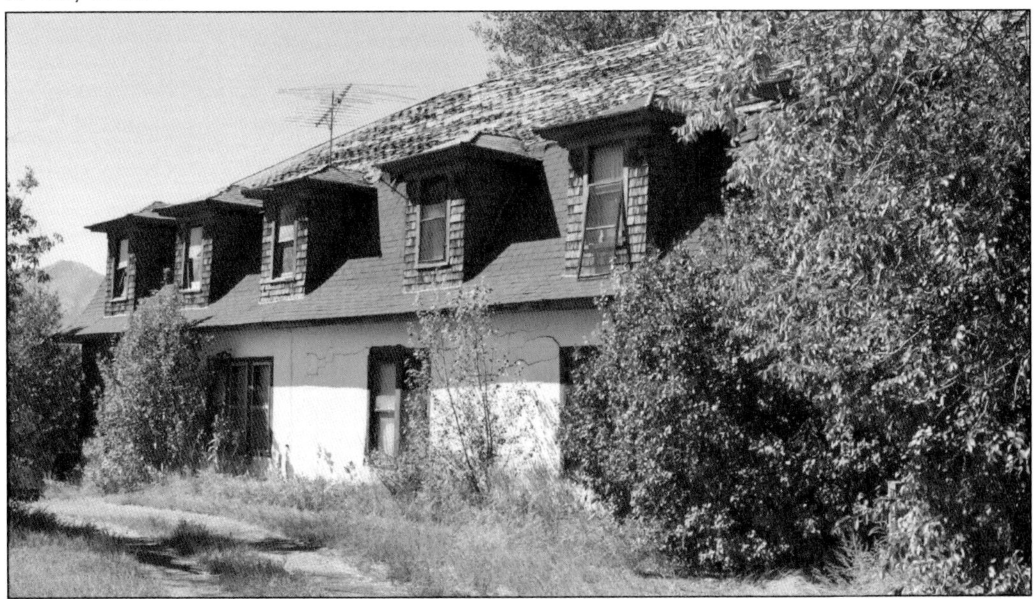

Gardner Hotel. Farmers and cattlemen found temporary lodging in the Huerfano River settlement of Gardner as early as 1863, the year Herbert Gardner opened a trading post and store at this site. The adobe-and-frame hotel pictured here was built in 1915 by Dan Costello to replace an earlier hotel that burned down.

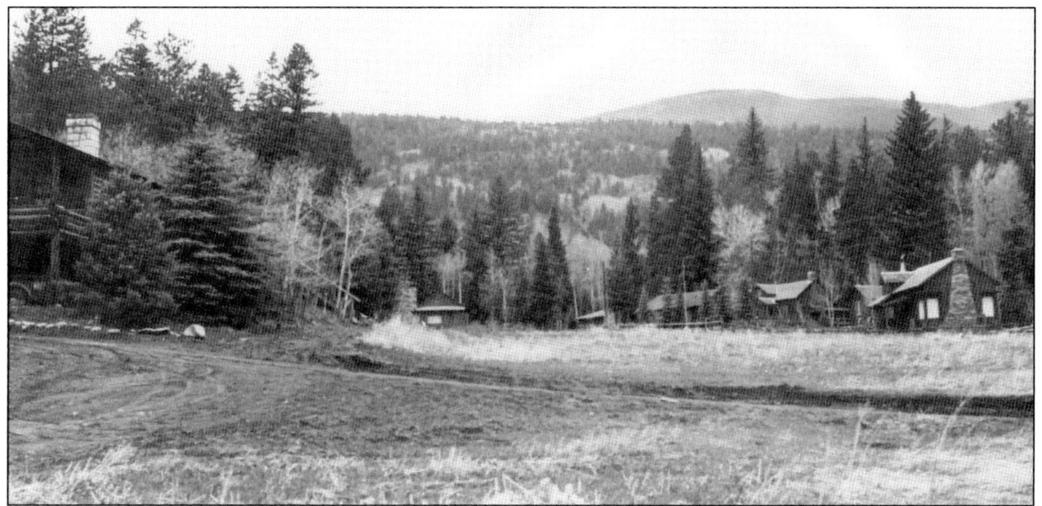

CUCHARA CAMPS. Cuchara Junction (old Cucharas), six miles east of Walsenburg, became a ghost town in the last half of the 20th century. The new Cuchara on the Upper Cucharas River started out as the settlement of Nunda in the 1870s. By 1916, the community had become known as Cuchara Camps. It was a seasonal resort with a hotel, restaurant, commissary, campgrounds, post office, and one-room log school. (PCCLD, no. Ph-C-400-06_002.)

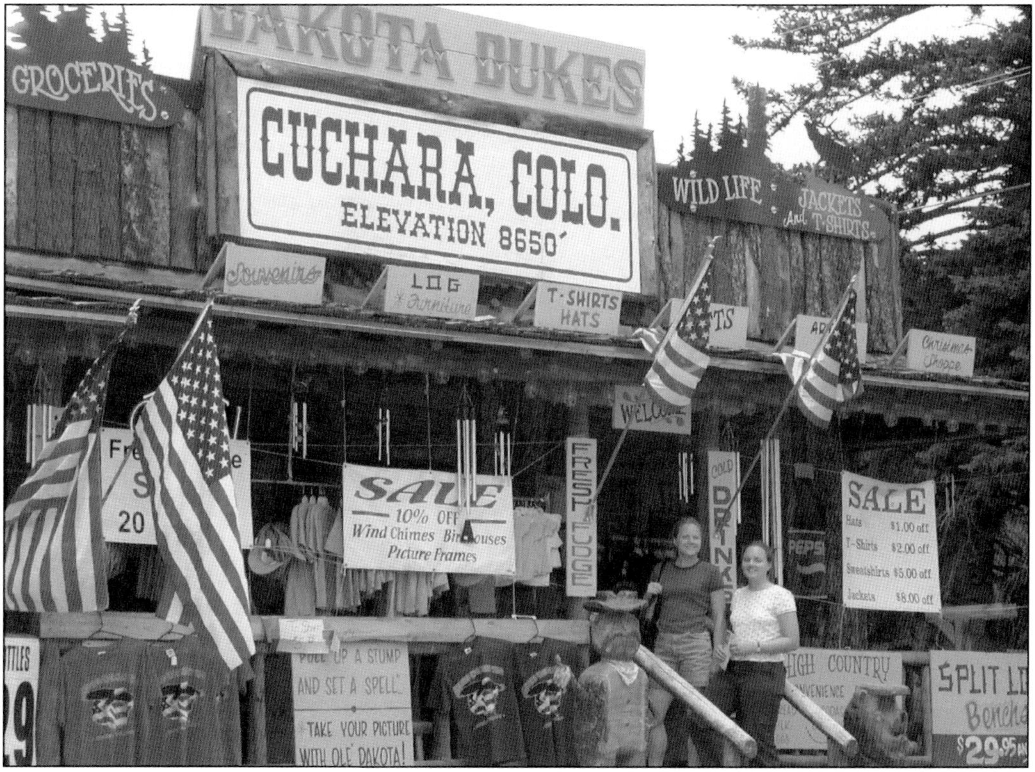

DAKOTA DUKES. The Cuchara Association was formed at Cuchara Camps in 1952. The community continued to grow steadily after the Cuchara Valley Ski Resort opened in 1981. The resort operated intermittently until 2000, when it closed for good. Dakota Dukes is one of the stores located in the town of Cuchara.

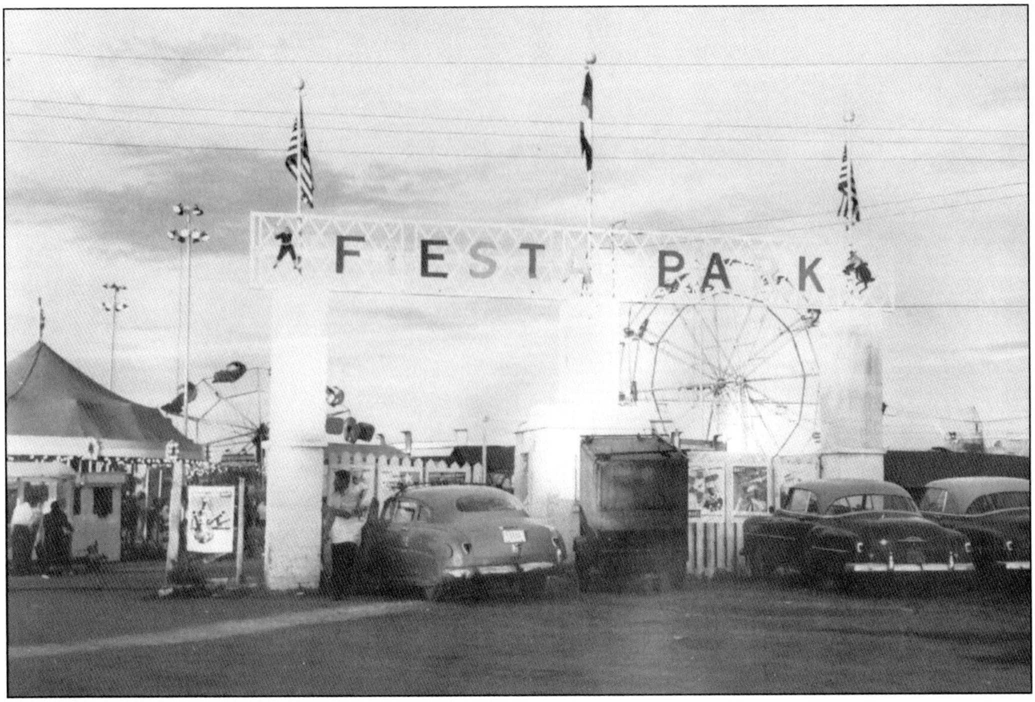

Fiesta Park in Walsenburg. During the 1940s, this recreational area drew large crowds to rodeos, carnivals, and horse races. Then it became the county fairgrounds. Now it sports two grassy ball parks and a children's playground on acreage adjacent to government buildings that are part of a complex known as the Huerfano County Community Center. (PCCLD, no. Ph-C-400-11_005.)

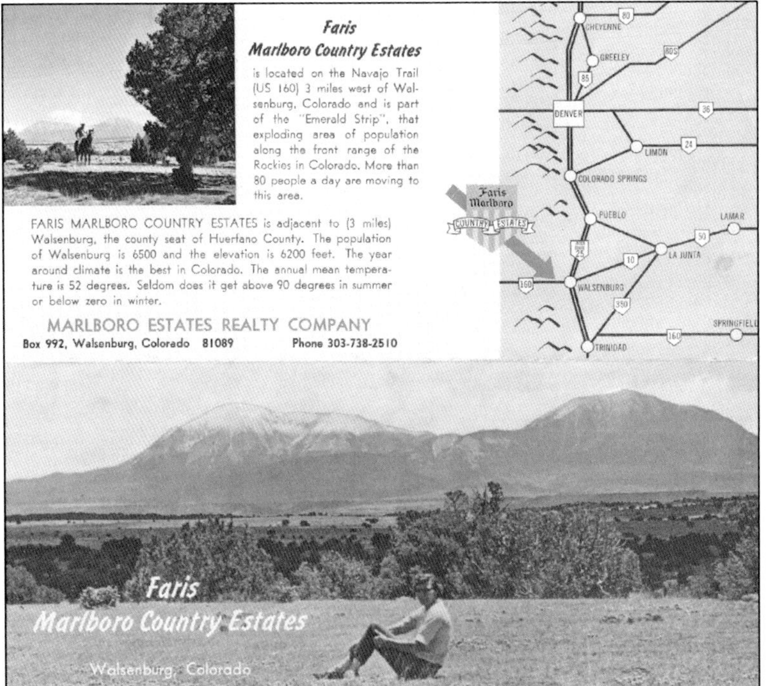

Faris Marlboro Estates. This glossy brochure from the early 1960s advertised a suburban development located just west of Walsenburg. It reads in part: "The population of Walsenburg is 6500 and the elevation is 6200 feet. The year around climate is the best in Colorado. The annual mean temperature is 52 degrees. Seldom does it get above 90 degrees in summer or below zero in winter." (Joe Edward Faris family.)

Eight

Believers, Past and Present

Religion has always played an important role in the daily lives of the people dwelling in the Huerfano River Valley. In the minds of many, it provided a path to eternal life. It also furnished lessons for maintaining a virtuous existence, developed community cohesiveness, and insured a social safety net for families in need of temporary food and lodging.

Certainly these reasons for being devout proved true for the Roman Catholics immigrating into southern Colorado during the last five decades of the 19th century. The incoming Hispanic settlers arrived without ordained priests because there was a shortage of officially trained holy men in northern New Mexico. A Catholic lay organization informally called Los Hermanos Penitentes (the Penitent Brothers) helped to fill the vacuum by offering both spiritual guidance and organizational structure to each new settlement.

The Penitent Brothers built *moradas*, small, windowless adobe structures where members gathered to offer songs of praise and worship. During the days leading up to Easter Sunday, the Penitentes practiced self-flagellation in private ceremonies and organized public reenactments of Good Friday so that everyone residing in the village could participate in Jesus' march to Calvary. In the summer, the brotherhood planned a festive day to honor the village's patron saint. Each *dia de fiesta* included a holy procession, morning mass, and afternoon sporting events, such as baseball games, horse races, rodeo events, and cockfighting. Los Hermanos Penitentes also practiced everyday acts of charity and contributed to their community by donating food items, free labor, and even use of their horses and wagons to provide firewood for the needy.

As Anglo American settlement increased in the region during the late 1860s, other denominations within the Christian faith began to appear along the Huerfano River. At first Episcopalian, Baptist, Methodist, and Presbyterian missionaries held services anywhere they could find shelter: trading posts, canvas tents, schoolhouses, town halls, and even saloons. Over the next 150 years, the number and variety of churches grew to reflect a plural society with changing attitudes and changing beliefs.

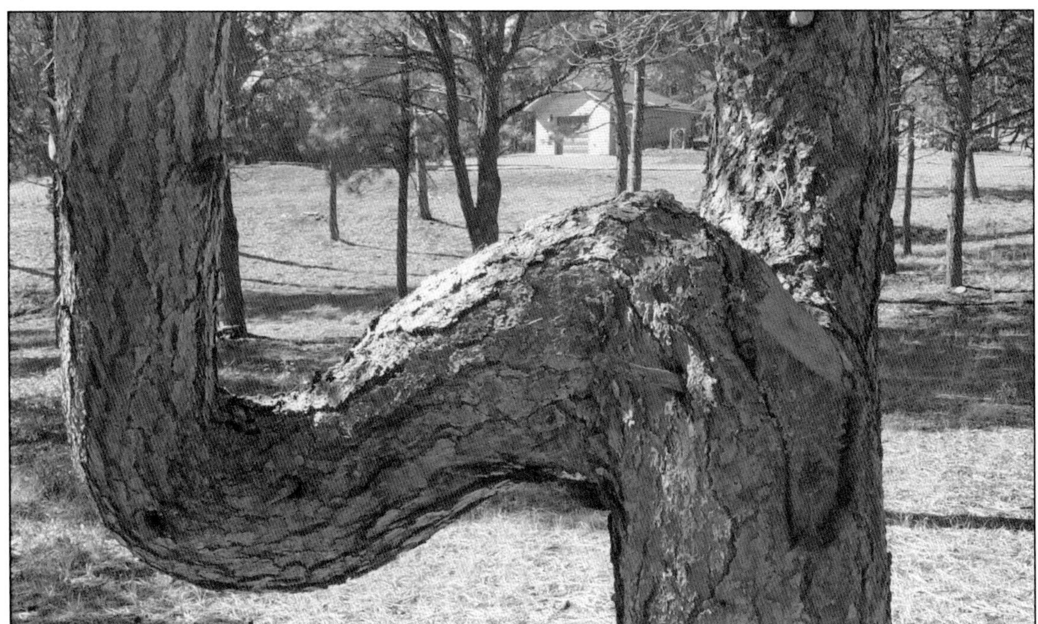

Ute Prayer Tree. Hundreds of culturally scarred trees have been identified throughout traditional Ute ancestral lands, including some in Huerfano County. These trees fall into different categories: peeled bark trees for nutritional and medicinal purposes, trail marking trees, burial trees, message trees, prophecy trees, and prayer trees to hold prayers for up to 800 years. (Olan and Lois Adams.)

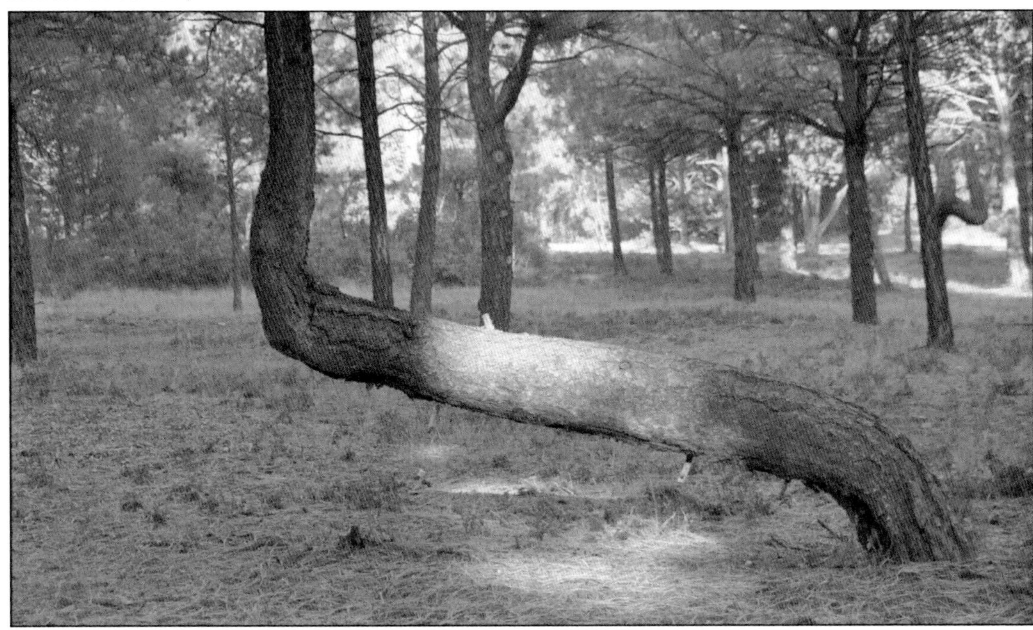

Burial Tree. To shape the trees, the Utes tied them in the way they wanted them to grow using ropes made from yucca fiber. This tree on Blackhawk Ranch is a burial tree. A burial tree can be identified by its two 90-degree bends and ligature marks that are clearly visible. Burial trees suggest that we were born of the earth, walk the earth during our lifetime, and then walk with our creator. (Susanne and Terry Bloomfield.)

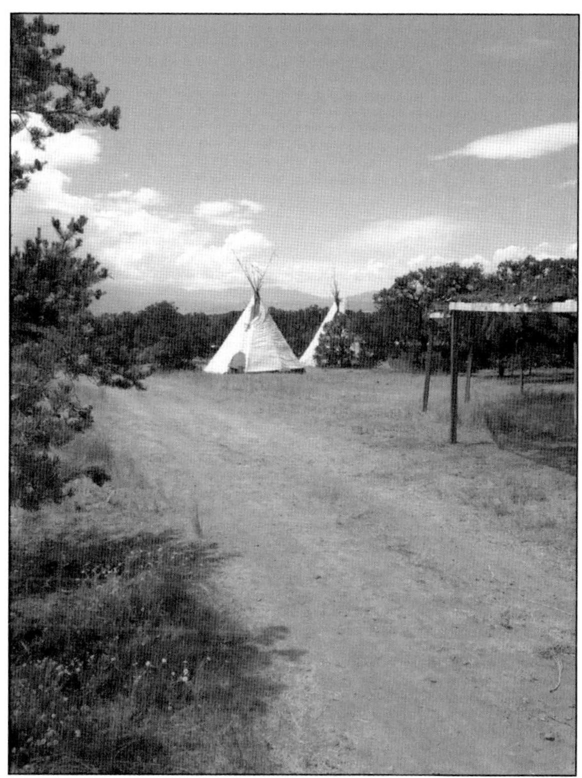

Ancient Rites of the Aztlan Sun Dance. Held in the mountains near Gardner, the Aztlan Sun Dance Ceremony attracts performers from the Lakota Sioux, Apache, Ute, and Navajo tribes during the summer solstice. On grounds belonging to the Native American Church, an Apache Shaman named Tomas Shash guides the dancers through the four-to-eight-day ritual full of spiritual and physical sacrifice. (Clint Boehler.)

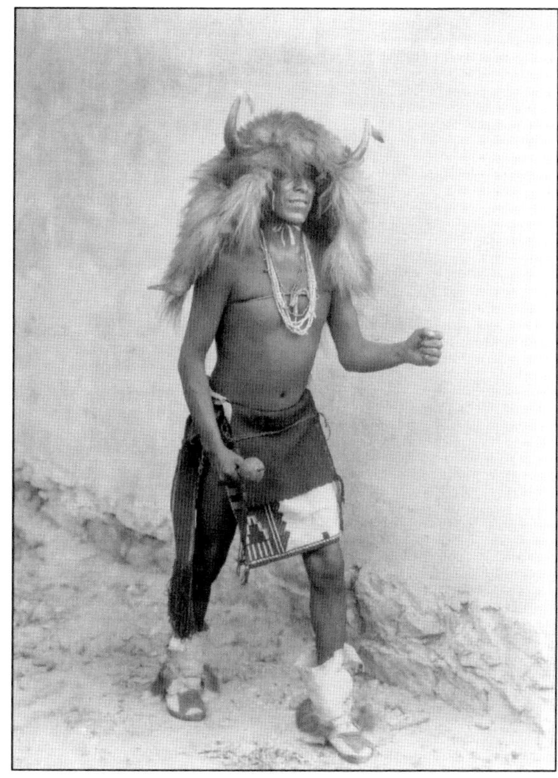

Sia Buffalo Dancer by Edward S. Curtis, c. 1926. The US government outlawed the Sun Dance in 1904, but the tribes still secretly kept it alive until it became legal again. Currently, respectful non–Native American visitors are allowed to attend the Huerfano County ceremony, but only the performers can enter the sacred inner circle to pray or dance or attach themselves to the Sun Pole. (Shutterstock.com.)

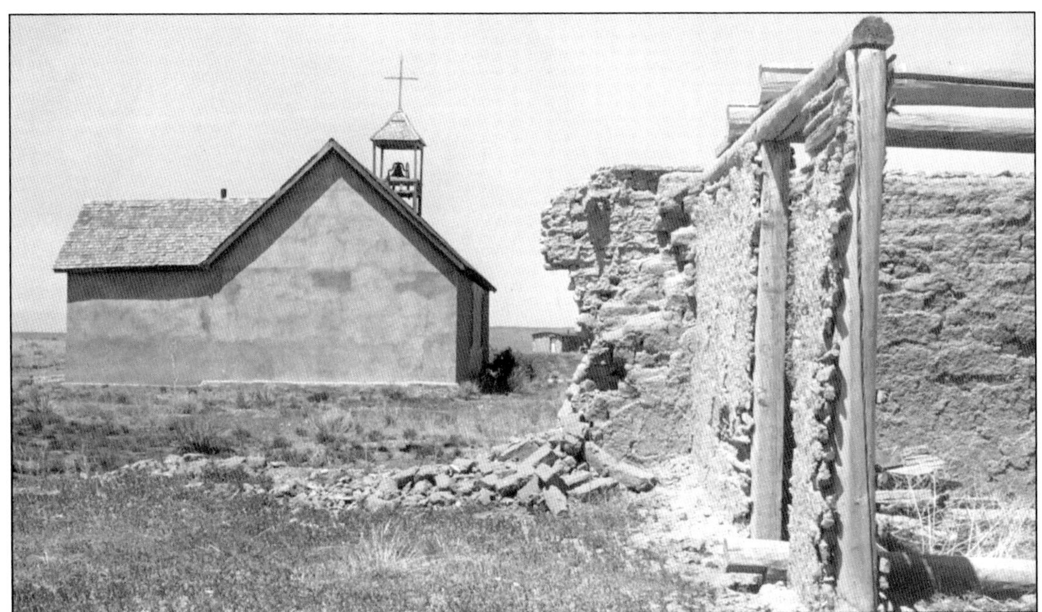

Church and Morada on the Lower Huerfano, near Avondale. Los Hermanos Penitentes are Hispanic Catholic laymen devoted to the teachings of the Catholic Church and Jesus Christ. They belong to a religious order that, translated into English, means "the Pious Fraternity of Our Father, Jesus the Nazarene." Women are also involved in the society but mostly as auxiliaries who support the men's activities during Holy Week. (PCCLD, no. PH-C-270-04_001.)

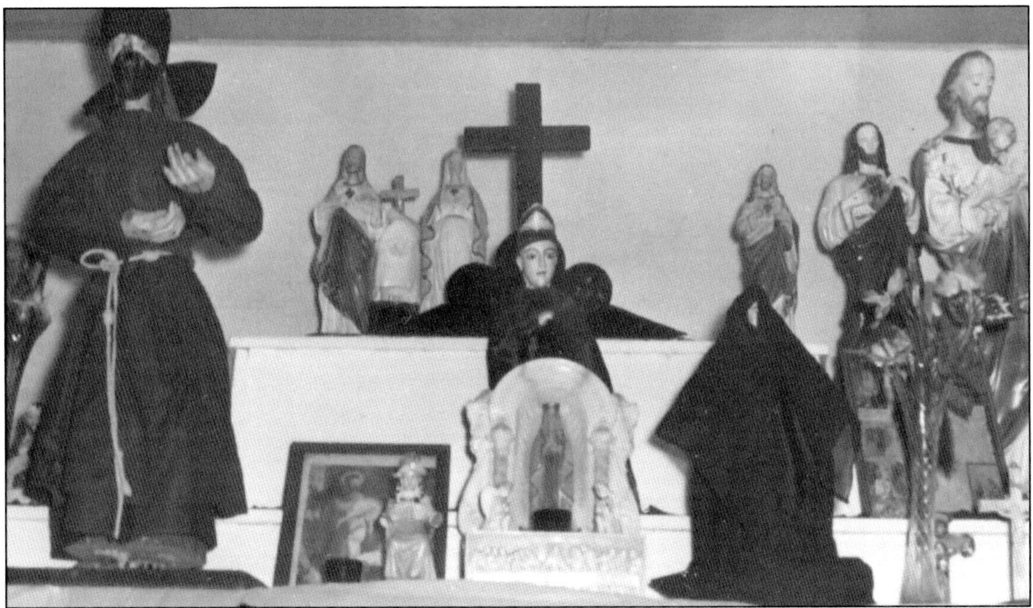

Altar inside a Penitente Morada, near Avondale. Self-floggings and other forms of physical penance earned the Hermanos a notorious reputation and formal banishment by the Vatican until 1947. Yet the good done by this order has been underrated. For centuries, the Brotherhood fed the hungry, attended to the sick, buried the dead, and supplied the spiritual glue that held together rural Hispanic communities throughout southern Colorado and northern New Mexico. (PCCLD, no. Ph-C-270-04_004.)

La Veta Baptist Chapel. This frame building was originally known as the Spanish Peaks Baptist Church. In 1877, it was moved from the north side of the Cucharas River to its present site on Main Street and renamed La Veta Baptist. The congregation built a new addition and weather-boarded the exterior in 1883. The structure has been altered several times since then.

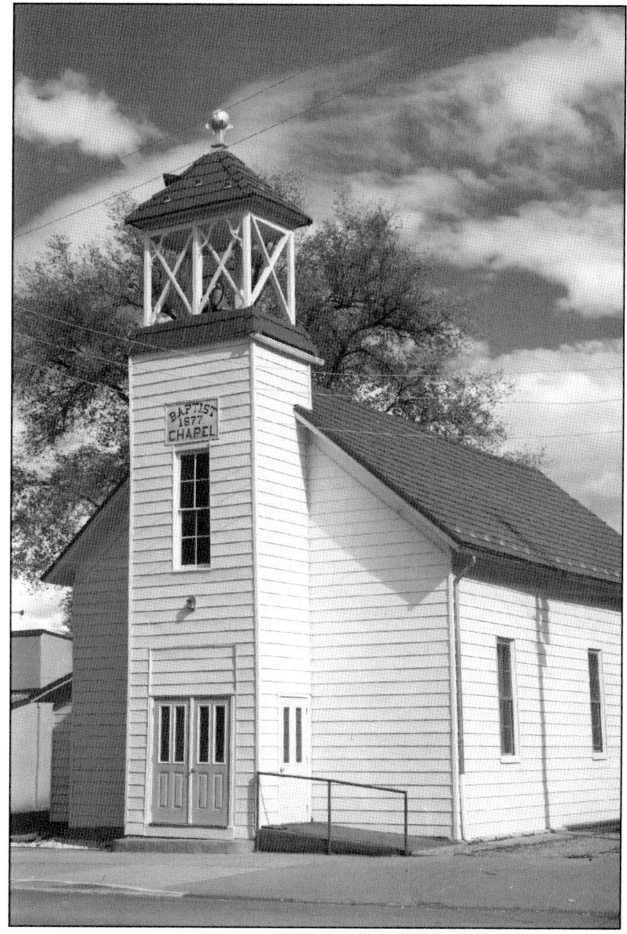

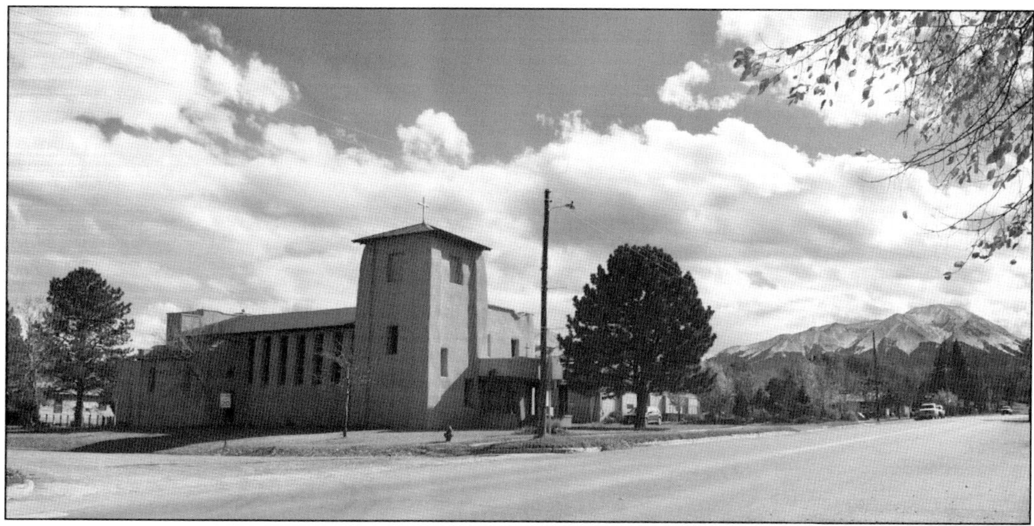

Christ the King Church, La Veta. Prior to the 1940s, Catholics living in the La Veta community did not have a church of their own. Formal plans for this building were drawn up in 1945. However, it was not officially dedicated until October 26, 1952.

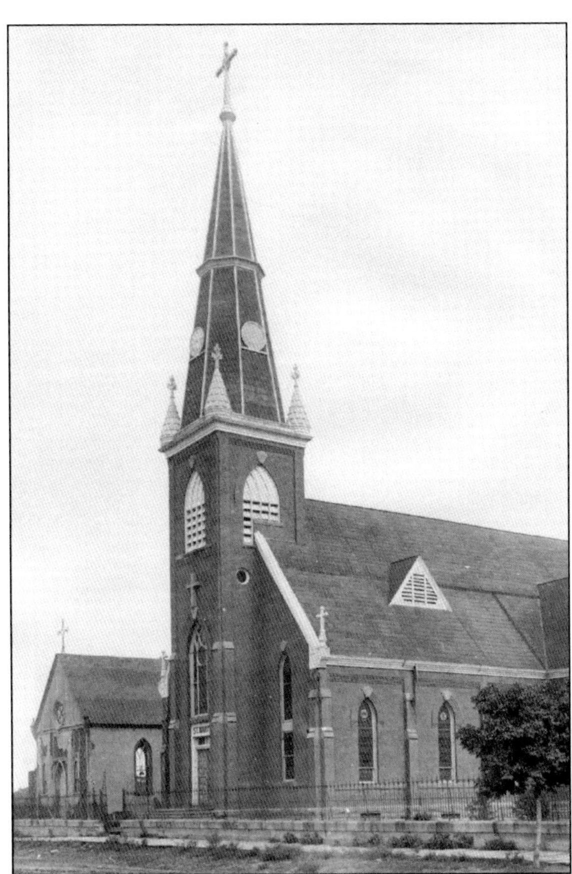

Our Lady of the Seven Sorrows, Walsenburg. This parish was established within the settlement of La Plaza de Los Leones in 1869. The little wooden hut that served as the town's first church burned down in 1871. The second church, an adobe chapel, was situated so close to the river that it was destroyed by the 1878 flood. For the next two decades, Fr. Gabriel Ussel labored to raise funds for a more substantial structure. St. Mary's Church, at 121 East Seventh Street, was begun in 1892 and dedicated in 1900. (PCCLD, no. Ph-C-400-12_001.)

Sacred Heart Church, Gardner. The construction effort on this place of worship was led by Elias Martinez, Catedra Garcia, and the Catholic Union Society. The entire Hispanic community, even the children, participated in making adobe blocks for the church walls. The building was completed in 1912 and extensively remodeled in 1961.

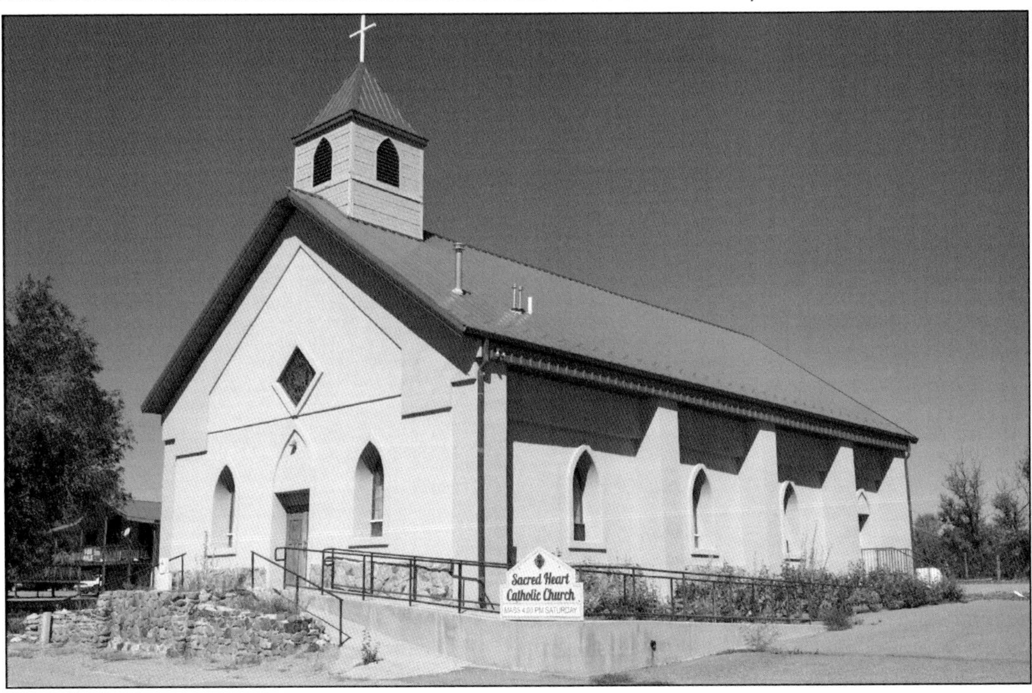

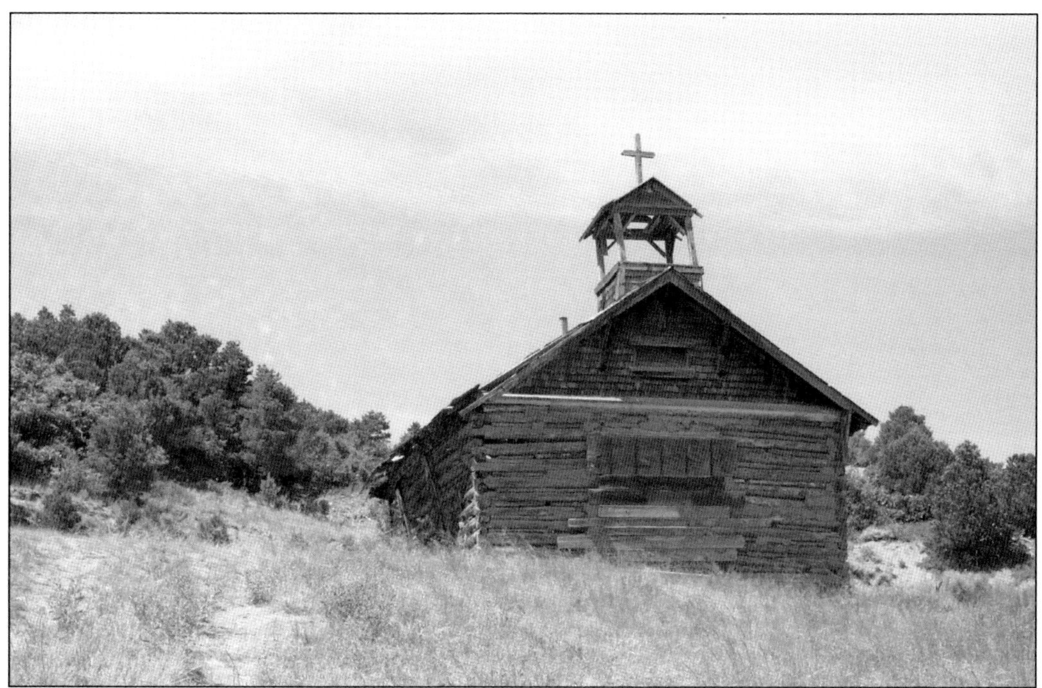

Abandoned Church on Yellowstone Creek Road. According to some sources, this log structure, completed in 1915, may have served as both a sanctioned church and a Penitente morada. At the time it was built, dozens of families lived near it, and they frequently attended mass here.

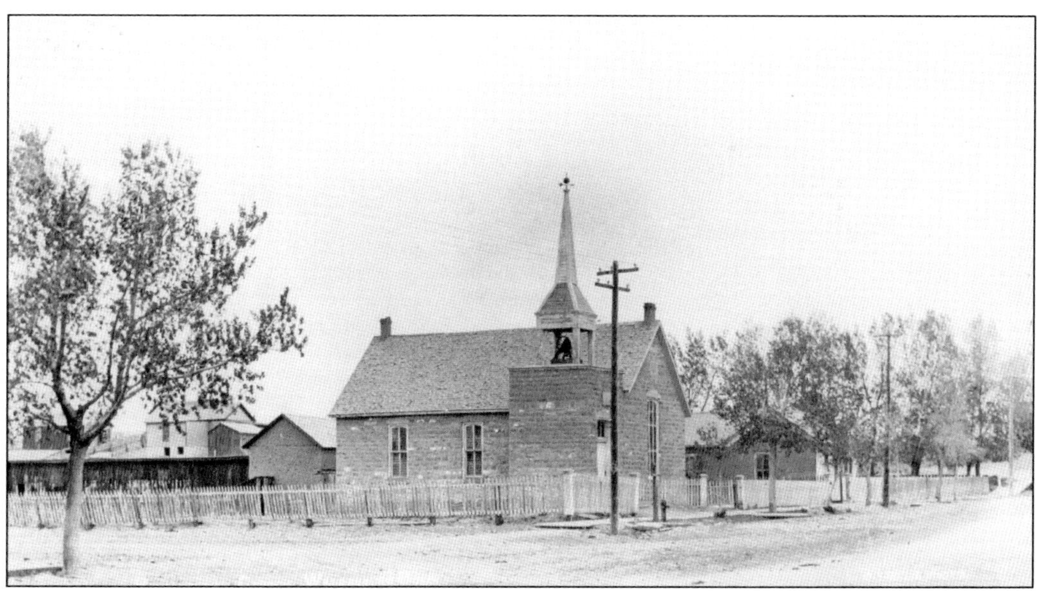

Presbyterian Church, Walsenburg, 1896. The building at 603 South Leon Avenue was built by members of the Spanish Presbyterian Church. Later, the Mennonites purchased this property. Another Presbyterian church was constructed at the corner of Kansas Avenue and Russell Street. In the 1920s, it served as the first meeting place of the Congregational church. This second site is now a parking lot for the Spanish Peaks Outreach Clinic. (MVHS/O.T. Davis Collection.)

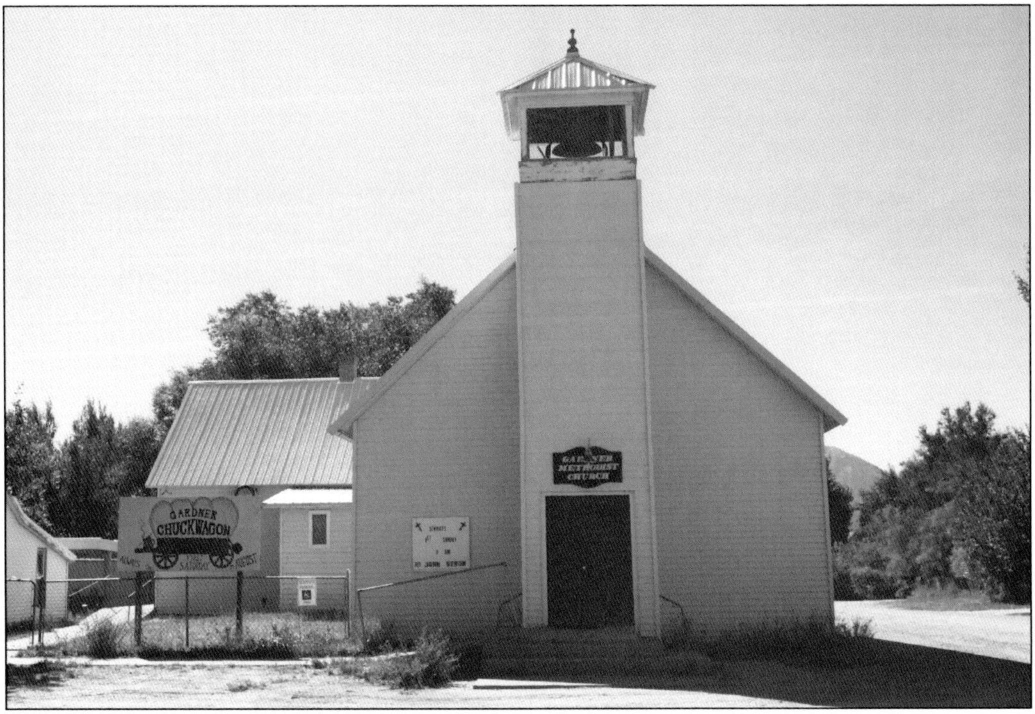

Methodist Church, Gardner. Asbury Quillian worked as a circuit rider for the Southern Methodist Conference when he began holding weekly services in a one-room schoolhouse on the Joshua Bains Homestead. From 1870 to 1889, Quillian catered to the spiritual needs of Methodists in small settlements like Gardner, Beulah, Hardscrabble, Rye, and Butte Valley. After he retired, his son continued to raise funds for a permanent church at Gardner. It was completed in 1901.

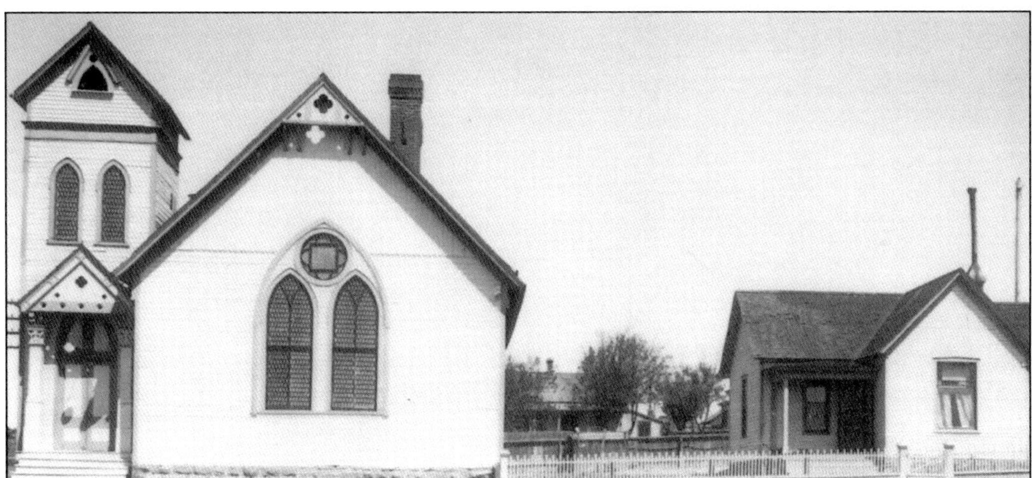

Methodist Episcopal Church, Walsenburg. In 1889, Pastor J.E. Squires and the church membership built the "little white church" on the northeast corner of Walsen and Pennsylvania Avenues. It was replaced by a large brick church in 1929. A 1961 union of the Community Congregational and United Methodist Churches led to a new name for the brick church. It is now called the United Church of Walsenburg. (HCHS/ATC.)

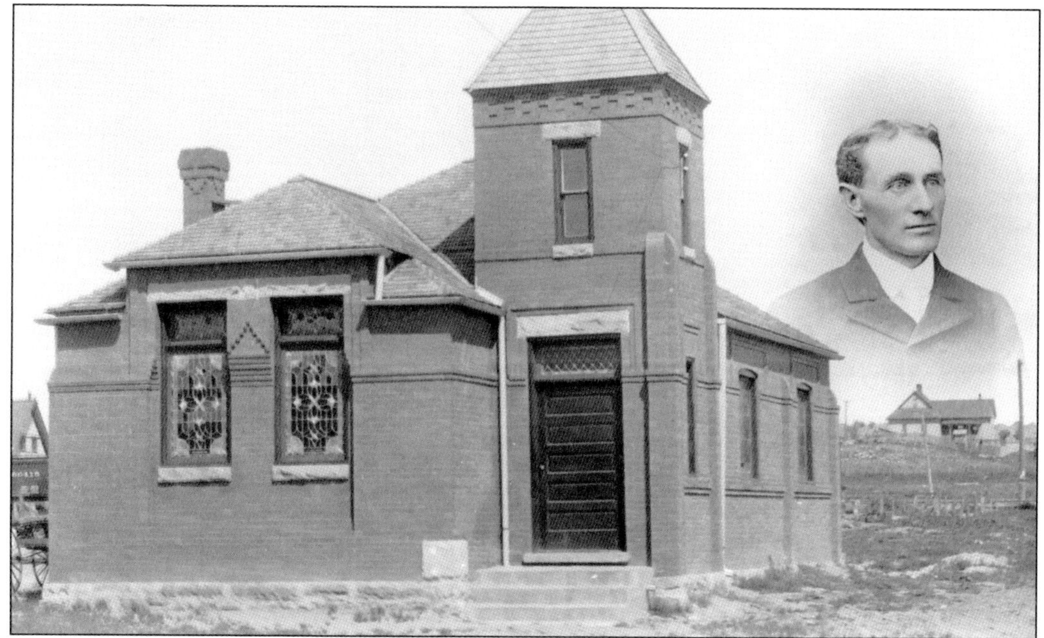

First Baptist Church at Walsenburg and Pastor M.B. Milne. The following news item was published in the September 1903 *Huerfano World*: "Reverend M.B. Milne, with the Baptist congregation in La Veta the past two years, has moved to Walsenburg where a $3,000 chapel is being erected on West Sixth Street. CF&I donated the lot for the church, which will accommodate 100 people." (MVHS/O.T. Davis Collection.)

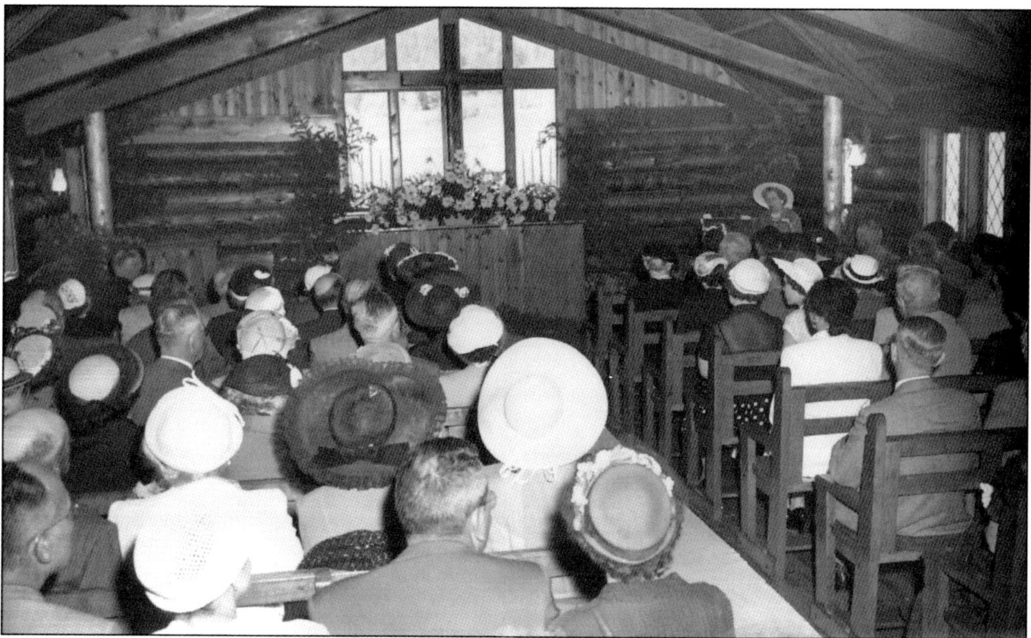

Cuchara Chapel, c. 1949. The settlement of Cucharas that was located six miles east of Walsenburg no longer exists. However, in the 20th century, a beautiful resort village called Curchara developed along State Highway 12 in the mountains south of La Veta. The nondenominational church pictured here sits in the center of the new Cuchara. (DPL, no. X-14002.)

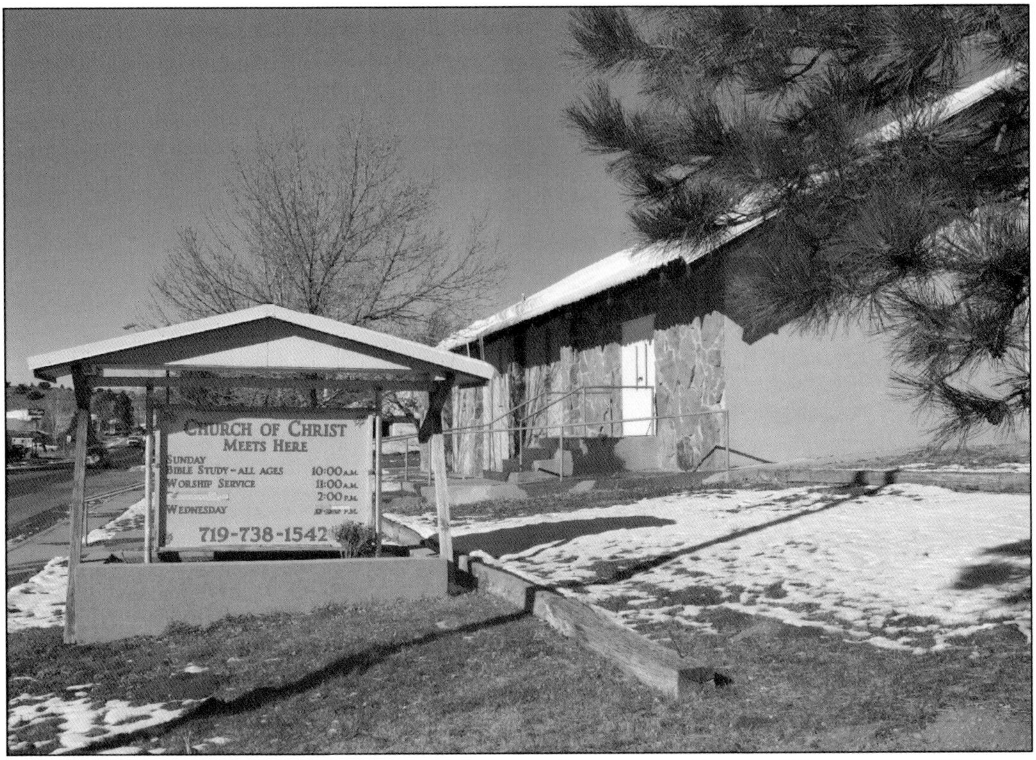

Church of Christ, Walsenburg. Today there are many Christian denominations in Huerfano County. A quick glance in the yellow pages yields a list that includes the Church of Christ, Assembly of God, Jehovah's Witnesses, St. Benedict Episcopal Mission, Emmanuel Apostolic Temple, Seventh Day Adventist, New Hope Community Church, Feed Store Church, Holy Cross Lutheran, Huerfano County Bible Church, and Church of Jesus Christ of Latter-Day Saints.

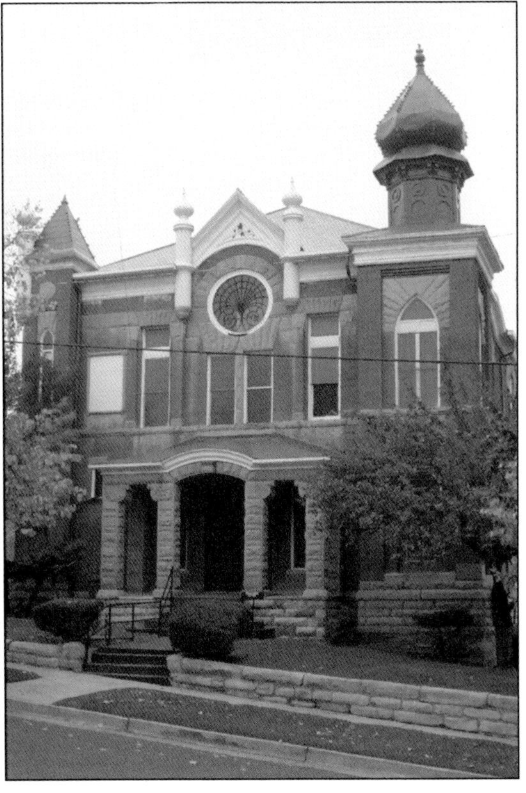

Temple Aaron. The German Jewish merchants who settled in Huerfano County in the last quarter of the 19th century tenaciously clung to their faith and their traditions. For high holidays they loaded their families into wagons and drove 40 miles to Trinidad to attend services at 407 South Maple Street. Temple Aaron, which was built in 1889, retains the honor of being the oldest synagogue in Colorado located on its original site. (DPL, no. AUR-3420.)

Nine

Counter-Culturists and Beyond

In the spring of 1965, four art students from Kansas and Colorado Universities decided to purchase seven acres of goat pasture near Trinidad at a cost of $450. Their first structure at Drop City was built with tar paper, bottle caps, roofing nails, chicken wire, scrap lumber, a couple of bags of cement, and silver asphalt roofing compound. Over the next two years, Las Animas County's artist colony continued to grow until a core group of 12 people were working together to create a live-in work of "drop art." Their geodesic domes and zomes covered in colorful automobile tops earned the Buckminster Fuller Dymaxion Award and set a new standard for environmentally friendly architectural design.

Then in the summer of 1967, the Joy Festival and accelerating media attention thrust Drop City into icon status, thereby attracting young men and women from the centers of the counterculture, east and west, who were identified by the locals with one brush: "hippies." As recreational drug users, disaffected Vietnam vets, teenage runaways, and other "dropouts" from mainstream culture swelled the transient population of Drop City, many of the original resident artists moved on to new opportunities.

Peter "Rabbit" Douthit, his wife, Judy, and two New York artists named Dean and Linda Fleming migrated to the southern slope of Greenhorn Mountain in the Huerfano Valley, where they established Libre on 360 acres of scenic alpine woodlands. The poets and artists who settled here christened their intentional community with a Spanish term that means "free," as in free to think creatively and step out of old social constraints.

Between 1968 and 1970, four more counterculture communities were established in the Huerfano River Valley: the Triple A (Anonymous Artists of America, in the shadow of Slide Mountain), the Red Rockers (in Red Rock Canyon west of Badito Cone), Ortiviz Farm on Turkey Creek, and Archuletaville (on rancher Dan Archuleta's land near the old town of Red Wing). Each of these intentional communities was unique. Yet each was filled with the energy of youth and the promise of a lifestyle dedicated to personal and artistic expression unhinged from old conventions.

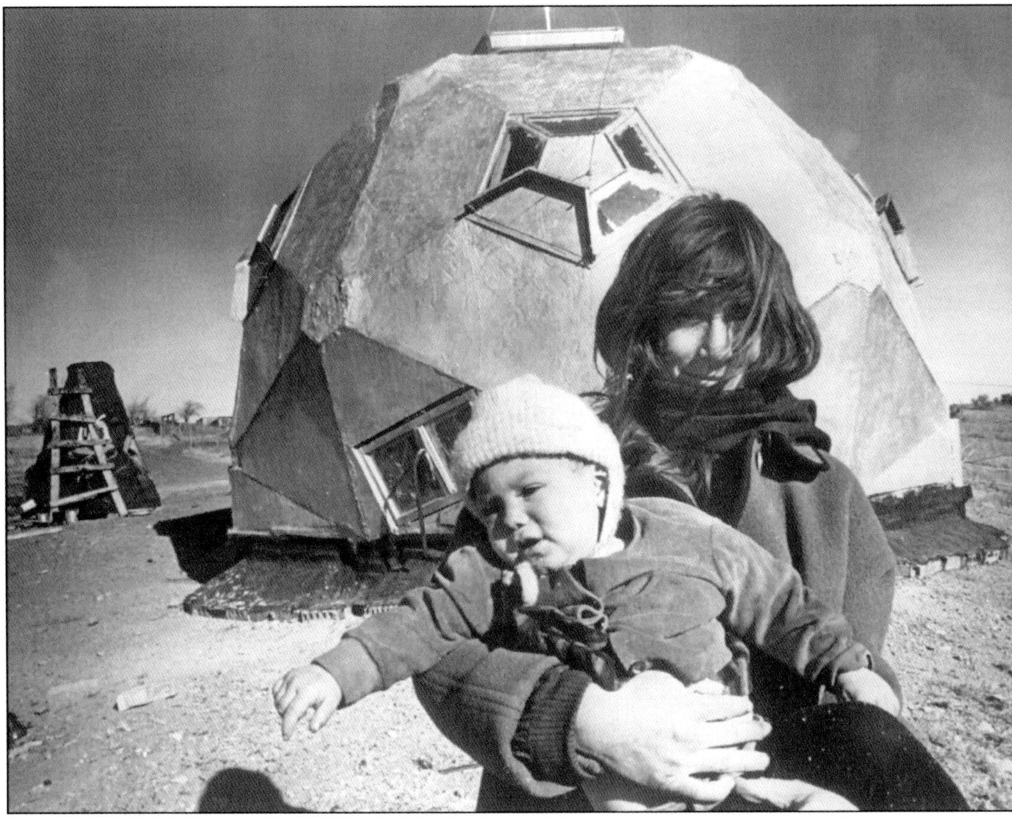

JoAnn Bernofsky and Child in Front of Early Geodesic Dome at Drop City, 1965. Gene Bernofsky, JoAnn Bernofsky, Clark Richert, and Richard Kallweit were students at the University of Kansas in 1962 when they coined the word "drop art." They created their "droppings" by tying a rope to interesting objects, lowering the objects down from a second-story apartment window to street level, and interacting with passersby to develop time-lapse collages. (DPL, no. X-7737.)

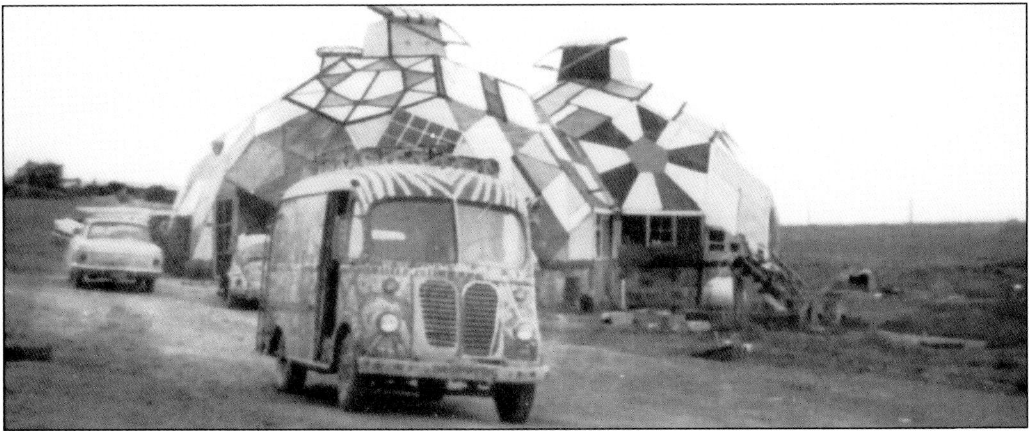

Las Animas County, 1968. Drop City's impressive structures were based on Buckminster Fuller's geodesic domes and the crystalline designs of Steve Baer (founder of Zomeworks Corporation, a pioneer company in geometric structure and passive solar energy). Drop City was abandoned in the early 1970s and torn down in the late 1990s. A truck repair facility now occupies a portion of the site. (Irene Guilly.)

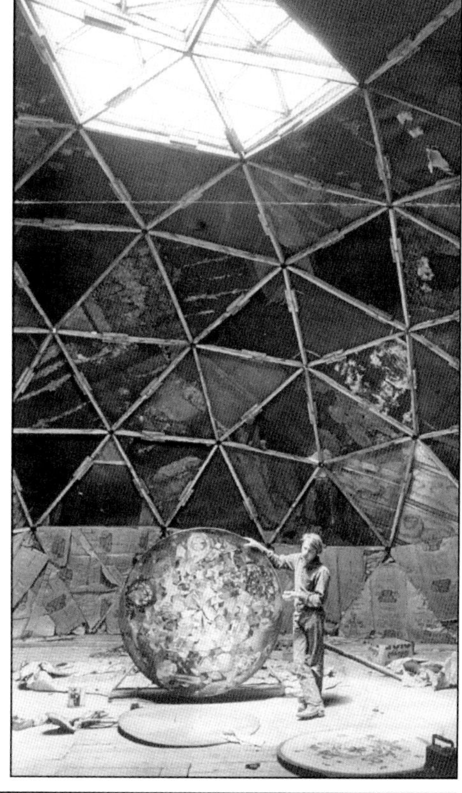

Clark Richert Stands near "The Ultimate Painting" within Dome Theatre. Drop City's early experiments with recycled materials and solar collection paved the way for today's green energy industries. Some of the other innovative artworks produced at Drop City include the original "Ultimate Painting" and a cooperatively written and illustrated comic book entitled *The Being Bag.* (DPL, no. X-7739.)

Peter "Rabbit" Douthit and His Zome in Libre, 1969. This home, like most of the houses in Libre, was built with the help of all residents in the community, a tradition reminiscent of the old-fashioned barn-raisings of pioneer America. Peter Douthit lived in Drop City from 1966 to 1968. His 1971 book *Drop City* is a fictional account of his experiences in southern Colorado's first counterculture communes. (Carolyn Newman.)

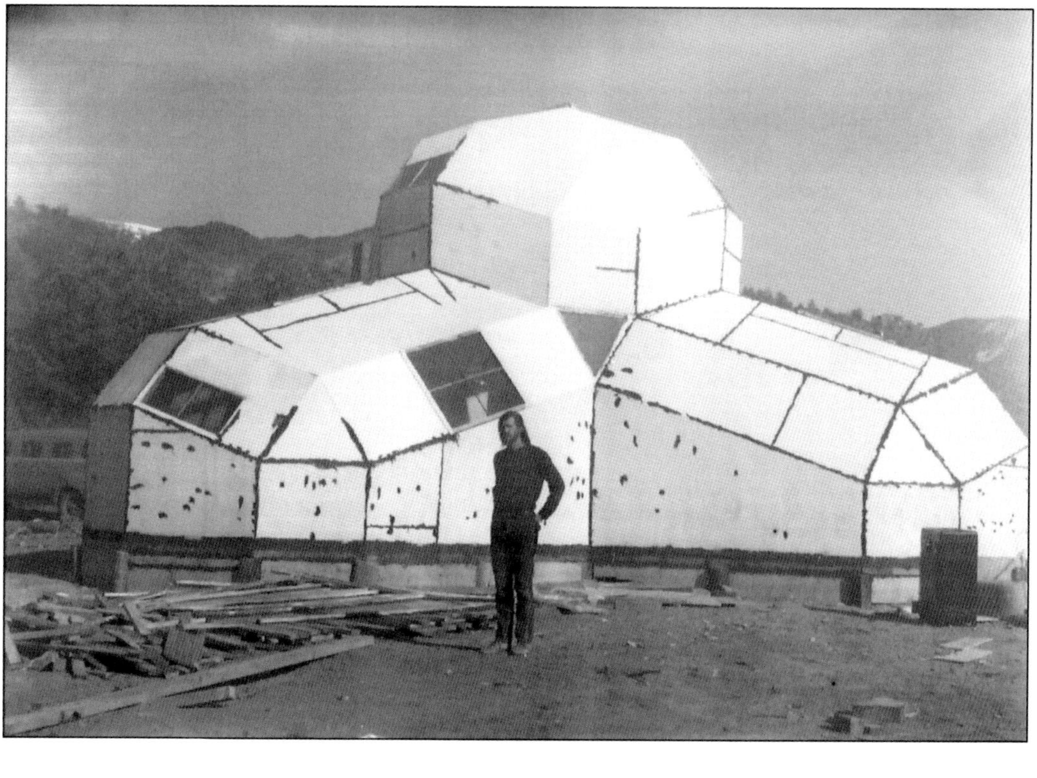

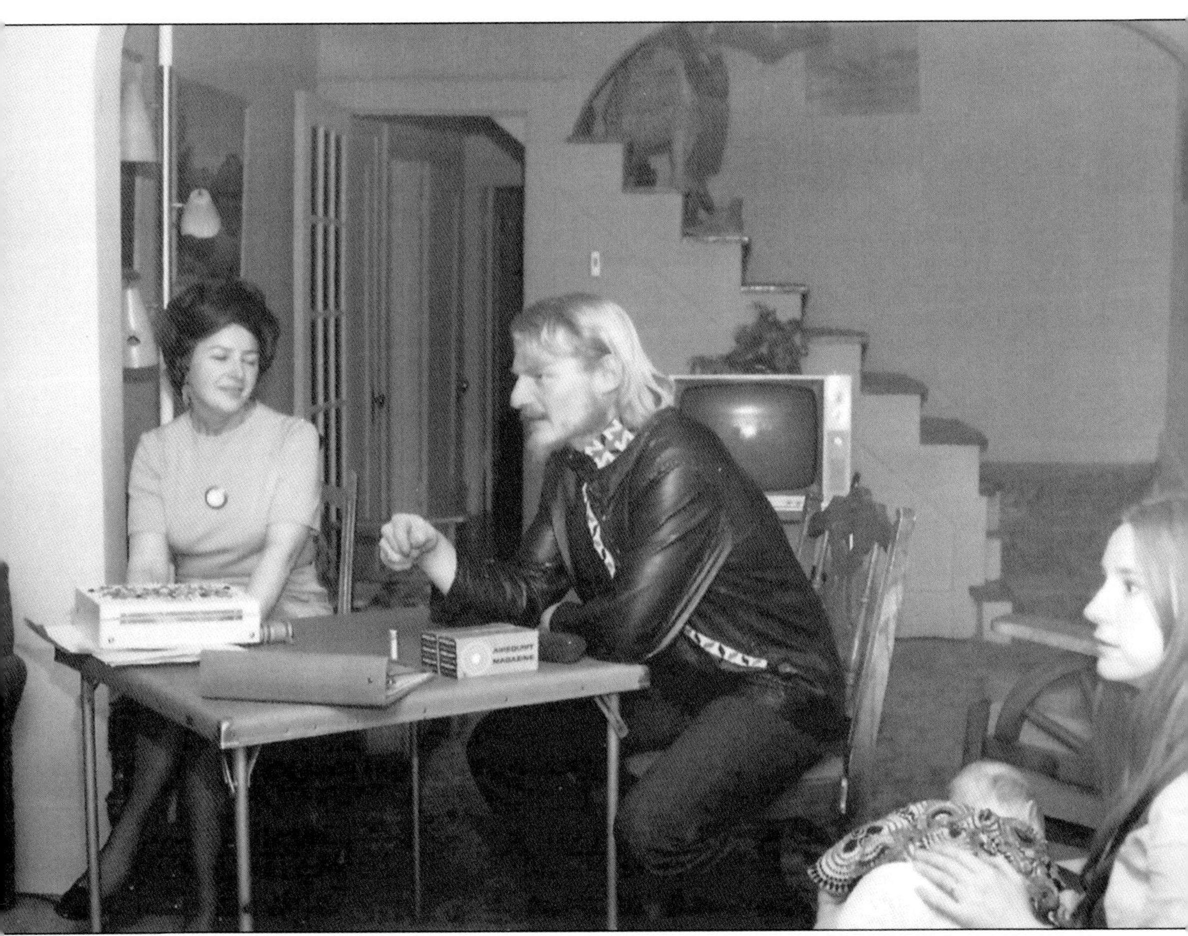

DEAN FLEMING, 1969. Accompanied by his wife, Linda, and their baby, Lia, Fleming presented a slide talk to the Walsenburg Junior Women's Club. Before moving to the Huerfano River Valley, Fleming served in the Korean War, taught art at the Carnegie Institute of Technology in Pittsburgh, and participated in many contemporary art shows in New York City. Dean and Linda were driving forces behind the purchasing of 360 acres of forested mountain land for $35 per acre in 1968. The founders of Libre chose to organize their intentional community as a nonprofit corporation and to establish a few ground rules: 1) members paid nominal dues to the corporation for basic expenses like taxes on the land or a pump for the spring box; 2) each adult member could vote, and on major issues, such as who would be allowed to join the commune, decisions had to be unanimous; and 3) Once accepted into the group, new members had to agree to build their homes a comfortable distance from the dwellings of other homeowners. (Carolyn Newman.)

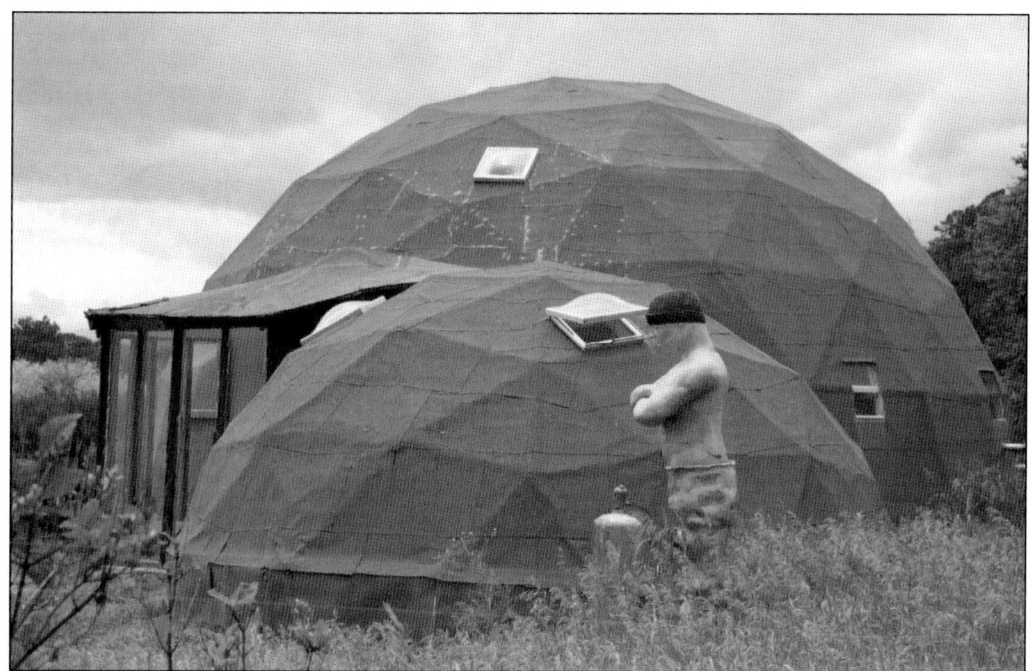

Dean Fleming's Residence. During the decade Libre was formed, a dozen communes and artist colonies sprang up between Pueblo, Colorado, and the New Mexico border. Today, Libre stands alone. Most of the dwellings at Libre are nearly a half-century old, although improvements have been added, including indoor plumbing, electricity, and more living space.

Dean Fleming, 1976. By August 1969, there were 15 individuals dwelling on the Libre property, including talented painters, sculptors, jewelers, weavers, potters, photographers, poets, and musicians. Five decades later, Dean Fleming continues to be a leader at Libre and an internationally renowned artist who has exhibited in Japan, Mexico, New York City, San Francisco, Austin, Santa Fe, Taos, and Denver. (Roberta Price.)

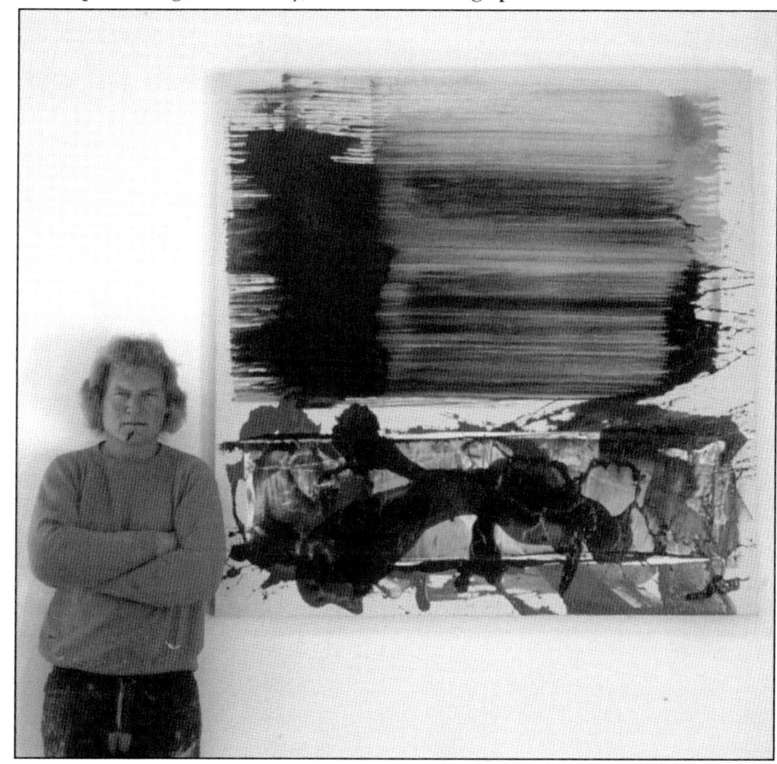

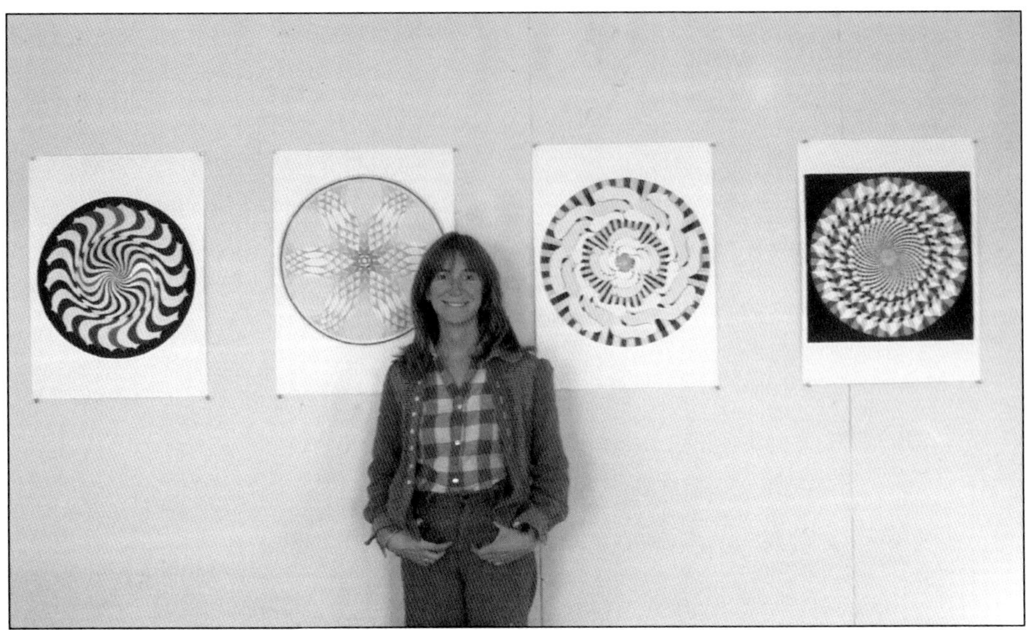

LINDA FLEMING WITH DRAWINGS, 1976. Linda is a professor of fine arts in sculpture and graduate studies at California College of the Arts in San Francisco. She has exhibited widely throughout the United States, and her works are in international collections in Moscow, Russia; Baghdad, Iraq; Sydney, Australia; and Seoul, South Korea; as well as many cities in the United States. (Roberta Price.)

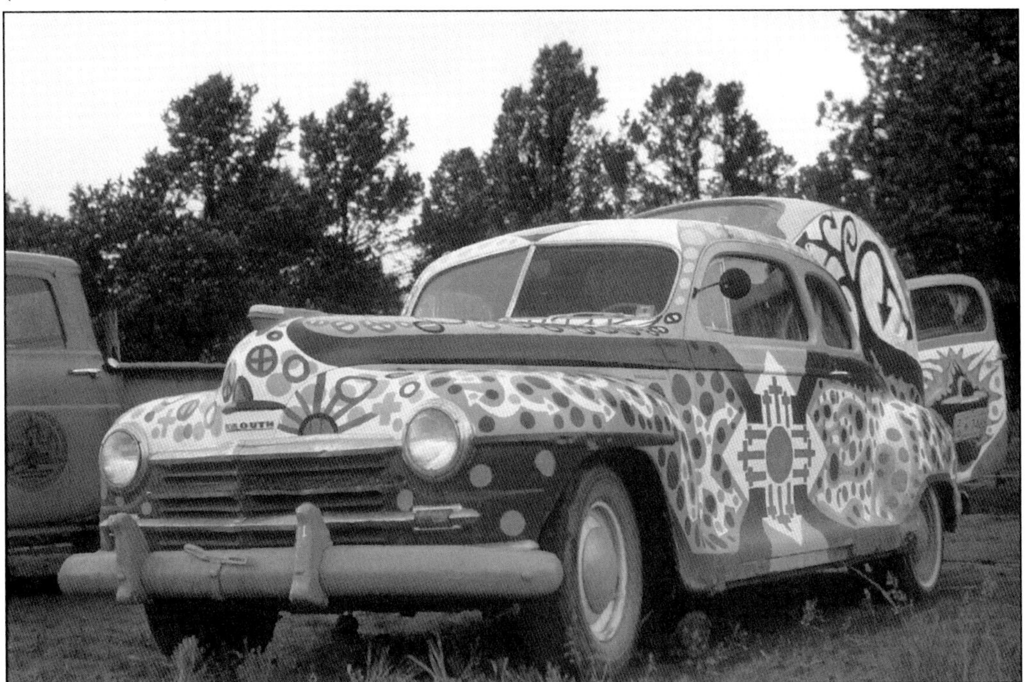

THE HUMPMOBILE. The Humpmobile was a 1947 Plymouth two-door sedan upon which Jim Fowler welded the back of a 1940 Chevy panel wagon to convert the vehicle into an art car. He and his first wife, Sandy, slept in it while they were building their home at Libre. (Jim Fowler.)

Jim Fowler's Artwork. Fowler has remained at Libre these past five decades and continues to produce art. He is best known for his sculptures, including this carving, which stands in front of his home. For years, he served as Libre's main mechanic because he could fix almost anything, from old truck engines to washing machines.

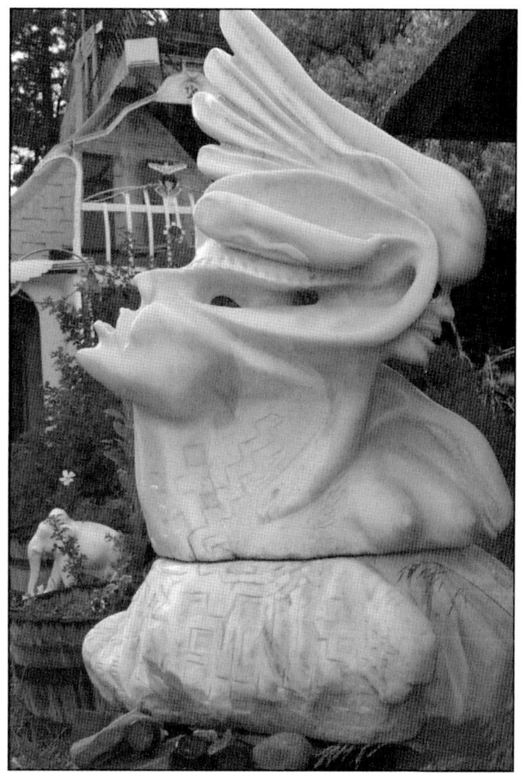

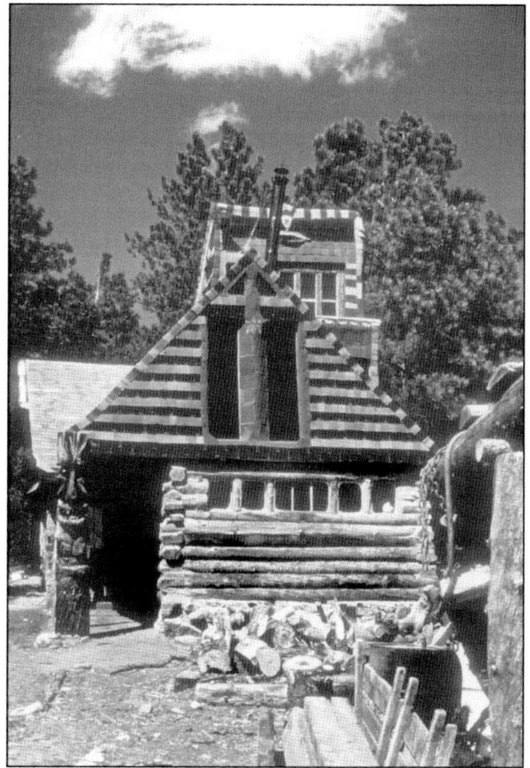

Jim Fowler's House, 1975. Jim and his current wife, Sesame, would eventually raise four children within this house. One of Jim's daughters became a Ford Agency model and is now an architect. Another became a doctor. Other children raised at Libre have become filmmakers, computer wizards, teachers, environmentalists, health care workers, and skilled technicians in various high-paying industries. (Jim and Sesame Fowler.)

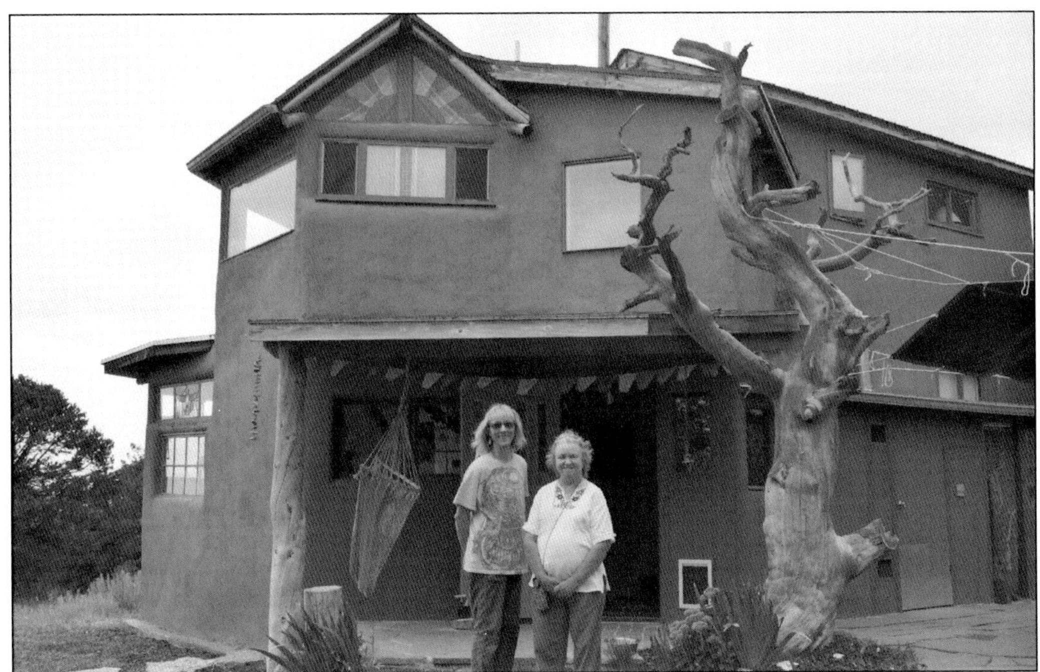

Home of Bill Haynes and Muriel Fibelkorn. Muriel (left) and a visitor attending a Huerfano County Historical Society tour stand before this house at Libre. Muriel still tends a garden and cooks healthy meals with the produce she grows in it. The residents of Libre believed in living on less in order to preserve the earth for future generations. In between their artistic endeavors, they stayed busy baking bread, raising livestock, making goat cheese, sewing homemade shirts, and canning hundreds of jars of tomatoes.

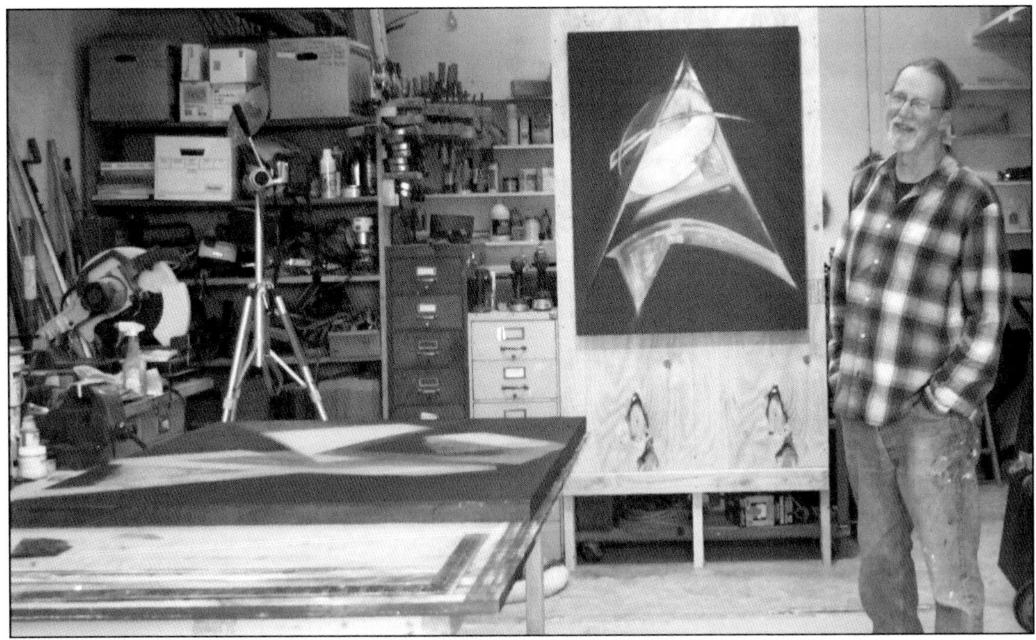

Bill Haynes's Workshop/Studio. Haynes displays two paintings scheduled to be on exhibit at one of the art galleries in La Veta during the month of August 2015.

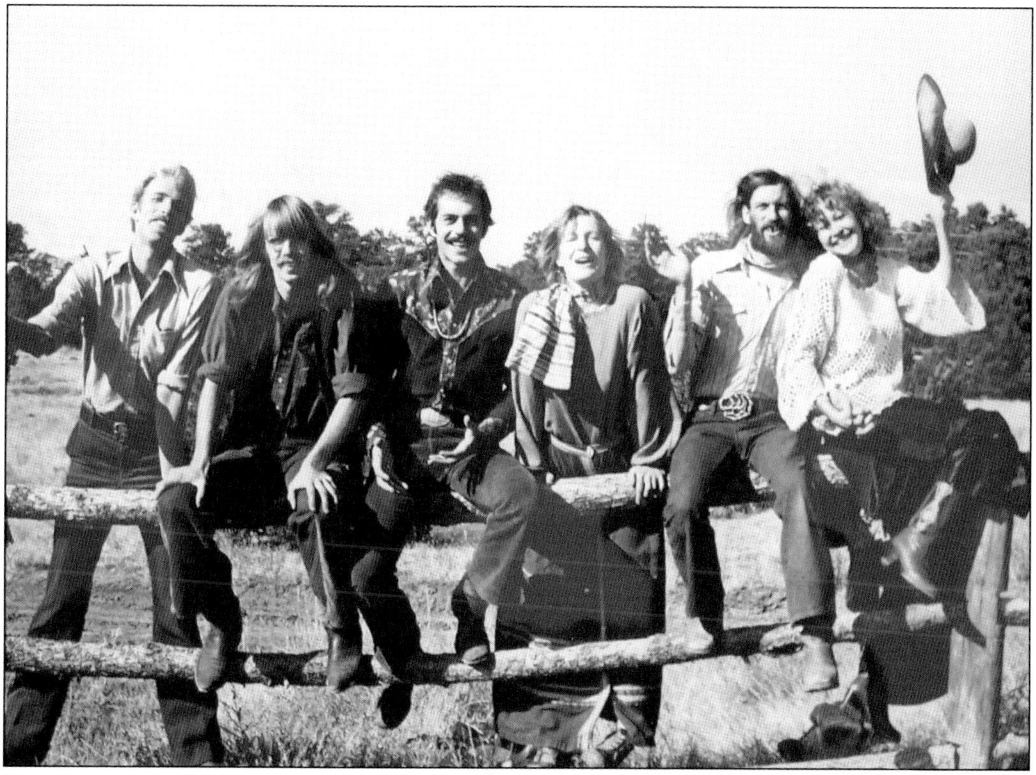

Dog Brothers Band, 1974. The members of this group are, from left to right, David Henry (lead guitar and vocals), Jim Fowler (bass guitar), David "Izzy" Perkins (guitar and vocals), Peggy Abbott (piano), "Daddy" Dave Gordon (drums), and Cari Seawell (vocals). David Perkins and David Henry wrote many original songs for the band. (David Perkins.)

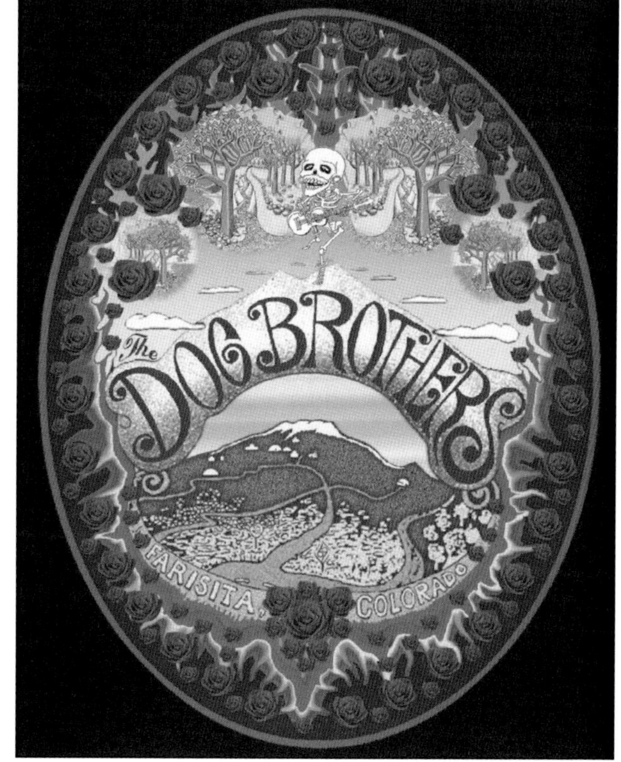

A Dog Brothers Band Logo. Both the Dog Brothers Band and the Triple A (Anonymous Artists of America) performed throughout southern Colorado and northern New Mexico. The Triple A got its start as an opening act for the Grateful Dead in the Bay Area during the late 1960s. (Jim Fowler.)

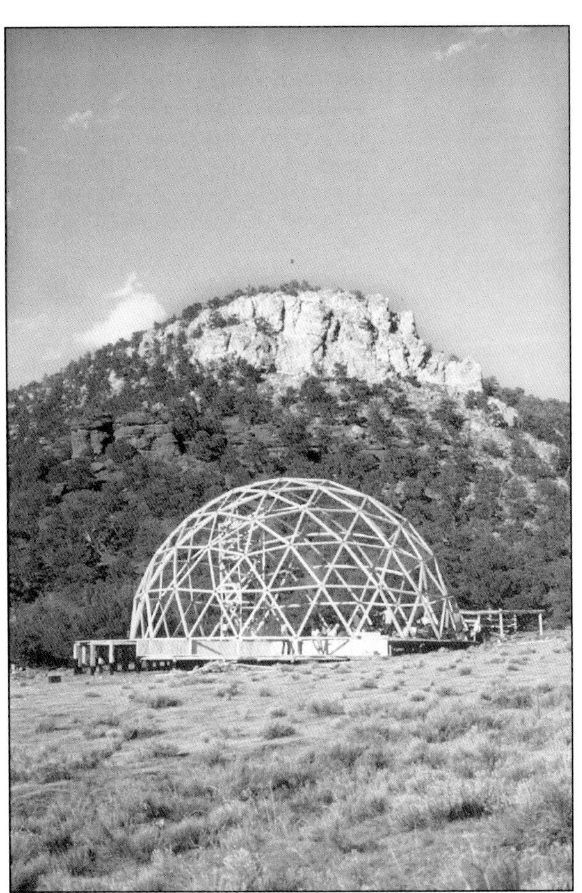

Red Rocker Dome, 1970. Winnie, Larry, and Vicky Laszlo; Nancy Moore; David Anson; Terry Bisson; Mary Corey; and eight other young innovators migrated to Red Rock Canyon between 1969 and 1970. The dome they built was 30 feet high and 60 feet in diameter. As believers in pure socialism, the Red Rockers shared food, shelter, household duties, a communal closet, a sleeping loft without partitions, and the land itself. (Roberta Price.)

Party in Red Rock Canyon. As soon as the frame of the dome was in place, the Red Rockers threw a party. Among the guests attending the celebration were Bessie from Red Wing plus members of the Triple A community, including Ellie Linke, Elaine Baker, and their children. Most of the original Red Rockers had abandoned the Huerfano Valley by the late 1970s. Their land is now privately owned. (Roberta Price.)

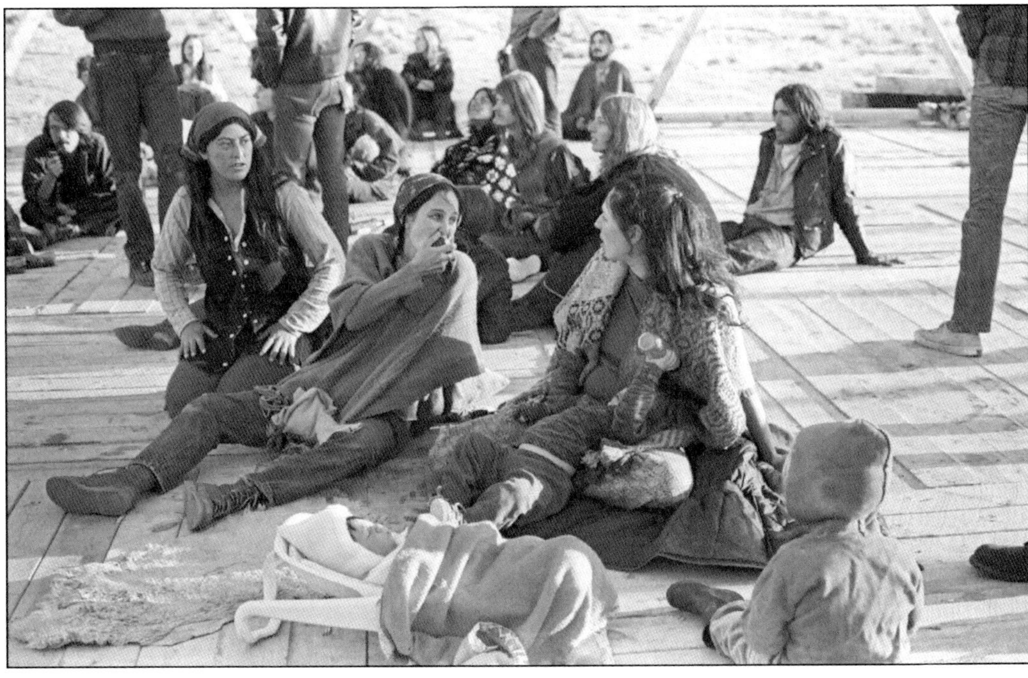

JOHNNY BUCCI. Bucci sold the Red Rockers a couple hundred acres of land east of the Valdez Cemetery for $135 per acre. He and his wife, Alta May, always had a pot of coffee on the stove and served it hot and strong to his neighbors from Red Rocks, Libre, and Ortiviz Farm. This is a print created by Ken Martinez, owner of the Darkwood Studio in Walsenburg.

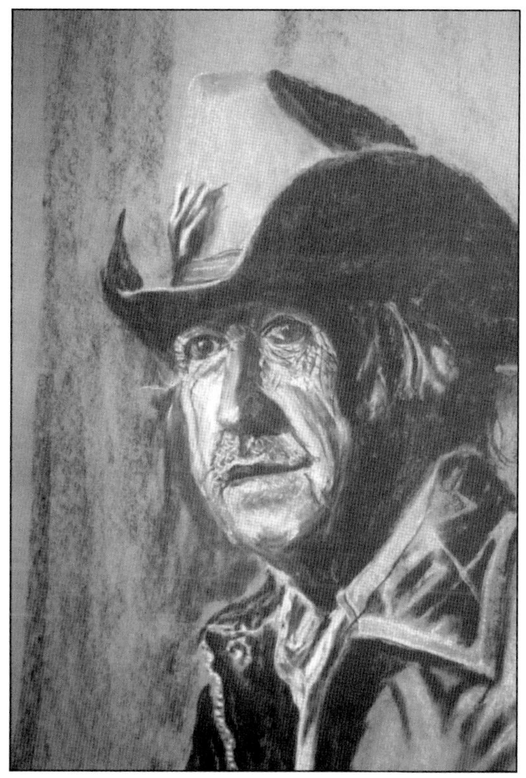

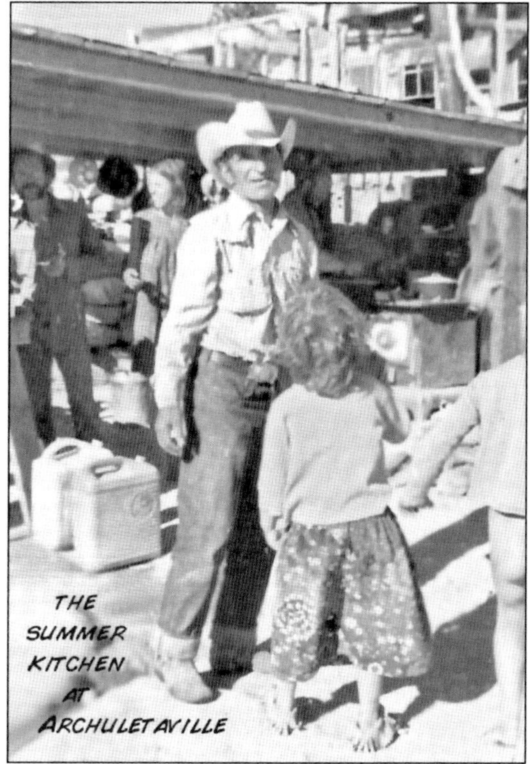

DAN ARCHULETA. Archuletaville was the smallest counterculture commune in the Huerfano Valley and the least formally organized. Dan Archuleta owned the sheep barns and dirt root cellars where the six families resided. He provided free rent in return for free labor during spring plantings and summer harvests. (Jim Fowler.)

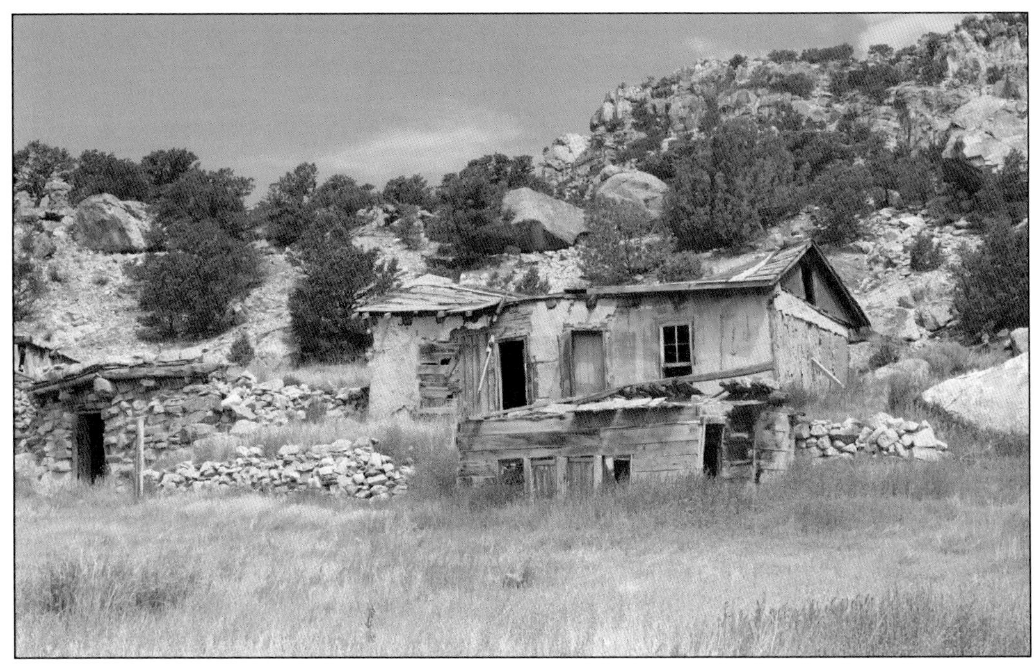

ARCHULETAVILLE. Accommodations were quite rustic. Muslin stretched under the ceilings caught the dirt drifting down from the ceiling and the insects. At least one teepee was added along with a gypsy wagon. Over time, Archuletaville has become a village of abandoned ruins.

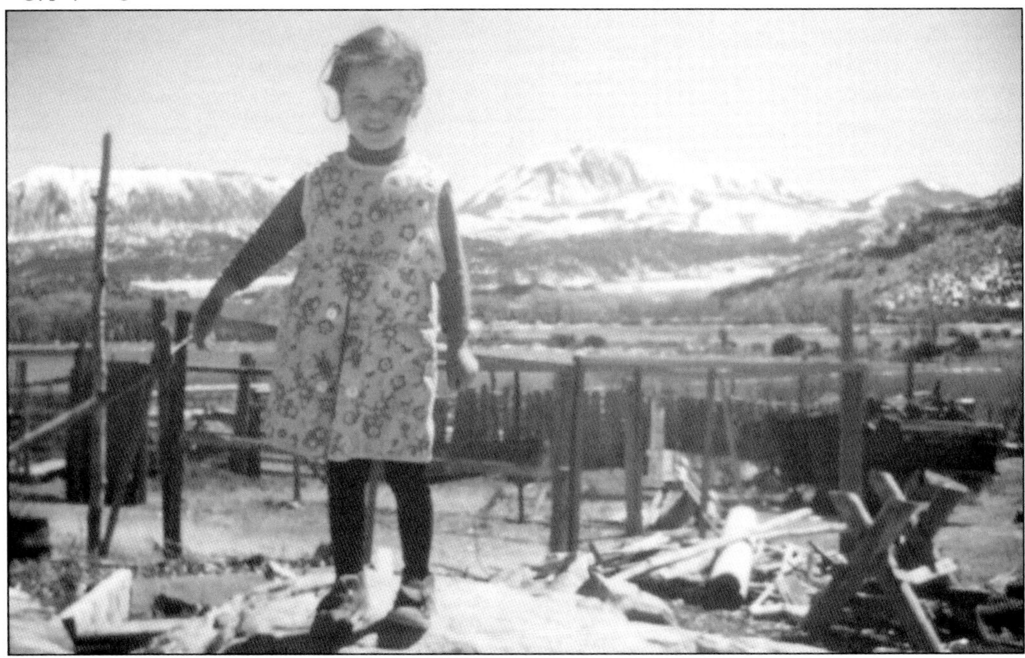

TALA AT ARCHULETAVILLE. Waska, son of Sesame Fowler, was born at Archuletaville in 1974. Tala, pictured here at Archuletaville, was born in a teepee near Truchas, New Mexico, in 1971. The scenic background illustrates the fact that the counterculture communards who came to Huerfano County had quite a knack for choosing beautiful sites for their group living experiments. (Jim Fowler.)

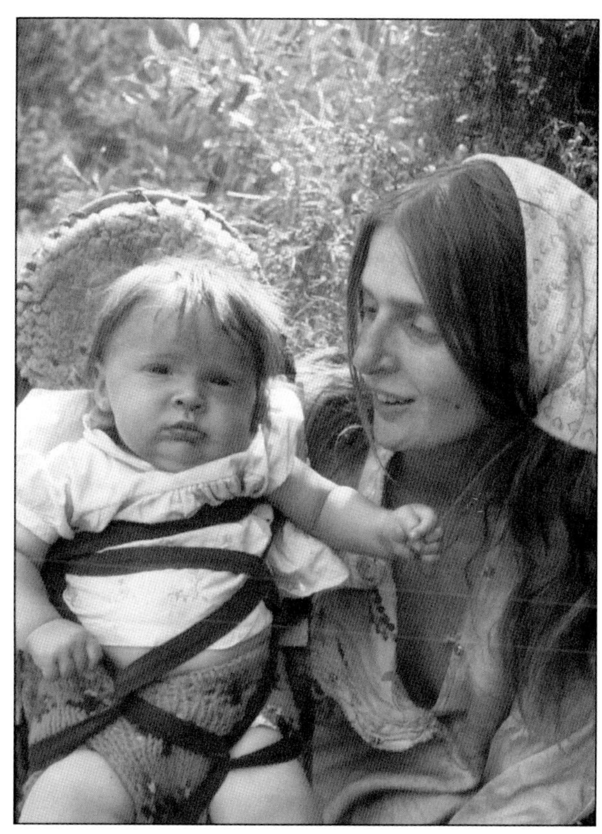

Mother and Child. Susie Cotcher from the Ortiviz Farm community holds her daughter, Rahil, during the summer of 1976. For several years in the 1970s, the denizens of Ortiviz Farm provided the other four communes with organic produce and dairy products. Unfortunately, the mountain valley's short growing season and clay soil proved quite challenging. (Roberta Price.)

Anonymous Artists of America Bus. The Triple A band and commune, born in the early San Francisco counterculture, moved to the valley in 1969. They soon became part of the county's culture, their exuberant music resonating with the local populations, harkening to a time when the live music of the mining camps and Hispanic celebrations was a feature of Huerfano neighborhoods. (Adrienne Berkun.)

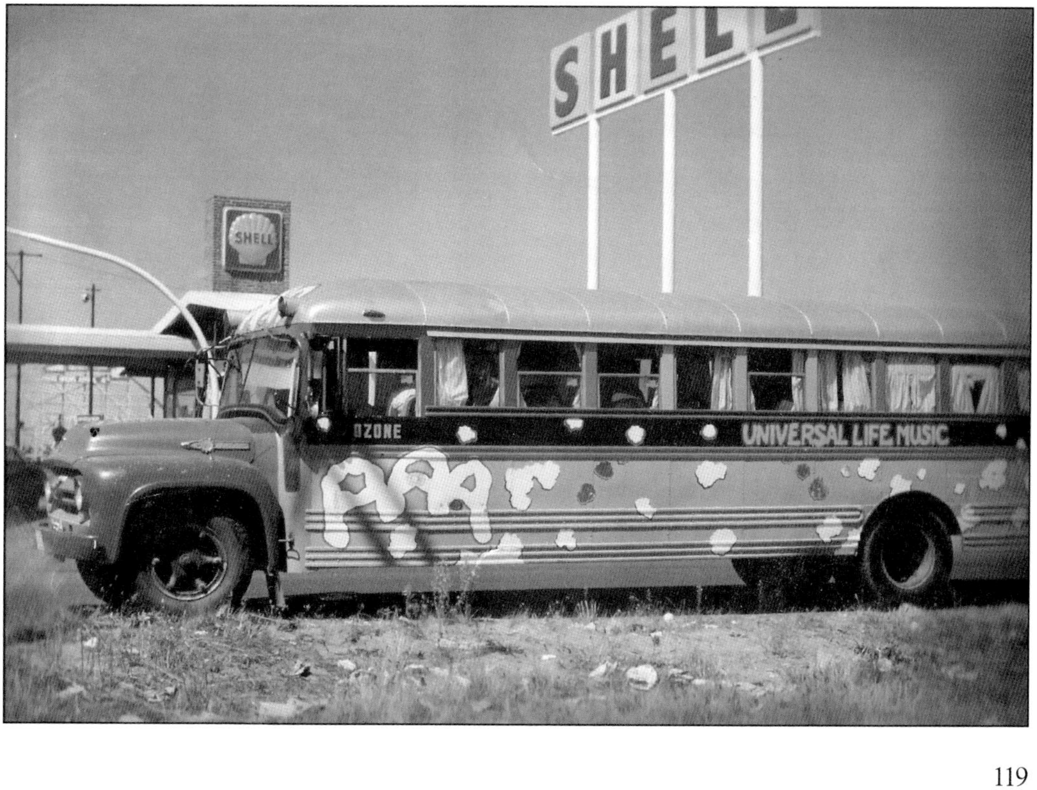

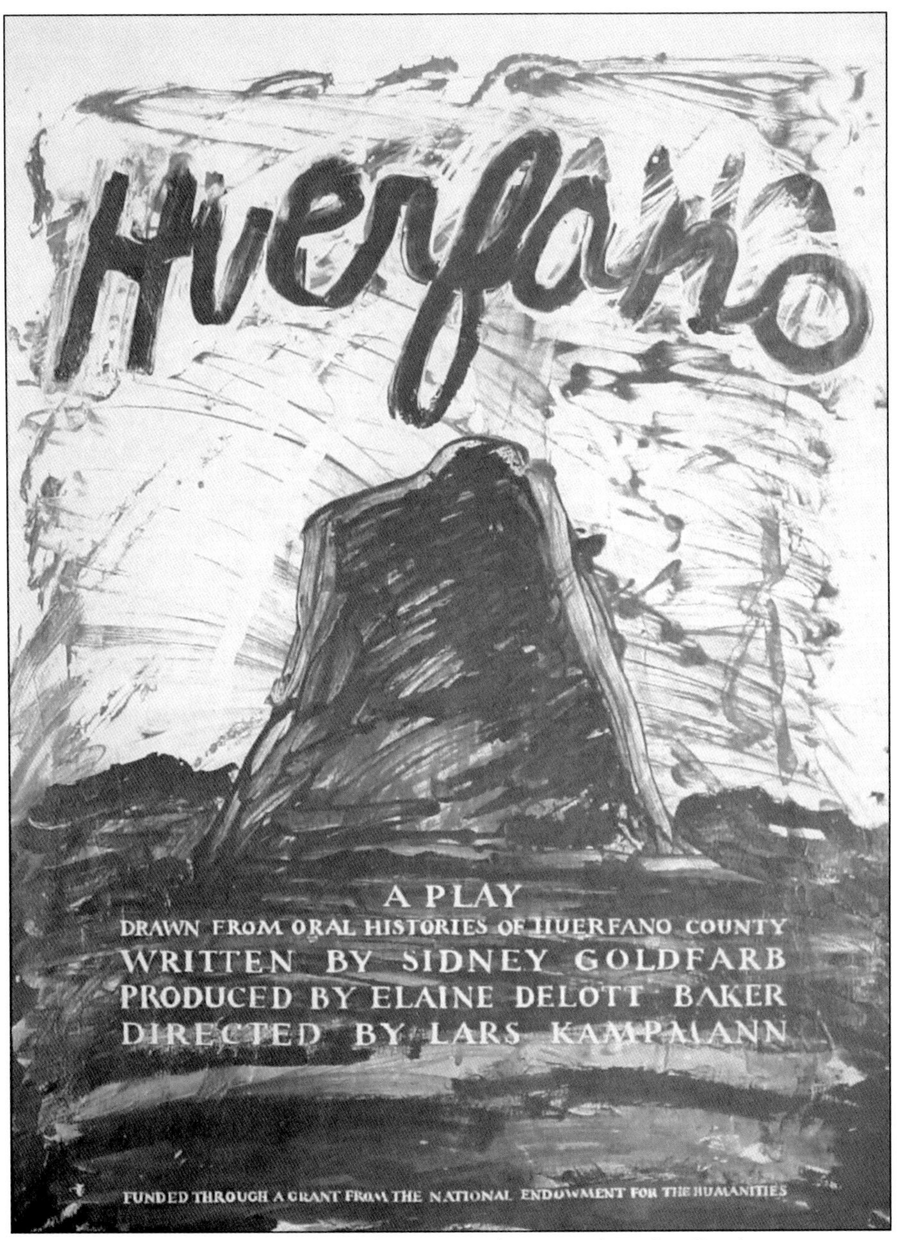

HUERFANO PLAY. The communards of the 1960s who moved to the Gardner area were proud to identify themselves as doers and innovators. They gained the respect of the locals who had settled here before them by contributing both socially and economically to the larger community. These are just some of their achievements. They started the first free medical clinic in the upper Huerfano Valley; initiated a food cooperative; provided artwork for the playground at the Gardner Community Center; recorded the oral histories of septuagenarians who had survived the 1913–1914 Coalfield War; drew up the architectural plans for the Gardner School Annex; supplied much of the physical labor to build this annex; founded the Huerfano County Arts Council, which sponsored many cross-cultural events; composed the first bilingual preschool curriculum for the area; and added teachers, veterinarians, lawyers, writers, artists, and builders to the professional labor pool. (Roberta Price.)

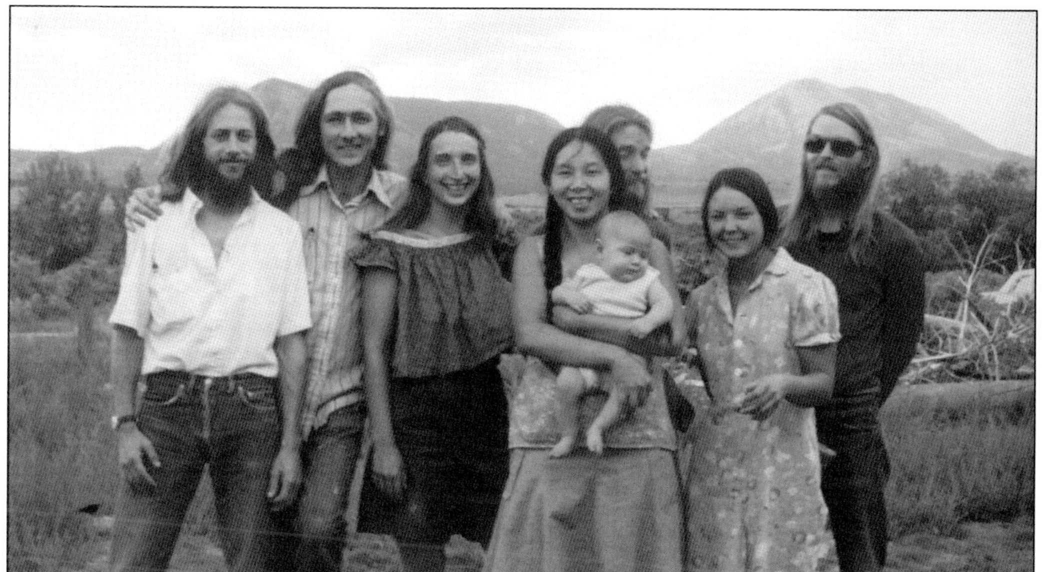

Medical Opera, 1977. The medical personnel who staffed the Gardner Clinic provided affordable health care to upper Huerfano Valley residents from 1975 to the mid-1990s. Before coming to southern Colorado, most of this group had worked at free clinics in New York City or San Francisco. Pictured here from left to right are Bobby Jones, Leonce Evans, Jill Gruenberg, Mat Ting holding baby Willie Mushen, Nikishan Stewart, Lena Reese, and Owen Cookingham. (Roberta Price.)

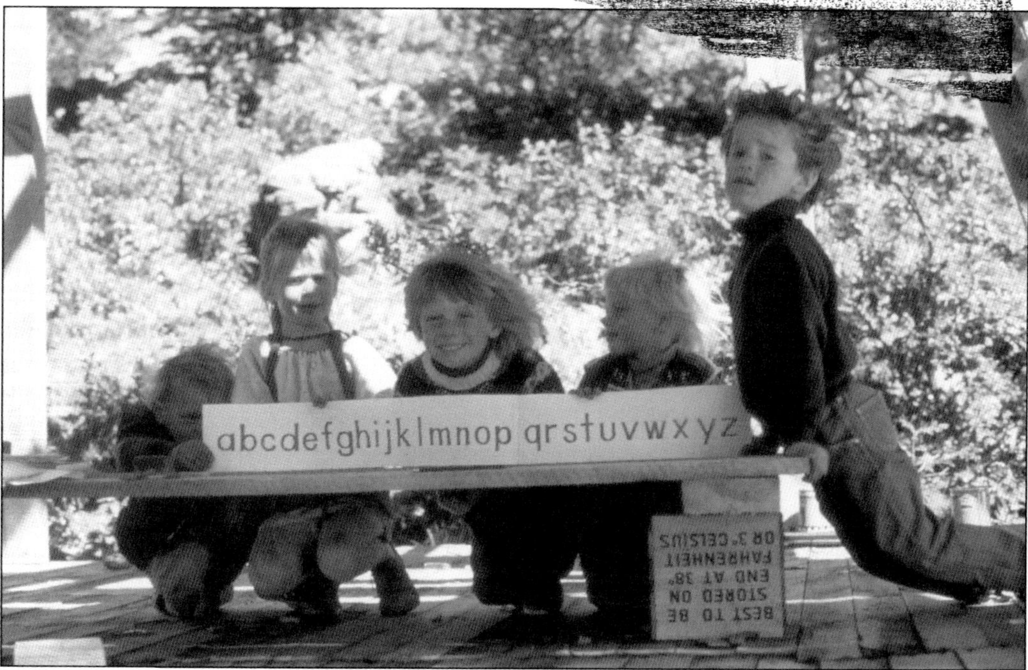

Libre School in Session. Because many of the adult residents had college degrees and sufficient courses to meet state requirements for teacher licensure, the community of Libre boasted its own elementary school. On this particular day, the children were learning measurement lessons and carpentry skills at Bill Keidel's house construction site. From left to right are Travis Gonzales, Lori Ksander, Aaron Wehrman, Aricia Wehrman, and Jason Gonzales. (Roberta Price.)

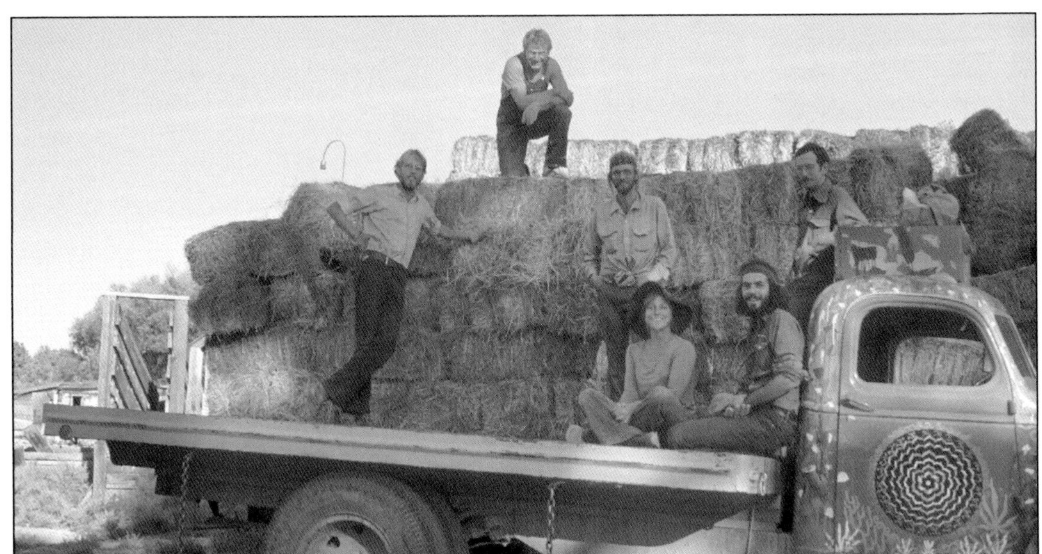

Libre Flatbed, 1972. This truck was often used for hauling logs off the top of Greenhorn Mountain, but on this particular day, Libre livestock growers were hauling hay for their horses and goats. The communards pictured here are, from left to right, David Henry, Dean Fleming, Jim Fowler, Roberta Price, David Perkins, and Richard Wehrman. (Roberta Price.)

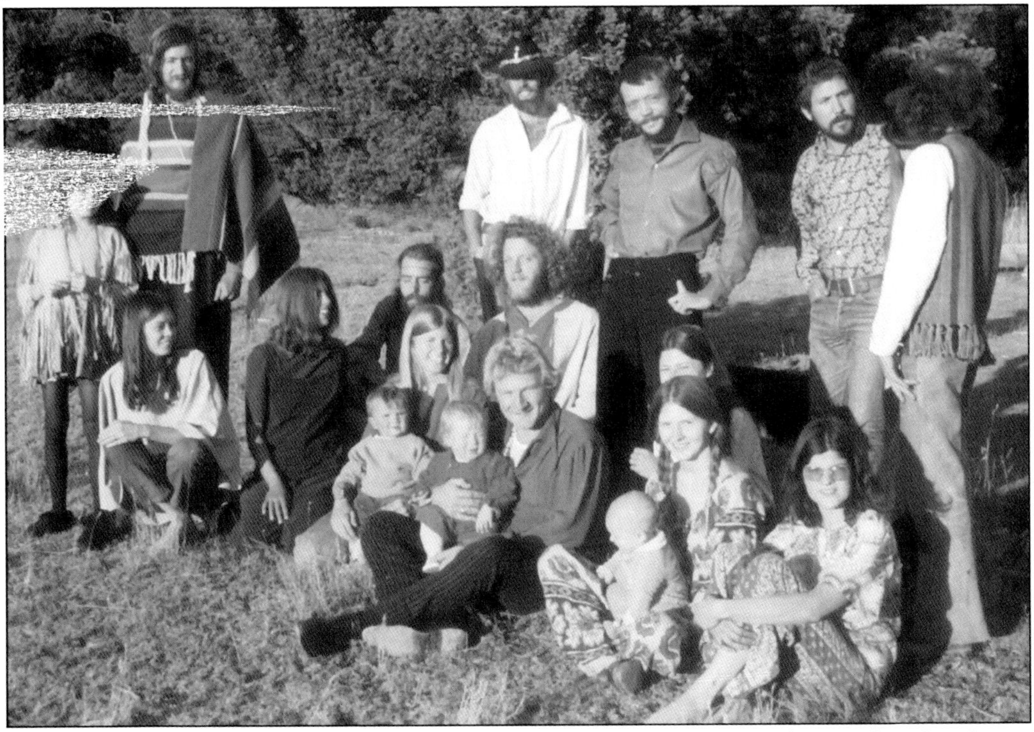

Libre Group and Guests, 1969. From left to right are (first row) Judy Douthit, Stephanie Aisenstein, Pat McMahon with baby Nanda, Dean Fleming with baby Lia, Ginger Smith with her baby, and Sandy Fowler; (second row) Dallas Haynes, Steve Raynes, and Harriet ?; (third row) Kathy Douthit, Peter "Rabbit" Douthit, Jim Fowler, Steve Vesey, Jim Szilagyi, and Gene Smith. (Linda Fleming.)

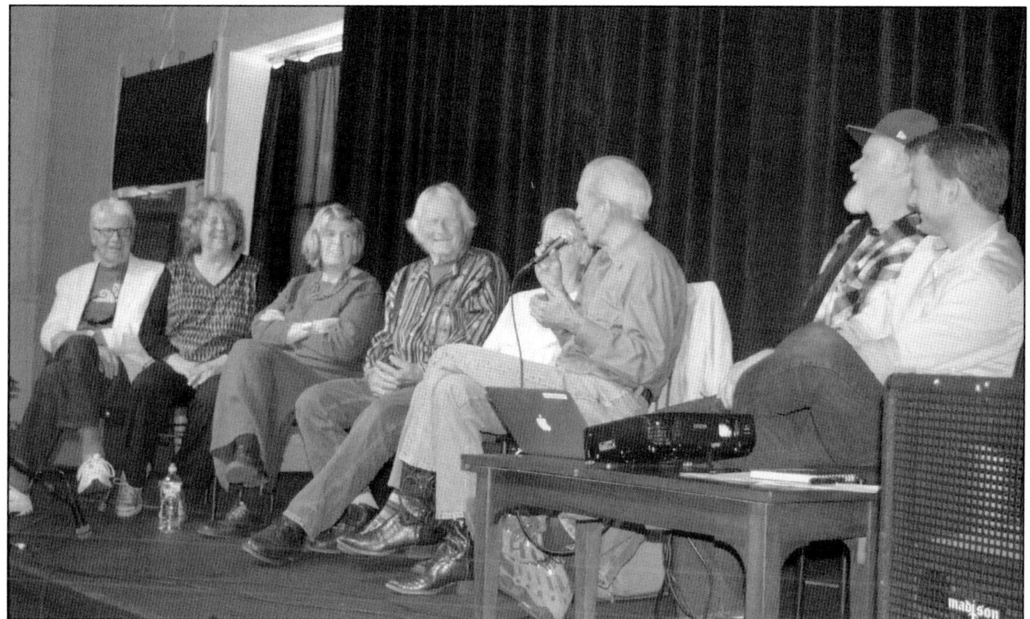

Communes of Southern Colorado Panel. In May 2015, the Francisco Crossing and the La Veta Library sponsored a series of presentations to commemorate the 50th anniversary of Drop City. One performance featured a panel discussion that included past and present residents of area communes. Pictured from left to right are Chip Baker, Elaine Baker, Pat McMahon, Dean Fleming, Nancy Brooks, David Perkins, Jeff Briggs, and Bobby Jones's son, Brook.

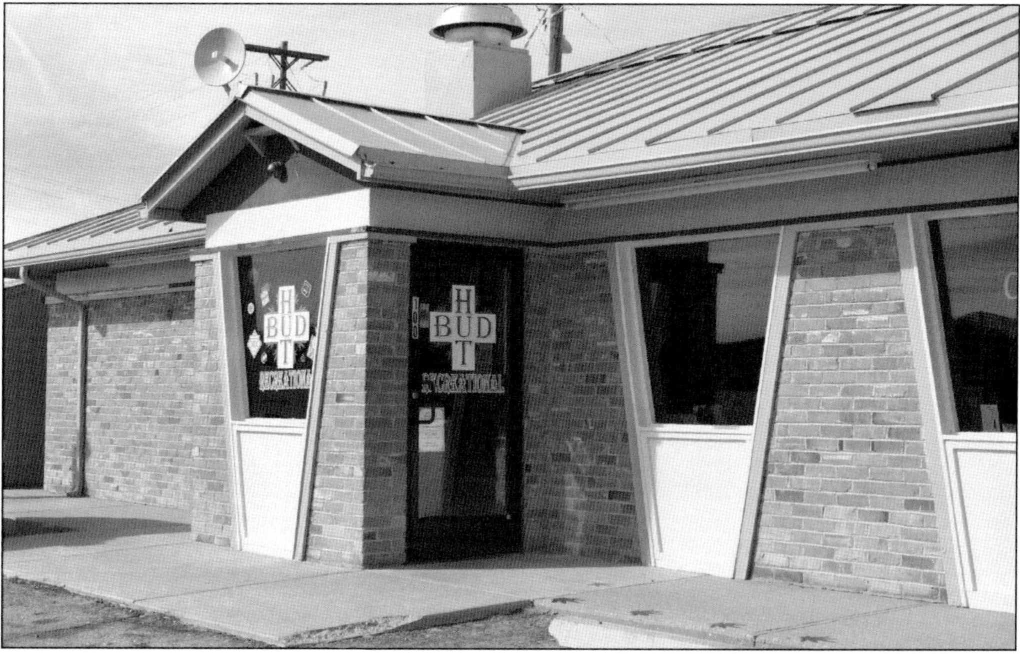

Repurposing the Old Pizza Hut. A 2012 state statute legalizing marijuana added a newly taxable product to the list of items sold within Walsenburg's city limits. Increasing tolerance for counterculture ideas plus a need for additional revenues helped to bring about a change in zoning laws.

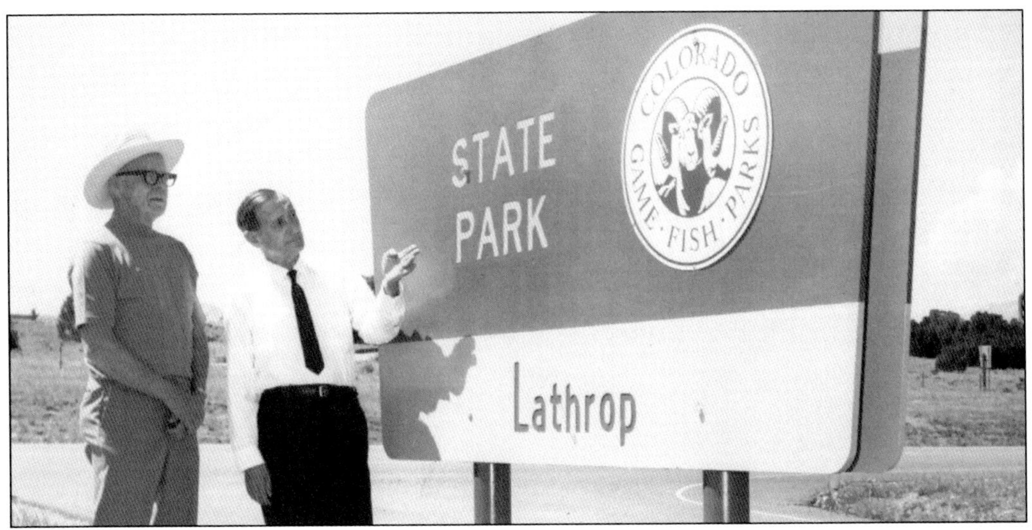

LATHROP STATE PARK. Lathrop opened in 1962 as Colorado's first state park. This recreational area is three miles west of Walsenburg. It offers a wide variety of boating, hiking, fishing, and camping opportunities, as do many other scenic retreats within Huerfano County. (HCHS/ATC.)

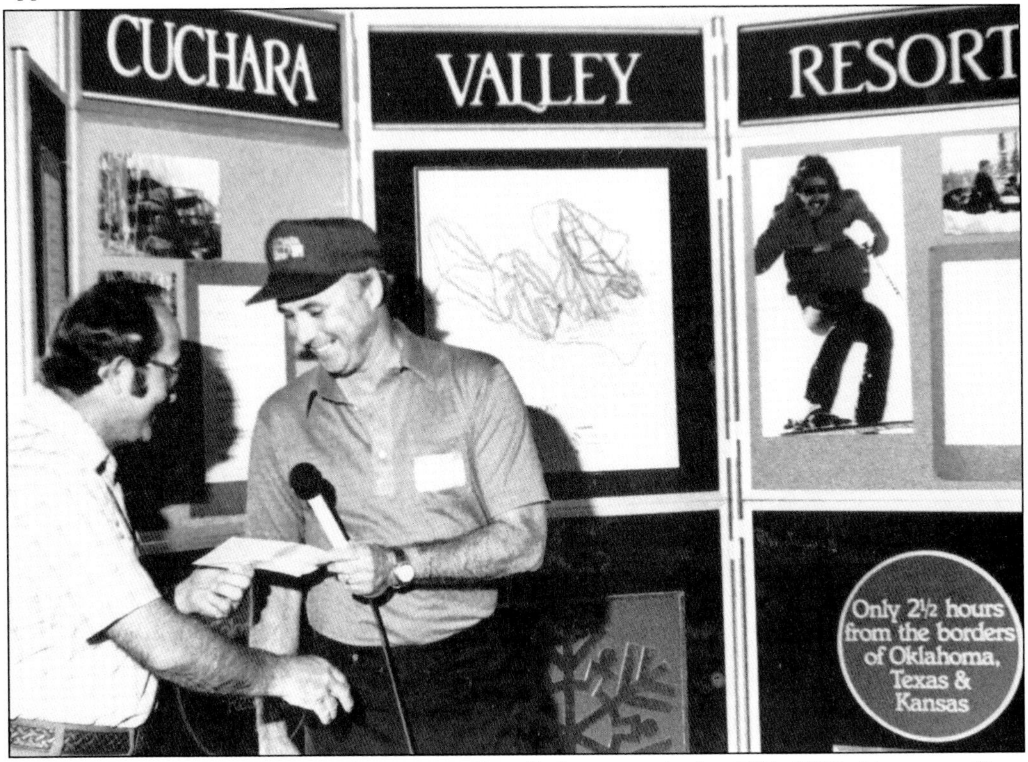

CUCHARA VALLEY SKI AREA. This resort officially began with the 1981–1982 ski season. Over the next 20 years, it suffered from a lack of winter snowpack plus inadequate funding. The US Forest Service decided in 2001 that the owners were in violation of their special use permit and revoked their ability to operate. Several attempts have been made to convert Cuchara into a year-round recreational facility functioning as a nonprofit agency. Thus far, nothing has panned out. (HCHS/ATC.)

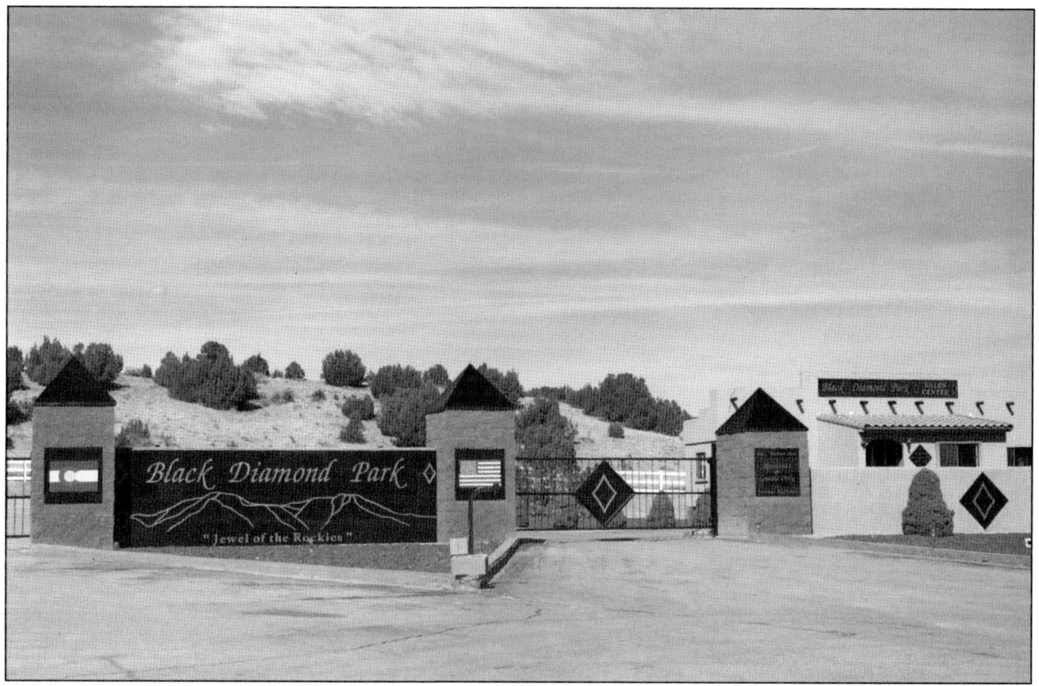

Black Diamond Park. This attempt at developing a master-planned, 21st century neighborhood is a gated community situated next to the Walsenburg Golf Course and Lathrop State Park. It provides scenic home sites and extraordinary outdoor recreational opportunities for all seasons.

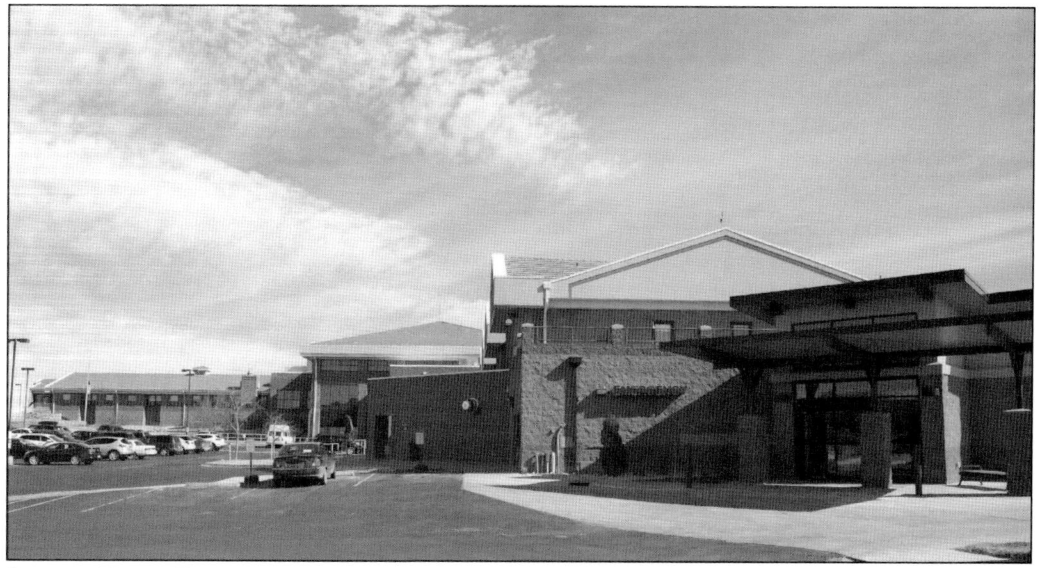

Spanish Peaks Regional Health Center. SPRHC is a general medical and surgical hospital in Walsenburg. It is a 20-bed, full-service hospital providing laboratory, radiology, surgery, and therapy services, a dialysis center, and a Level IV trauma and emergency room. It is adjacent to the Spanish Peaks Veterans Community Living Center. Both facilities offer scenic views of the Rocky Mountains and Lathrop State Park.

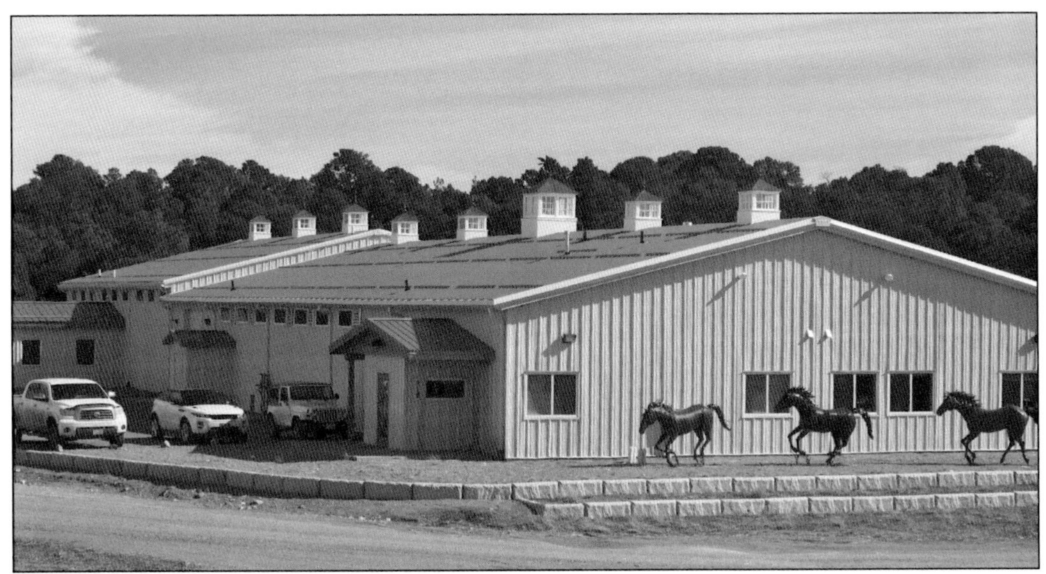

Chae Organics Manufacturing and Distribution Center. Chae Organics makes perfumes, cosmetics, skin care products, and toxin-free household cleaners. This building is located west of Walsenburg, across from Lathrop State Park.

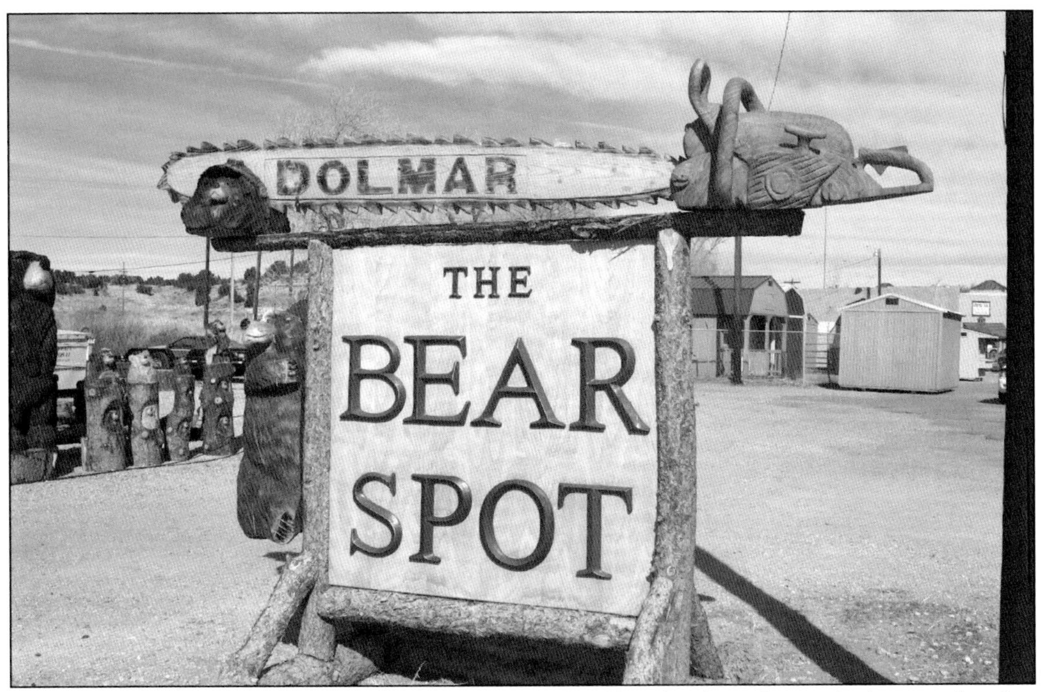

The Bear Spot. Although many businesses have abandoned Walsenburg during the last two decades, this shop that sells wood carvings continues to remain afloat. Improved infrastructure within a subdivision bordering Interstate 25 also provides hope that the town will soon attract new restaurants, motel chains, and industrial park franchises. Meanwhile, the residents of Huerfano County cling stubbornly to the beautiful region they love and await the next economic recovery.

Bibliography

Anderson, John Wesley. *Ute Indian Prayer Trees of the Pikes Peak Region*. Colorado Springs, CO: Old Colorado City Historical Society, 2015.

Archuleta, Ruben E. *Land of Penitentes, Land of Tradition*. Pueblo West, CO: El Jefe, 2003.

Beasley, Conger. "Among the Penitentes: Remembering an Ancient Holy Week Tradition in Southern Colorado." *Colorado Springs Independent*. Colorado Springs, CO: April 20, 2000.

Boehler, Clint. "Sun Dance of the Aztlan." *Huerfano World Journal*. Walsenburg, CO: August 1, 2008.

Butler, Mike. Images of America: *Southern Colorado O.T. Davis Collection*. Charleston, SC: Arcadia Publishing, 2014.

Christofferson, Nancy. *Coal Was King: Huerfano County's Mining History*. La Veta, CO: Self-published, 2000.

———. *La Veta, The First 40 Years: A History of La Veta, Colorado*. La Veta, CO: Self-published, 2001.

Clyne, Rick J. *Coal People: Life in Southern Colorado's Company Towns, 1890–1930*. Denver, CO: Colorado Historical Society, 1999.

Lecompte, Janet. *Pueblo, Hardscrabble, Greenhorn: Society on the High Plains, 1832–1856*. Norman, OK: University of Oklahoma Press, 1980.

Manos, John W. *The Orphan: Do You Know Huerfano?* La Veta, CO: Rinehart Publishing, 2012.

Mitchell, Karen. *Welcome to Huerfano County, Colorado Resources Page*. www.kmitch.com/Huerfano/resource.htm.

Murray, Robert A. *Las Animas, Huerfano and Custer: Three Colorado Counties on A Cultural Frontier: A History of the Raton Basin*. Cultural Resources Series: No. 6 Historical. Denver, CO: Bureau of Land Management, 1978.

Price, Roberta. *Across The Great Divide*. Albuquerque, NM: University of New Mexico Press, 2010.

———. *Huerfano: A Memoir of Life in the Counterculture*. Boston, MA: University of Massachusetts Press, 2004.

Ree, Dorothy Rose. *Walsenburg: Crossroads Town*. Walsenburg, CO: Nocturn Independent Publishing, 2006.

Taylor, Ralph C. *Colorado South of the Border*. Denver, CO: Sage Books, 1963.

Thomas, Douglas B. *From Fort Massachusetts to the Rio Grande: A History of Southern Colorado and Northern New Mexico from 1850–1900*. Washington, DC: Thomas International, 2002.

Wolf, Tom. *Colorado's Sangre de Cristo Mountains*. Niwot, CO: University Press of Colorado, 1995.

Consistent with our mission to preserve history on a local level, this book was printed in South Carolina on American-made paper and manufactured entirely in the United States. Products carrying the accredited Forest Stewardship Council (FSC) label are printed on 100 percent FSC-certified paper.

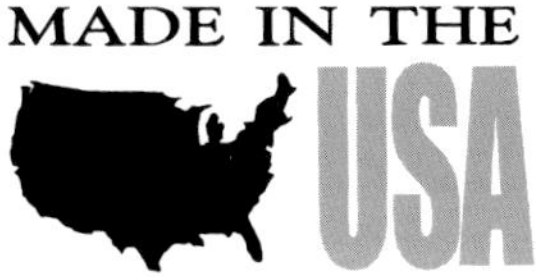